SIMON PETER:
The Reed and the Rock

SIMON PETER:
The Reed and the Rock

DAVID PAWSON

Anchor Recordings

First published in Great Britain in 2013 by
Anchor Recordings Ltd
72 The Street
Kennington, Ashford TN24 9HS

ISBN 978-1-909886-23-0

Printed by Lightning Source

Contents

This book is based on a series of talks. Originating as it does from the spoken word, its style will be found by many readers to be somewhat different from my usual written style. It is hoped that this will not detract from the substance of the biblical teaching found here.

As always, I ask the reader to compare everything I say or write with what is written in the Bible and, if at any point a conflict is found, always to rely upon the clear teaching of scripture.

David Pawson

1

SIMON IS RENAMED

"You are Simon the son of John. You will be called Cephas"
(which, when translated, is Peter).

Of all the apostles, Peter is the most loveable. He is such a transparent character. His virtues and vices are in the shop window for all to see. His strengths and weaknesses are so apparent that we see ourselves in him. Things we have thought of saying and doing he just came right out with. He was so impulsive. We have a sneaking sympathy with someone who rushes in where angels fear to tread and who is always opening his mouth and putting his foot in it.

Simon Peter was a key figure in AD26 to 36, that vital decade of the history of our human race. Peter saw so much happen – as an ordinary man – and if we study his life we will see it happening too. We get a firsthand witness of the events that changed the world.

We will study his life partly so that we may see what happened in the three years of our Lord's public ministry and the first seven years of the church's life. That ten years really turned the tide in human affairs. But we will not only use Peter to look at the events, we will use the events to look at Peter. This is the second reason for this study: here we see how an ordinary man was transformed by these events. We shall see what can happen to very ordinary people right now – they, too, can be changed by the same events.

You see, Peter was changed radically—he started out with the name Simon, which means a "reed", which is not a very complimentary name to give your boy I would have thought. Straight, upright, but easily swayed and in fact that's exactly what he was by nature and by temperament. If ever there was what we call a sanguine temperament, it was Peter. If you want a good book on the subject read Tim LaHaye's *Transformed Temperaments*. The sanguine temperament is the easiest one to spot in anybody else and the hardest one to spot in yourself. A sanguine man is someone who is very impulsive, talkative, emotional, easily swayed, responds to his environment immediately, and therefore of course depends very much on the company he is in for the kind of thing he does and says. Jesus took this 'reed' and changed him into a rock. Who says you can't change human nature? That is the devil's own lie – but, of course, apart from Christ you can't and that's why people think you can't be changed and say that you stay the character you are until your dying day—but that is not true. I could make it even more startling by saying the coward became a martyr. The man who would swear and blaspheme, and say that he didn't know his best friend to save his skin, became a man who asked to be crucified upside-down because he was not worthy to be put to death in the same way as our Lord. Now what got into this man? What happened to him?

We begin at the very beginning: Simon Peter's baptism. We are going to look at his call, at the first three things that Jesus said to him, and we are going to see in each of those three things a double emphasis.

I don't know much about Peter's birth, but I know that he is not dead. We are talking about someone who is very much alive right now. Somebody said they dug up his bones under the Vatican – and they may have done, but what do his bones matter? I'm talking about someone who is very much alive, who was born as we are born. Just as during his lifetime he met two men who had been dead over a thousand years, Moses and Elijah, so today Peter is very much alive. He is one of those I am looking forward to meeting in heaven.

I get the impression (I don't know where from) that he was a very big man – the big fisherman, great big hands and great big shoulders, and I am looking forward to looking up into his face and shaking his hand and meeting him. Now if he was born (as many babies seem to be!) in the middle of the night, his dad would not have been there to see him into the world. He would be out on the Sea of Galilee fishing, and maybe his future mother-in-law was the midwife; she lived nearby anyway. But when Jesus was a boy maybe about ten years of age in Nazareth, Peter cried his first cry.

It is interesting that his parents gave him that name "Reed". Maybe the temperament ran in the family. But he was born with this loveable but erratic and unreliable temperament – he is the man who will keep opening his mouth when he should be quiet. On one occasion God spoke from heaven and shut him up so that Peter would stop talking and do a bit of listening for a change.

But this man who would always have friends, who excites his company, who is stimulating and joyful, who gets over his bad moods very quickly, can also go right down to the bottom and weep his heart out over something he regrets. This is the man we are looking at—the reed. Upright, but slender and bendable, that's Peter; so they gave him his name and I am afraid he lived up to it.

But environment plays as much a part as heredity. If we look at this man's environment we find first of all that it must have been tough. I began my ministry in the Shetland Islands many years ago and found that fishermen are strong people. They have to wrestle with the sea and storms, so they get tough that way, and Peter was in such an environment. His would have been a family that lived close to the breadline and close to natural forces.

In the Shetlands I found that many fishermen were superstitious (they wouldn't take a parson or a pig on board when they were sailing out of harbour to go fishing). But I also met some fishermen in those islands who were deeply religious, and Simon Peter's family was religious too. When you are battling with the forces of nature you are aware of the powers greater than yourself – much more aware than if you just catch a train to the office in the morning.

Simon lived in Capernaum, nowadays just a few little ruins and a monastery, but then a busy little town. It was situated on the Via Maris, a road stretching from Asia to Africa, and the world and his wife went up and down that road. Soldiers and tradesmen went up and down that road. Little Simon would have met many different people in the main street in the little town where he lived, and it gave him a vision of the world. No doubt he watched the Roman soldiers marching up and down that street, little dreaming that one day a Roman would nail him to a cross in the distant city of Rome. But the little lad grew up in that town on the edge of a lake, seeing the world—that was his background.

Some time in his late teens he got religious. There was a revivalist preacher, a "Baptist evangelist", about fifty miles away – a man called John. Crowds were heading off down the Jordan River to the lowest point on the earth's surface (and the dirtiest river). They were going to hear the preacher. They hadn't had a preacher like this in four hundred years, and that was a long time to wait. They had been waiting for God to speak to them again. The young people were getting excited, and older people too.

I have the feeling that Peter's older brother Andrew said, "Have you thought of going to hear the revivalist preacher?"

Peter, then in his late teens, agreed, little dreaming that the trip would be the turning point in his whole life. So he went, and for the first time in his life he realised he was a dirty young man and that he needed cleaning up. As soon as you realise that, you are on the way to glory.

So he responded to the appeal of the preacher and he got baptised to wash way the past – in that muddy river we call the Jordan. He went down into that water, and as the water closed over his head he just knew that he would never be the same again, that he was saying goodbye to the life he had lived as a teenager, and that he was now going to try and live a clean life.

So far he thought that was all that was going to happen, but in fact for him there would be something more. John kept saying when he preached: I am not the Christ; I am preparing the way for someone else, someone who is somewhere in this crowd and you don't know who he is or where he is, but I know that there is someone who is going to be the Christ, the King.

If you said that today to a British audience it would not interest them, but say it to an audience of Jews and it could get them excited one way or the other. Say, "The Christ is somewhere in this crowd," and there would be thousands there. John said, "There is the Christ and I am not fit to tie up his boot laces, but he is going to do more for you than I can. I can baptise you in water but he is going to baptise you in the Holy Spirit." Simon and Andrew listened.

Probably a few days later, while they still attending the meetings, Andrew pushed through the crowd, grabbed Peter by the arm and said, "Peter, we've found him." Peter's heart missed a beat, "The Christ, the King!"

"Yes, we found him, Simon, come and meet him. I'll introduce you to him. I've been talking to him," and they went. So memorable was that moment that sixty years later one of the men there said it was four o'clock in the afternoon. He could remember the time vividly. Peter came, and for the first time he met Jesus. What a moment!

You know, there must have been something about the eyes of Jesus. When Jesus looked at people and they looked into his eyes, something happened. Jesus had "x-ray eyes". By this I mean by that he didn't look at people the way others look at people. We look at each other and we look at the outside and we say, "Well, that's a funny shaped nose and he's grown a beard, hasn't he?" We look at the outside. The Lord doesn't look like that, he looks at the inside, and he looks right through people. He doesn't look at their face so much as their heart.

Jesus looked at Simon that day, looked right through him, and could see both the person he was and the person he could be. When Jesus looks at anyone's life he sees two people: the person who is, and the person they could be. Often there is a great big gulf between the two. We cannot always see these two people when we look at someone. Alas, we most often look at the person who is, and we don't see them as they could be. How often we write them off because of this.

Jesus saw two people and said, "You are Simon, but I'm going to give you a new name; I'm going to call you Cephas." That was in the Aramaic, which Jesus spoke. It is the same as our word "Peter" and it means "rock".

The first thing you realise when you come to Jesus is that when he takes a look at your life he sees everything that is there already. You can't hide anything from him. You may have hidden things from other people but you can't hide them from the eyes of Jesus. He looks just straight through and he sees the person you are – you are Simon, you're a reed; you are weak, unreliable, emotional, impulsive, talkative; you are Simon but I am going to give you a new name because from now on you are going to be different.

Do you realise what Jesus sees when he looks at you? You may know how he sees you as the person you are, but do you realise he sees your new nature that deserves a new name? Maybe not yet—those of us who have known Christ for some years would never have dreamt in our wildest moments that we would be doing and being what we are now, but he saw it. Furthermore, Jesus can not only see two people, he can see how to change the one into the other—that is the glory of it.

Most of us have had dreams, most of us have caught a vision of what we could be and what we would like to be. Most of us have started out in life with great desires to make of this one life that we've got – and we have only got it once – something worthwhile. Alas, those dreams get pushed down by hard experience of life—we lose the vision, and in middle age we settle for who we are, we give up so easily, but Jesus looks at everybody and says "You are [*put your own name in*]"; I'm going to call you...." Do you know your new name yet? He's got one for you. You see, Jesus, when he gave the name, was always accurate. He always summed up the new person very well.

When he met James and John, they already had a nickname. People used to call them "Boanerges", and that was not very complimentary. To paraphrase, it is, "Blow your top", but Boanerges means "thunder". Really it means: "to let fly, to blow up, to let off steam". Yet Jesus looked at James and John too, and he could see John, who would become a most beloved, gentle man.

So we look to Peter, and that was the first moment: "You're going to be Cephas, a rock" – the man as he could be. Now as soon as you become aware of the gap between the actual and the ideal, as soon as you become ashamed of that gap, as soon as you think there is hope of closing the gap, then you have taken the first step in the Christian life. You have realised truth—about the present and about the future.

The time came for Peter to go back home and it was over. I expect he went back to Galilee wondering, "Will I ever see him again? I have seen in his eyes reflected my dreams. I want to be that rock." I have no doubt that when he got back home they just laughed their heads off when he said, "Don't call me Simon, call me Cephas."

"Oh why?"

"Well, I'm going to be a rock."

"You are going to be a rock? Come on. How do you think you're going to be a rock?"

Can't you hear the banter at home about this new name he had been given? But Peter went on hoping and dreaming.

We now come to the second point at which Jesus spoke to him. It is fascinating. One night, Peter had been out fishing. James and John were out there too, and they had caught nothing, having laboured all night. They had tried the shallows, they had tried the deeps, and the fish were not rising. They rise at night, and if you can hang a lamp over the water to create an artificial moon, the fish come up to you. You still see fishermen on the Galilee today with hurricane lamps hanging over the stern of their boat to draw the fish up. They tried everything that night and the fish were not biting.

So they were coming sadly back towards Capernaum at night when they saw a big crowd on the shore. They turned just a little aside from their course toward Capernaum and came to a horseshoe-shaped bay, like a natural amphitheatre – you can still see it today – pointing out to the Sea of Galilee. There was a man talking to the crowd and, when they got near, Simon knew it was Jesus. He had come north and was preaching.

They pulled in to hear. As they approached, Jesus turned around and asked to borrow Simon's boat. He got aboard and used it as a pulpit. Peter's heart must have been bursting with pride – his boat, the pulpit of the king; that back seat was now a throne! Then, after he had finished preaching, Jesus said, "Now let's go and get some fish."

At this point there was the real possibility of a conflict of wills. Who knows best how to fish – a fisherman or a carpenter? Peter could so easily have opened his mouth and let fly at that moment. He could have so easily said, "Who do you think you're talking to? You may know how to preach but fishing is my business." After all, he said some pretty blunt things to Jesus later, so he could have said that now. He was weary, he was a skilful fisherman, he had tried every way he knew, but had not caught anything, and here was a preacher telling him how to do his job! I can imagine the little battle going on in Peter's heart as soon as Jesus said, "Let's go out and get some fish. We'll go out into the deeper water." But Peter surrendered to the Lord, and the first time he put the situation into the Lord's hands something extraordinary happened. He called Jesus "Master". That still wasn't enough yet, but it was heading on the way. It was at least a token of surrender. So they headed out for the deep water again. It was now broad daylight, when fish don't rise, for a start, and you find them in the shallows not the deep water anyway – just crazy but, "Master, if you say so."

Sometimes the Lord tells you to do crazy things, but the test of our faith is whether we say, "Master, if you say so" – and you know the results if you know your Bible. It says that the nets were breaking and the boats were sinking because of all the fish. Immediately, Peter was in a situation he couldn't cope with. It is like the farmer who prayed so earnestly for rain that when he came out of the church door it was bucketing down, and he just stood there and said, "Nay, Lord, this is just ridiculous." Peter might have said that: Lord, you're going to wreck the whole business – the nets, the boats! It is a lovely touch, but Peter was afraid. That was his first reaction because something was happening that was unnatural. When anything supernatural occurs, people get afraid. Have you noticed that? Whenever something is happening that you can't account for in any other way than that a miracle is taking place, fear is the first reaction of the natural human heart. We can cope with the natural, but we cannot cope with the supernatural. Our nets break, our boats sink! Peter couldn't cope and he was afraid naturally, but then the fear moved from his mind to his heart – and he became afraid *morally*.

It's interesting how often when God is at work people get afraid morally. Being afraid mentally leads to being ashamed morally. Peter, in the boat, in front of his friends, dropped on to his knees and said, "Get out of this boat, get away from me, please. I just can't cope with this kind of thing. Get away from me for I am a sinful man, O Lord!" Not just mental confusion but moral shame had come into his life. I believe it was at this point that Peter really realised he was a sinner – how bad he was. He had responded to John's preaching but now he really felt it.

Sometimes we come to Christ without feeling too deeply our sins, and maybe later the Lord challenges us and we go deeper, and we feel ashamed then. "Get away from me!" The Lord said the second thing to Peter that is recorded in the Gospels – it is a lovely thing and I paraphrase it so that you get the feel of it. Jesus said, "All right, Peter, I'm going away but will you come with me?" He said, "Follow me and I will make you fishers of men."

When Christ really speaks to a sinner, he makes both a demand and an offer. The demand here is: "Follow me." The offer is: "I will make you...." These are the two sides of the gospel. The gospel is a demand; it demands not that you follow a system, not that you follow a church but that you follow a *person* called Jesus. It is a demand that you follow him all the way. You go with him. There is nothing that Jesus asks anyone to do that he asks them to do without him. It is to stay with him.

The offer is: Peter, I will make you the kind of fisherman you never dreamt you would be. How often our Lord was able to meet somebody with language and an offer that was just right for them. I let my imagination run away with me now: what would he say to a farmer? Well, since I did a bit of farming, I know. He says, "Follow me and I will make you a cultivator and harvester of souls." What would he say to an engineer? "Follow me, and I will enable you to build bridges between men and God." If you are a doctor he may say to you, "Follow me and I will make you a healer of hearts." If you are a dentist: "Follow me and I'll help you to fight decay." I want you to put into your mind right now what you believe Jesus would say to you. Think of your job, think of what you have done up till now. What is Jesus saying to you? "Follow me and I will make you...." What an offer! What confidence he has. He doesn't say "I'll try" or "We'll see what we can do," but "I will make you...." That is a promise. Only the Creator who made people in the first place could promise to make them again.

You may be able to give a testimony that Jesus made you that promise and he kept it, and he made you what you never thought you could be. The demand and the offer was the second time Jesus spoke.

Now we come to the third time Jesus spoke to them, to Peter particularly, a few weeks later. The crowds were coming and it was an exciting period in Peter's life. We will look at some of the things that happened, but his relationship to Jesus is getting deeper and deeper. It began by calling him "the Christ", it moved on to calling him "Master", and then it was, "Depart from me for I am a sinful man, O Lord." When you start using the word "Lord" for Jesus you are getting very close.

Now the crowds were coming, miracles were happening – but one day Jesus left the crowd down by the lakeside and announced publicly, "I'm going up into the hills. Anyone can follow me, but I am going up there." He started up the hills behind Capernaum, and so many people did not follow – quite a lot didn't bother. They would wait where they were till he came back, but Simon Peter was one of those who climbed up after him.

Up they went into the mountains until Jesus turned, sat down—they all sat down, and then if I may paraphrase freely again, Jesus said, "Now of all of you who followed me up this hill I'm going to choose just twelve. I have a very special task for you." Again there are two aspects to what he said, two parts of the task: one, he said, "I want you to be with me"; and two, "I want to send you out to preach and to have authority to cast out demons." In other words: I am going to concentrate from now on. I am going to leave the crowd and I want just twelve men. Of course, Jesus was a master strategist and could do more by concentrating on the twelve.

So Jesus was saying to the twelve: I want to bring you out of your jobs and out of the world, to be with me, to spend all your time with me, to eat with me, walk with me, talk with me, work with me – and then, when you have learned to do what I do, I am going to send you out to do it. You are going to preach and you are going to release. As Peter listened, I can just see his mind saying, "Oh could I be one? Would he choose me? Will he?" Then Jesus stopped and he began to look around to choose—what a moment, very intense. There must have been a large crowd there because we know that later he sent at least seventy disciples out two by two. So there must have been at least seventy and maybe more there.

He looked around, and for the third time he looked at Peter. You know those eyes just went through you – they could break your heart, and later they would. The Lord turned and looked at Peter. "Simon, you are the first; come and join me." Oh, what a moment! You know the glory of it is as Jesus later said to his apostles, "You didn't choose me, I chose you." Whatever we think at the time, we may drop our nets and follow him, and we may think we made the big decision and decided to be a Christian, but you know at a later stage Jesus just says gently, "You know I chose you." You are baptised not because you chose to be baptised but because the Lord chose you to be baptised. It is his choice and you respond to it.

So he said, "Simon, I want you and James and John. Simon, we'll have your brother, too – Andrew." Isn't that interesting? Andrew found Christ first but Simon was chosen first and Andrew came along fourth, and then the others came. "I'm going to have a tax collector – Matthew, won't you?"

To another Simon: "I want you." How remarkable: a tax collector, a collaborator, traitor and zealot (a man ready to kill, to try and get the land back for his own nationality).

So it went on—Thaddeus, Bartholomew, and Philip. Got eleven now, then Jesus looked rather sad and said, "Judas Iscariot, I'll have you" – knowing what that would involve. So he chose the twelve, but of those Peter was the first. Why twelve? Well, in order to start a synagogue you have to have at least ten men. Jesus, making sure, knowing that he would lose one, made sure that he would have at least eleven, and he started a synagogue which is why from then on he kept being called "Rabbi" – because he gathered a synagogue around himself and was a teacher of Jewish men.

But that was not the final reason. I believe it entered into it. Why twelve men? Because way back at the beginning of the history of Israel there had been twelve brothers, twelve sons of Israel. Those twelve began the twelve tribes. I believe that Jesus, in choosing twelve men, was starting a new humanity. Now the world was to see a new race, a new humanity, and Simon Peter was the first to be chosen.

So, with heart bursting, he began to follow Jesus. He little dreamt the final outcome. He did not know it would mean great glory for him. He little knew that his fame would spread throughout the world for two thousand years. Little did he know when he set off after Jesus that his name would one day be engraved on a gigantic pearl, and that pearl made into a gate for the heavenly city, the New Jerusalem. So that anybody who went in and out of that gate would read "Peter" on the gate. He didn't know (I think he may have guessed) that to follow a king would bring glory.

What he did not then realise is what we may not realise fully, and that is that there is no crown without a cross, and that the path to glory lies directly through the valley of suffering. He was going to be put in prison because he became one of the twelve. He was going to be on trial for his life. He was going to be executed as a common criminal. In fact, out of those twelve only one was going to die a natural death, one would commit suicide, the other ten would all be martyred for the faith. Peter did not know this when he set off, any more than any of us realised what it would mean to follow Christ, but this is the path to which we are called through suffering to glory. The important thing is: both will be shared with Jesus. You share the cross with him and you will share the crown. You share his death, his burial, and his resurrection. As you are baptised, you share his risen life from then on. One day you will share his heavenly radiance, sit with him on thrones.

There will be time to be separated from the world; and there will be time to go into that world and tell others. It is all part of our life – to come into Jesus and to go out to a lost world – and that is just the beginning.

2

PHYSICAL HEALING

Read Luke chapter 8

Still today people are finding that the Lord Jesus Christ can reach down from heaven and touch bodies (not only souls), and touch them for good.

In Peter's day life expectancy was short. Infant mortality rates were high and that was part of the problem. There were doctors. Indeed, Luke was a doctor, but their methods were crude and primitive by comparison with today. So if you survived childhood you had to be tough. I imagine Peter as a man's man. He knew how to swear like the rest of them. In fact, that came out a little later – and he was in strong health. Therefore it comes as a bit of a surprise that when he left his fishing to follow Jesus, on the next three occasions we read of him, he is involved with women and with sick people. What a total change of way of life for Peter.

Not that he was always a great help! In fact, Peter had an awful lot to learn about the ministry of healing, as we shall see. Let us go through three incidents and then draw some conclusions from them about the ministry of healing. The thing that is going to hit us very hard is this: too often we spiritualise our religion and we talk about saving souls. The New Testament never uses that expression, it talks about saving men and women – people. That is about the whole person, which includes the body. According to the Bible, my body is my soul and my soul is my body and God took the dust of the earth and breathed into it and the dust became a living soul.

We could say that Jesus heals us spiritually and then physically – that is the order because the redemption of our spirits has already taken place. The redemption of our bodies we are still waiting for, but he is going to save the whole of us because the soul includes everything. So now we are going to look at the redemption of the body as a vital part of the soul.

Here are the three incidents, all concerned with women. Firstly, there is an old woman (or certainly older); secondly, a woman in middle years; and, thirdly, a little girl. Peter was involved in all three cases. There is not only a progression downward in age, there is a progression upward in seriousness of condition. The first condition was a high temperature, a fever; the second, a twelve-year-old haemorrhage; the third, a dying person. It is as if the Lord was teaching Peter gently, step by step, to enlarge his faith and his confidence in the Master he had begun to follow.

Let us see how the first case happened. It took place in the middle of a very busy day, in Capernaum, which can be hot. It is 620 feet below sea level, down in the Jordan Valley. In the summer that can get blistering hot temperatures, lying as it does in a hollow. It had been a very busy morning. Jesus had preached most of the morning and given the most famous sermon ever – the Sermon on the Mount. On the way back down to Capernaum, as they walked, Christ had been busy healing people. He met a leper and healed him of leprosy. Then he met someone else, who said, "My servant is sick."

Without even going to visit the servant, Jesus said, "It's all right, from this minute he's well" – and he was.

About midday, Jesus arrived in Capernaum, and here,

when they got to Peter's house, his mother-in-law was ill. So there was a real crisis in that home. Going into that dark inner room – the windows were small, of course – it would have been dark, but you could just make out the shining face and the restless body of someone who is running a high temperature, tossing and turning. They were putting cold cloths on her brow.

Jesus went into that dark little room and when he went in it seems he just took Peter's mother-in-law by the hand and said, "Come on, get up." She got up and shook her head a bit. Her temperature went down and she was well again. There is a lovely sequel to this – such a simple little event. The mother-in-law then waited on Jesus. She became a waitress and showed her gratitude. That doesn't always happen. I visited a man in hospital and he said, "Look, if God will only heal me of this trouble and bring me out of hospital and restore me to my wife, I will be in your church every Sunday from then on." The Lord did bring him out of hospital but we never saw him at church. Nearly two years later, I went to see him again in hospital. He said, "Oh, I really mean it this time: if God will get me out of this I'll really live as he wants me to live." God did get him out of it – but he didn't. Christ healed ten lepers and only one came back to say thank you. All health is a gift of God, all healing is a gift of God, whether it comes through the hospital, the doctor, the nurse or medicine. But how many wait upon the Lord after they are healed? Doesn't it so often just give them the chance to go right back to the life they lived before and forget about those deep thoughts they had when they were sick? Sometimes God has to put you flat on your back before you look up and think about him.

Now one little bit of sheer speculation at this point (it is pure speculation and therefore you can forget it if it doesn't appeal to you), but I found myself wondering what Simon's mother-in-law thought about her son-in-law dropping his job and wandering off after a preacher. It is a sort of thing that a mother-in-law could react against, don't you think? Here I've given my daughter this man, and the first thing he does is drop his job and go off into the blue as some wandering evangelist. I wonder if there had been that kind of tension in that home, but I know that after this healing any such tension would disappear. That mother-in-law would be so proud and so glad that her son-in-law was with this man. If you have had the touch of the Lord upon you, it does something to your attitudes. You think differently. So that was the first incident, let's move now to the second.

It happened a few weeks later. There was a very lonely middle-aged woman. Jesus had been on a boat trip across the lake, and he had gone there to get a rest. It had not been terribly restful, there had been a storm in the middle of the lake for a start, and Jesus had had to tell that to stop jumping up at his disciples. Translating the command literally, he told it to get muzzled. To the wind and the waves: "Stop behaving like a puppy dog and jumping up. My disciples are getting worried. Stop it." The wind and the waves obeyed him. Then they got to the shores and in the middle of a cemetery they found a naked maniac. Not a very peaceful trip, then. Jesus had to deal with him until he was clothed and in his right mind again. So they got back in the boat to go back to where they had come from. It hadn't been a very successful holiday from that point of view, though it had from other points of view. As soon as they got back, there was a terrific crowd. This was in the days when Jesus was a superstar when he had the biggest fan club there had ever been in that country. It was in the days before that dreadful thing happened – that occasion when a crowd of five thousand plus dropped to twelve in just one sermon. This was still in the days when Jesus was mobbed by fans wherever he went. I call them fans because that was about the level of the crowd devotion that he had in those early days.

It says they were jostling him, pushing him, in fact the literal word translated in the New International Version says, "They almost crushed him." You can imagine the disciples in that, trying to keep up with him trying to get a bit of breathing space and being jostled and crowded. Suddenly, within that crowd, something happened. There was one woman in it. We need to know a little about her background. She suffered from perpetual menstruation. Now that had a double effect, which we need to realise. It not only meant considerable physical debilitation and discomfort constantly, it meant social ostracism. It meant she was unclean and could not mix in the synagogue.

That is why I say she was a lonely woman – not just suffering physically but suffering socially and indeed spiritually. This woman had tried every doctor she knew, and she had spent every penny she had on them. Doctors are never paid by results. It would be quite a revolution in the National Health Service if they were! So she had spent all her money on doctors and had nothing to show for it. So she tried Jesus as a last resort and got the first result. It is a pity when people regard Jesus as the last resort, though many people come to him that way. He doesn't turn them down because they have tried everybody else first.

I think there is a lesson here. When we are sick, should we not go to Jesus first and ask him what to do about it? I believe that he may sometimes still tell us to go to the doctor, but isn't it important to go to him first, and say, "What do you suggest I do?" Anyway, she came to him last. She was the kind of woman who did not want to be noticed. There may be one or two in any congregation just like this: scared stiff of doing anything public. She was shy – understandably, for twelve years she had been in this condition.

So she thought, "While there's a big crowd I'll just edge through and I'll touch the tassel of his cloak – not the hem. You see very often in those days the outer cloak was a big square of nice linen with a tassel at each of the four corners, which you threw around your shoulders. In fact Jesus had a rather special one. Some dear lady must have put all her love into it and sewn him a very special one. It was seamless, it was made out of one large, woven piece of cloth. When they came to crucify him and they took it from him, they wanted to keep it in one piece so they gambled for it you remember. It would have the four tassels hanging down. She said, "You know if I could just get through and in between someone's legs and just touch that tassel...." Superstition to believe that a bit of wool could cure you? — no, not superstition but faith, because anybody's tassel would not do. It had to be the one worn by Jesus, and that's faith.

Oh I know her ideas were not very sophisticated. I know that it was rather simple to think of touching his clothes, but nevertheless it was simple faith not superstition because it was directed to the right person. So she reached through between two people and she just touched. Immediately, she knew her body had dried up. She felt it, the flow stopped, she knew. You could imagine her being so thrilled with her blessing that she was going to creep away through the crowd. She had received health, which is perhaps one of the greatest practical blessings in life. If you have got your health, you can cope with most other things. If you lose that, everything else becomes a burden.

So she was just turning around to creep away when a voice rang out, "Who touched me?" Can you imagine her heart at that moment? The joy was replaced with horror, and the crowd were all turning around to look. What's going on? Dreadful moment! Now, if only Peter had kept his big mouth shut! Peter said, "Don't be ridiculous Jesus.

Everybody's touching you." An implied rebuke or criticism, and Peter was not above criticising our Lord in these early days. It comes out again and again but you know, it is just as bad to think criticism as to speak it, and Peter was of the temperament that speaks it. At least you know where you are with that kind of a person, more than you do with the people who just think it.

But the kind of implication, if I may paraphrase it, was this: "You're a bit touchy today, Jesus, aren't you? Getting worried about people jostling you?" He just did not understand one vital truth about healing– that it is not magic. It's not like a conjuror. It is simply a transfer of strength from one person to another. Therefore, one can only gain at the other's loss. Now that's a truth about healing that we don't always realise. It is true at a very practical level. It can be true physically in ordinary medical and surgical treatment. But in spiritual healing it is true to a much greater degree. It was not magic. It is that Jesus has within him health – he is life, and in him is life. Therefore somebody could draw on his resources. But you see, Peter hadn't realised this yet. He thought that Jesus had a magic power. He didn't realise that when Jesus healed he was giving himself. He was transferring health and strength. Peter had not realised that Jesus' resources could be depleted, nor how Jesus himself replenished those resources.

If you read the Gospels carefully, you find out how he did so. He had to go and plug in and get recharged, sometimes all night, to keep those resources up and Peter never realised this. Before we leave this account, may I draw out one lesson for you here? Here you are, jostling together. You are a crowd, you've come near to Jesus because Jesus is right here by his Spirit. You are close to Jesus, but there is such a difference between jostling in a crowd near Jesus and an individual reaching out to touch him—that's totally different.

If you just jostle in the crowd you might be interested, you might see things that are interesting – but the people who go away different are not those who have just been near Jesus, but those who in faith have stretched out a finger and touched him, believing that is going to solve the problem and that you can draw resources from him. These are the people who go away helped. The jostling crowd around Christ is not helped but the woman who touches is helped. Do you come to jostle or to touch? There is a difference.

Now we come to the third event: a little girl. Now this third incident actually brackets the second that I have mentioned. It started before and it finished afterwards, and that is part of the key to the story. It started with a man who was an elder of the synagogue, who had a little girl of twelve, and she was dying. He came to Jesus. It sounds as if he came first.

"Can you do anything? Please come," he asked. So Jesus said, "Yes I'll come." That's when the crowd was jostling him and so the whole crowd came along. It was in the middle of that that the woman stopped him and there was this crucial delay.

If the elder knew the woman, I can imagine him feeling: she's been ill twelve years, she has plenty of time – my daughter just has a few hours, minutes maybe. Often we can feel our problem is more urgent than somebody else's. We look at it at a human level and we say, "Why doesn't everybody think of my problem? Mine's more serious." We forget that with God time is not so urgent as with us. But after the delay, as soon as Jesus resumed his journey, some people came from the house and said, "It's too late, she's dead."

Can you imagine the heart of that man at that moment? His feelings towards that woman? His feelings towards Jesus? But Jesus turned to him and asked two things of him. First: don't be afraid. Second: only believe. These are the conditions in which Jesus is pleased to operate: no fear, but only faith. So he came to the house and there were the professional wailers outside, wailing as usual – as you hear in the Middle East at a funeral. Jesus told them to stop it. He said, "It's alright, she's asleep."

You know I can see that he took steps to hide what he was going to do. First, by saying she was just asleep, in a coma. Second, he turned them all out. He only took Peter, James, and John. He didn't take the other nine of his twelve disciples at this point. He wanted the fewest possible people to be there, so that there wouldn't be gossip afterwards.

Third, he got the father and mother and he swore them to secrecy, and said, "Now you must never, never describe what happens in this bedroom." Peter was one of the three who went in. Jesus reached out a hand and said, "My little girl, get up." She got up. Now the parents would be so much in tension at that point that Jesus with wonderful consideration and sensitivity to their needs said, "Go and get something ready for her to eat." What thoughtfulness, what sensitivity! So they came out of the bedroom. I think it must have been the hardest thing Peter was ever told to do, to keep quiet about that.

Can you imagine it, going out, with people crowding around? Was she just asleep? –Yes. That wasn't a white lie because, to God, death is just sleep from which we wake up. He can wake the dead. But it was the first time Peter had seen anything like that. For all human purposes, to all human thinking, death is the end beyond which you cannot do anything. It's the point at which you say, "Don't bother the Lord any more." Now Peter knew that even death couldn't have the last word when the Lord was in the picture.

Those were the three occasions. Peter was left because he couldn't speak – it was all locked inside and he was left with an indelible impression with that third case, so much so that years later he could remember the exact words in the

Aramaic language which Jesus used.

I draw two conclusions from these three incidents. There is a sequel and we see it years later. We have looked at what Peter said and did at the time, now we look at what he said and did many years later. Firstly, Peter *remembered* what he had seen and he *preached* about it. In those early weeks with Jesus he had learned three crucial things about the Christian attitude to bodies. Christ has a compassion for the whole man or woman. He doesn't talk about "souls" or "bodies" he talks about people. He didn't heal bodies. He didn't save souls. He saved and he healed people. That's important. We have a long way to go to catch up with his thinking. Otherwise we split a person up and we say their body is the doctor's preserve and their mind is the psychiatrist's and the pastor can look after the soul. But Jesus has compassion on people, and a doctor needs to see his patient not as a body but as a person, and a psychiatrist needs to see a client not as a mind but a person and a pastor needs to see people not as souls but as persons. That's terribly important. Peter learned about Jesus' concern for bodies – for practical needs.

At two crises in my life I went to visit a very saintly man of God. I had a long car journey to go and see him. I just saw him twice. The first time I went, I thought: it's wonderful of him just to give me the time to talk over this problem. But his first words to me were, "Now you've had a long journey, the toilet's just down the hall." I thought how very considerate for me as a person. The second time I went he said, "That sounds a bad throat, just wait a moment." He went into the kitchen, got a liquidiser, put a lemon in it, poured that out and put some honey in with it, brought it back and said, "Now drink that first." I was deeply impressed with this spiritual man because he had a concern for bodies. There was something Christ-like about that. It gave me confidence to share the deeper issues. Peter could have said, "We've dropped the fishing, we've dropped all the practical things now we've become these super spiritual saints." But Jesus had a *concern* for bodies.

The second thing Peter learned was Jesus' *contact* with bodies. One of the big snags about British society is that we are scared stiff of touching each other. Some men touch their dogs more than they touch their children. It is peculiar to our culture, but that is how we can express love for our children. Then they grow up and they get self-conscious about it, but when they are little, and free from the social inhibitions that are passed on to them as they grow up, they like a hug, they like to be touched. Jesus said, using the words of the prophecy, "Lo, I come to do your will, a body you have prepared for me," and he used that body to help people's bodies. Have you noticed how often he used his body when healing? He touched a leper. He took the mother-in-law by the hand. He took the little girl by the hand.

Our reaction to this is so often the reaction of Simon Peter on one occasion: "Lord, you're not going to wash my feet." I know of one case where a husband and wife got the big breakthrough in their strained relationship when they washed each other's feet.

The third thing Peter had to learn in connection with bodies was Jesus' *control* over them. After all, he made them in the first place and therefore he could remake them. Jesus could put his spit on people, make clay with dust, and put it on the person to heal their eyes. He was just doing what he had done in creation. He really was creating, not just healing, when he did that. We don't have perfect control of our bodies but he did.

Peter remembered this. If you study his sermons in later years, how often he mentions these things. For example, when he preached to the Jews on the day of Pentecost, what did he say? "Jesus of Nazareth a man attested by God to you with many miracles, wonders, signs...." When he preached to the Gentiles in Acts 10, what did he say? "Jesus of Nazareth, a man anointed with the Holy Spirit and with power ... and he went around doing good."

That's a lovely phrase, isn't it? He went around doing good and curing those who were sick. Peter never forgot. He preached it and he remembered it.

Not only did Peter remember it and preach it, he repeated it and *practised* it. He had learned well from Jesus. When Jesus sent the apostles out, he said, "Go out and preach and heal." Have I given you a correct quotation there? I wonder if you know. I haven't actually. He said, "Go out and preach by healing." Not two different things but all part of the same thing. Peter, having gained the confidence and faith, having learned by his mistakes, having walked with Jesus for those years, then was anointed by the same Holy Spirit in power who had come upon Jesus. Now Simon Peter went about doing good himself.

Those three cases were almost repeated in his own ministry. He went to the temple to pray and there was a beggar at the gate, lame for forty years – a man who asked for alms and got legs. Peter just said, with sublime confidence, "I haven't any money to give you, but I have got something else and what I have is yours." We take that as just the statement "Such as I have I give you" but it really was a *gift* because Peter would be diminished in his own resources. To give to that man he would lose something. He wasn't just magically saying the name "Jesus". Goodness would go out of him. We need to remember this. That is why you need to have the resources first to be able to do it. You need to replenish them afterwards. But he reached out, and the beggar leapt for joy, ran around the temple. Not long afterwards something happened very similar to touching the tassel of our Lord's garment. When Peter walked down the street they brought sick people and they laid them on the pavement that the shadow of Peter might cross them. Superstition? No, faith in Jesus. Those people were healed by Peter's shadow. If your faith is directed towards Christ it almost doesn't matter what the means is through which Christ reaches you, does it? As long as it is Christ you are looking to.

When Paul was a tentmaker, because it was hot he used a sweat rag. Do you know what that is? I used one in Arabia. You just tie it around your forehead when you are doing dusty work, to stop the sweat from coming into your eyes. So it says in the Acts of the Apostles that they used to take Paul's sweat rag to the sick. Again, not superstition, but faith in Paul's Saviour.

Then came the memorable day when Peter was faced with his biggest crisis. He went to a little place called Joppa, and when he got there they told him of a lovely lady in the church whose hands were always busy making things for other people – one of those practical ladies, good with a needle, who do good. They said, "She's died, would you like to have a look at the remains? She's laid out in the bedroom."

Peter thought back to the day when he went into the bedroom of that little girl in Capernaum. He said, "I'll go in alone." He went in and shut the door. *Talitha koum*. He remembered the words: "Get up." She did. Peter not only preached what he had learnt, he practised it.

I believe that the Lord is calling his whole church throughout the world to learn the lessons Peter learned. We are slow to learn them. We have our difficulties. We have our fears. We have our failures. Because faith healing has been brought into disrepute by charlatans and exhibitionists, we tend to run away from it. We have even argued ourselves into theological positions that all these things were simply done in the days of the apostles to ratify God's word – as if God would only heal a person to make a point. That is almost blasphemy. God heals because he has compassion on a sick person. He is not trying to win an argument or prove a point. Healing the sick is an end in itself – worth doing or Christ would never have healed those ten lepers. Just helping someone who's needing help, making those whole who are broken.

We are sometimes put off faith healing by those who have oversimplified the teaching of the Bible, who have, for example, said that God has no place for medicine or surgery. That is an oversimplification. There are some who have said that no Christian has a right even to sneeze! So we have run away from something that I think the Lord wants us to learn, like Peter. Not that Peter went everywhere emptying every cemetery or every hospital or doing every doctor out of business—far from it. But nevertheless, Peter learned. He learned that what Jesus did in the flesh he can do in the Spirit. He ministered. I believe that the Lord wants to call us to rediscover this, and all over the world it is being rediscovered. *Healing*, by Roman Catholic writer Francis McNutt, is one of the best books I have read on the New Testament teaching. One chapter, headed 'Eleven reasons why people are not healed' is one of the most practical chapters in the book. I believe it to be the will of God that within every local body of Christ some should be given a ministry in this regard, and that we should pray for that ministry and pray that God will give it, and use it for his glory.

3

MIRACLES AND THE MESSAGE

Read Matthew 14:22–33; 17:24–26

Matthew 14:22 describes an incident after Jesus had fed the five thousand. Having sent his disciples away, he made the disciples get into the boat and go on ahead of him while he dismissed the crowd. Then he went up into the hills by himself to pray. When evening came he was there alone, but the boat was already a considerable distance from the land, buffeted by the waves because the wind was against it. In the night, Jesus went out to them, walking on the lake. When the disciples saw him walking on the lake they were terrified. "It's a ghost," they said, and they cried out in fear.

But Jesus immediately said to them, "Take courage it is I, don't be afraid."

"Lord, if it's you," Peter replied, "Tell me to come to you on the water."

"Come," he said. Then Peter got down out of the boat and walked on the water to Jesus. But when he saw the wind he was afraid and, beginning to sink, cried out, "Lord save me."

Immediately, Jesus reached out his hand and caught him. "You of little faith," he said, "Why did you doubt?" When they climbed into the boat the wind died down. Then those who were in the boat worshipped him, saying, "Truly you are the Son of God.

Then Matthew 17:24. A very strange miracle. After Jesus and his disciples arrived in Capernaum, the collectors of the two-drachma tax came to Peter and asked, "Doesn't your teacher pay the temple tax?"

"Yes he does," he replied.

When Peter came into the house, Jesus was the first to speak. "What do you think, Simon," he asked, "from whom do the kings of the earth collect duty and taxes? From their own sons or from others?"

"From others," Peter replied.

"Then the sons are exempted," Jesus said to him. But so that we may not offend them, go to the lake and throw out your line, take the first fish you catch, open its mouth, and you will find a four drachma coin. Take it, and give it to them for my tax and yours.

An intriguing little story, it takes me back to the days when I was a pastor in the Shetland Islands and learnt how the fishermen used to turn on their short wave radios and sing hymns when they were out at sea – which their wives would listen to with headphones onshore. The hymns were a kind of reassurance to the families that they were alright. There was one little village where most of the women wore black and most of the people there were women, because from that village thirteen boats set out fishing one night and got right into the eye of a hurricane-like storm. One of them ran against the wind and fought through, battering through the waves. The other twelve ran with the wind. One got back – the one that faced the storm and battled through. The village was bereaved of its menfolk.

We are looking at four miracles connected with the sea. In these miracles Peter is in an environment which he understands, or thinks he understands. The miracles are so remarkable that if you talk about them today you will have two opposite reactions. I have discovered that although I was brought up in an age that didn't regard the miraculous as believable, this situation is changed. There are two reactions to wonderful events like these. There are those who say, "No, I cannot believe that Jesus could tell Peter to go and fish, and he would find the tax in the fish's mouth." Even scholars said that. One very well known scholar wrote in his commentary that Jesus was in fact telling Peter to go and fish, and sell the fish and get the money and pay the tax. Those who cannot believe in the miraculous divide into two groups. There are some who say miracles *can't* happen and some who say miracles *don't* happen. These are two different objections to miracles. Those who say miracles can't happen say simply that this universe is a cast iron system of cause and effect run by laws – it is a machine, and you can't suddenly make the machine do something opposite to those laws. On their view, miracles can't happen. It is a closed system, like a watch—God may have made it and wound it up, but it must run according to its laws and nothing can change that. The weather goes according to meteorological laws and nobody can change the weather, therefore there is no point in praying about it. You can expect miracles in your heart but not miracles outside you—that is this viewpoint.

That view has been eroded through scientific discoveries which have really altered the picture. For example, the discovery that matter was not indestructible, but could be destroyed, that it could be turned back into energy. That made people think again of material miracles. Then the discovery that in the nucleus of an atom there are certain behaviour patterns there that are random and not mathematical ones, and that in the tiny universe we call the "atom" there are random facts which suddenly means it is no longer the fixed system that we thought it was.

There are other discoveries too, notably Einstein's theory of relativity (coming from a Hebrew mind). He realised that the universe is far more flexible than had been thought – not fixed. Wonderful possibilities were opened up, and terrible possibilities such as the atom bomb. So you don't hear so many people now saying that miracles can't happen. But you do hear still a lot of people saying they don't happen, that God could do these things but wouldn't, and that in fact they haven't happened.

Usually, people who say this do so on this ground: "I've never seen one." Just because you have never seen a thing doesn't prove anything, does it? In fact, if they did see one they would think there was some other explanation. But I believe that today the opposite viewpoint, the viewpoint of the credulous, is the greater difficulty. We have lived through the discovery of more wonders in my lifetime than in any previous era—so we have got to the point now where we believe anything, and we lose our critical faculty. We swallow whole the most fantastic things. It is partly due to the fact that we have become used to such things as landing a man on the moon. When it was announced that one of the astronauts had played golf there, people just said, "Mmm, interesting," and walked on. For by then we had had three or four moon shots and the thing had just grown stale. Many have lost their critical faculty. A credulous generation will swallow the most fantastic story without asking the right questions. Proof of this is the popularity of books and films which mix a little fact and a lot of rubbish and yet are believed – and the appeal of science fiction is also remarkable.

Now I thank God that I have a Bible to read which is not fiction but fact. It does not ask you to believe *anything*, it asks you to believe those things to be true which actually happened. One of the striking features of the Bible is that there is no trace of human imagination in it. Even the most extraordinary things are retold in such a matter of fact way that they might be describing hanging out the washing. You know: go and fish, Peter, and you'll find a coin in its mouth. So Peter went and he did. It is just so matter of fact. The word "fantastic" doesn't occur once in Scripture. The word "terrific" or "great" does, but in its true sense. The language of hyperbole – exaggeration – is just not to be found in scripture. In a matter of fact way, miracles are described quite factually by eyewitnesses who were there at the time and I reckon that a man who was there at the time is in a much better position to tell me what happened than a man who is writing about it two thousand years later. I am prepared to accept what was written because the reports, the records of these firsthand witnesses to these miracles, would stand up in any court of law.

In a court, if four different witnesses describing the same event do so in exactly identical terms, you can smell a rat straight away! They have got together and cooked up the story. But if four independent witnesses describe the same thing, then there will be apparent discrepancies due to them being truthful. There will be the slight differences that come from the difference of outlook of different people. The Bible has the ring of truth. Apparent discrepancies disappear on close examination of what actually happened. The testimony for the resurrection would be accepted by any jury in England if that kind of evidence were offered for any other event. The reason why people won't accept the evidence for the resurrection is that they don't want to, because if they did they would have to change.

Now look at the miracles connected with Peter here. We are going through the life of Peter to see Peter himself, and the Lord through Peter, and to get the feel of Peter's own reactions to what happened, and to see how he changed from the reed into the rock, from an unstable character, easily swayed, to someone absolutely firm who was prepared to go to his death for his faith – and the miracles were part of his education. First, we return to the miraculous draft of fish. Peter thought he knew that sea, he thought he knew fish, but he didn't. He had toiled all night and caught nothing and, as he came back to shore, Jesus was preaching to a crowd. He borrowed his boat for a pulpit and pushed out from the crowd so he could speak across the water to the people – and you know that acoustics are very fine bouncing across the water, and you can call a long way like that. At last Peter's boat was some use that day. If it was no use for fish it was for a pulpit.

We learn from this that obedience is vital to success. However crazy the command seem may be, however contrary to your experience and accumulated wisdom—to obey the Lord is the secret of success. Peter learned that lesson here, and later in life in the episode of Cornelius.

A second lesson he learned was this: Jesus calls his followers to live dangerously. He said, "Out into the deep" and that was not where they normally fished. They fished in the shallows where they could catch the fish between the bottom and the surface. To go out into the deep was to expose oneself to the possibility of storm. It was to get out of one's safe environment, and I believe the Lord calls us to do that. Time and again, when we have been discussing things to experiment with, in church and fellowship and evangelism, people said to me: "But isn't there a danger in that?" I say, "Well, yes, there certainly is and we make mistakes, but I'd rather live dangerously because that's where the Lord wants you to live." Once you get a phobia about the dangers of something, you really don't go any further. The Lord says: get out into the deep with me. It is more dangerous out there but I want you to live dangerously. In fact, it is safer out in the deep with Jesus than it is in the shallows without him.

The third lesson I learned from this, which Peter learned,

is this lovely theme: you can never get the Lord in your debt. Have you ever tried? Peter, alone in the boat, may have thought: well, that's rather nice of me to lend him my boat when, after a day's toil or night's toil, I should be going home to bed. Jesus, when he had finished preaching, said to Peter, "Now let's go and get some fish." He gave him more fish than he got for a whole night's labour, so much that he couldn't cope with it – the net was breaking and the boat was sinking. If you try to get God in your debt, owing you something – see what happens! The Lord will never allow himself to be in any man's debt, and you will find your nets will break.

Peter didn't learn the lesson thoroughly at this stage because later, as we shall see, he once said to Jesus, "You know, Jesus, we left everything to follow you." Rather proud of it – the sacrifice he had made.

Jesus said, "Peter, no-one has left anything for me, houses, lands, family, possessions, that will not be repaid one hundred fold in the world to come." Peter had to learn that the Lord owes us nothing; we owe him everything. He gives us far more than we deserve.

Now we return to the miracle of the coin in the mouth of the fish. At first sight it looks like a little tax evasion but wouldn't it be nice if we could go and fish for our tax just like that? It was a tax paid not to the civic authorities but to the religious authorities. It was a temple tax. It kept the temple going, which was a very expensive building to keep up, and all the priests and all the sacrifices cost a lot of money. So every male Jew over twenty years of age had to pay two days' wages (a drachma was one day's wage) to the religious authorities to keep the whole show going in Jerusalem.

There is no doubt that somebody was trying to trip Jesus up, and said to Peter, "Does your master pay the temple tax?"

In other words, can we find a loophole in him? Can we point out that he's a bit of a rebel, religiously speaking? Peter said, "No I'm sure he pays." Peter had met out in the street the man who collected this tax. Once a year they set up a booth in the middle of the street and collected these two drachma from every male. No doubt the man in the booth called out to Peter as he walked along the street, "What about your master, is he going to pay up?" The amazing thing is that when Peter walked into the house Jesus said, "They've been talking to you about our tax, have they?" Before Peter said a word. The thing that comes out in this story is the miracle of knowledge. Now it is one of the gifts of the Spirit – a word of knowledge, to know something that only God knows, to know what's happening in someone else's life or in some other place.

It can be a very simple and helpful gift. I remember one day that I called a lady whom I hadn't rung up for nine months or more. She said, "Why have you phoned?"

"I don't know, you tell me," I replied.

She said, "You know, I've been trying to get through to you for half an hour. I'm in real trouble and I needed you badly, and there's something wrong with the phone. So I just put the receiver down finally and said, 'Lord, get me through to Mr. Pawson.'"

And I knew I must ring her!

She said, "It took less than thirty seconds to get through with God."

How lovely to be given knowledge that God has, if it is going to help someone.

Jesus had this gift of knowledge supremely. He knew about things that were happening somewhere else; he knew about people. He knew when Lazarus died, even though he was miles away at the time. He said, "Peter, they're asking you about tax are they? Then let me ask you a question.

Do kings tax their sons or others?" This is a pretty relevant question. Jesus is saying that this tax is for God's house: I am God's Son, that is my Father's house. I'm exempt from this tax, I'm a Son in the royal family so there should be no tax to pay. That is a profound principle and Jesus shared it with Peter. Now comes the big shock in this – Jesus said that they were going to pay it anyway. He tells Peter to pay up for them.

Now before I deal with the miracle let me just underline this tremendous truth – that Jesus was teaching: I'm exempt. I have a right to claim that I have no duty to pay tax to the temple. It is my Father's house. I am his Son and therefore I should not be taxed to live in my own home. But in fact he said, "We're going to pay up lest we cause offence." Oh for the wisdom of Jesus, to know when to stand on principle and when to give way lest we cause offence. It is the most difficult part of the Christian life, isn't it? To know the principle but know when you don't need to apply it, and to know when to apply it would give offence wrongly. He doesn't mean simply that somebody would be upset. When he says, "Lest we give offence," he means: Lest we put a stumbling block in the way of someone, lest we make it more difficult for someone else to do the right thing. That is the important point.

A fundamental concern of a Christian should not just be my principles, and "I'll stand on my rights and my exemptions" – but if I do so will I make it more difficult for someone else to do the right thing? A profound principle which led Peter years later to write in 1 Peter, "Be subject to every human institution for the Lord's sake." Now there are times when we could stand on our rights. The day is coming when churches will not be looked upon favourably by the authorities. It may be right for us then to say, "Yes, lest we give offence, we will not stand on our rights or exemptions."

We don't want to make it more difficult for anyone else. What a profound truth there is here: you should consider other people as well as your own principles when you are considering a course of action. Will it cause them to stumble? Will it trip them up? Will it make it more difficult for them? You can still hold to the principle and not practise it. You can still hold your own conviction but consider other people.

Let's look at the miracle. If you go to Galilee today and cross the lake to a little café on the far side in the little kibbutz of Ein Gev, you can sit on the seashore on a lovely terrace looking down into the waves. You can see the fish, and they will give you fish and chips and they are delicious. The fish will be a rather flat fish but quite a deep one. If you can imagine an oval shaped fish about nine inches long. It's called to this day, "Peter's fish". It's quite a well-known species in the Sea of Galilee. There are many species in there. It is a very rich freshwater lake, but this fish is a mouth breed or with a large mouth, which is almost a pouch, which serves in the same way as a kangaroo's pouch, and they carry their young in their mouth. The young swim in and are protected within the mouth of the mother fish, then swim out again to find food. It is quite remarkable to see this. I have seen photographs of it close up through a microscope, tiny fish making for the mouth of the parent fish. Now when a fish is feeling particularly motherly or fatherly and has no babies, their mouth feels empty. So they have the practice of picking something up to fill their mouth. It is a kind of dummy family, a sort of compensation. They pick up bright stones and all kinds of bright objects, and indeed they have been found to have picked up rings and other objects that have been dropped in the water. Anything that sparkles or is bright, they pick up and carry around in their mouths. No doubt this is what had happened here.

Do you think I have explained the miracle? Nothing of the

kind. It is only one fish in a thousand that is doing this. Jesus said, "You take a line, not a net. Take a line, catch one fish and that fish will provide our tax," and sure enough it did. It is a miracle of the knowledge of Jesus. He knew that fish had that coin in its mouth, and he knew how much the coin was worth too. It was worth four drachmas and he got that coin, exactly the amount. Now he said, "Pay up for you and me," which brings me to another lovely truth in this miracle and it is that God can shift money about like nobody's business, and he does so in the most unexpected ways.

He meets our material needs in extraordinary ways. In the middle of the jungle, there was a man of God, C.T. Studd, on missionary work, and he broke his dentures. He needed them to survive because he was struggling with chewing the local food. He just could not eat without his teeth. So he got on his knees in the middle of the jungle, miles from anywhere, and he prayed for a new set. The very next day he ran into a geographical expedition of about a dozen men, and among them was an equipped professional dentist who gave him dentures, enabling him to go on working for the Lord in the middle of the jungle. How God answers prayer!

Tom Rees, was seeking to buy Hildenborough Hall, a beautiful home, high on the North Downs overlooking Sevenoaks. It was built and owned by a knighted man of the name of Lyle, of sugar fame. Tom had a gap of just ten thousand pounds. He tried to get the price down but there was still a gap, so he prayed. A few days later, a friend of his called him and said, "Tom I have you very much on my heart and my prayers this morning; I felt burdened for you. Are you in need?" Tom said no because he knew this man was not in a position to help him as much as he needed. The friend said, "Tom, I think you are. Is it money?"

"Well yes, it is, but it's more than you can help me with."

"Tom what would you say to an interest-free loan of ten

thousand pounds?"

Tom replied, "I didn't know you had that."

"A member of the family has died and I've been left a little farm, a smallholding, and I already have one which I work. I don't want another. I'm going to sell it and I'm prepared to lend you part of the proceeds."

A few days later, he called Tom again. "Tom, the loan is off."

Tom's heart sank, and he said, "Well never mind. Thank you for making the offer."

"No," he said, "the loan is now a gift."

"A gift?"

"Yes, you can have it."

"Why is it now a gift?"

"Well," he said, "the smallholding has been sold and it was sold for ten thousand pounds more than it had been valued at, so I feel that I must give away the difference, and so the ten thousand pounds is yours."

"Oh," said Tom, "tell me why it was sold for ten thousand pounds more?"

"Well it was bought by a big firm and not just a private buyer and they want it for their purposes."

"Oh, what was the name of the firm?"

"Tate & Lyle."

It is only God who can shift money around from the seller to the buyer in order to buy, but I find that no different from telling Peter to go and fish for it – do you?

Thank God that he is the God of the miraculous today. Whatever your need, God can meet it, maybe in an extra-ordinary, unexpected way – but he is a God who knows where all the money is, and all the silver and gold is his. That is why, years later, Peter could say quite calmly, "Silver and gold have I none" – because all the silver and gold belongs to his Father, and it is great to be the son of a multi-millionaire.

Now let's go back to the miracle of walking on the water. Our Lord was defying not only gravity but specific gravity for the specific gravity of the human body is a good deal greater than the specific gravity of water, and water cannot support a human body under normal circumstances. It shows the total control that Jesus had over nature. There was a full moon that night. It was Passover time. The wind was high, the waves were high, the disciples were beating against that storm in their little boat.

Can you imagine the scene – waves rising up, and just as a wave went down one of them said, "Look, there's someone coming," and they looked. The wave rose again and then went down. They caught a glimpse of a figure, a bit eerie in the bright moonlight, walking on the water. It was enough to unnerve anyone, and they were terrified.

Jesus called out, "It's alright, don't be afraid." How many times Jesus said "Don't be afraid" – and he still says it, because fear cripples. How often fears of all kinds of things get us down, spoil us, cripple our witness. "Fear not. It's I." Now it is in that situation, when your fear goes, you tend to be over bold. Peter again, literally, put his foot in it – and found it supported him. He said, "Jesus, if it really is you, I'm going to come and meet you on that water. Could I do what you do?"

Jesus did not come near the boat, take his hand and help him. He just said, "Peter you step right out of that boat and come along." Peter was going to learn some profound lessons on faith. Number one, he was going to learn that faith has to *act* first before it can prove. Now that is so important with almost every supernatural ability, every gift of the Spirit: you don't know you have got it until you *use* it. You have no assurance that you are able to use it until you actually do. That is what holds up many people from exercising gifts of the Spirit – they just don't realise that they have to *do* it.

They must step out of the boat before they can discover that they can. Jesus said, "When you pray, believe that you have what you've asked for and you'll get it. In fact you have it as soon as you believe."

Faith must *act*. It's no good saying in my mind: well, I accept that Jesus could help me to walk on the water. That's no use at all. It's no use my mind saying, "I believe in miracles." In fact, that kind of faith the devil shares with you. He believes that there is one God, and he trembles! In James chapter 2, where that statement is made about Satan, James takes one of the best men in the Old Testament and one of the worst women and says that they both had faith because they both acted on their faith. They both stepped out of the boat. It is only when you really burn your boats, when you cut your past, when you launch out in real faith, that you discover that you are upheld. Peter did not have faith until he stepped out of the boat.

The second lesson that he had to learn about faith is that it has to keep its eyes on Jesus and off everything else if it is going to continue working. Peter learned the lesson which most of us learn the hard way: as soon as you get your eyes off Jesus, things go wrong and down you go. The fact is that Peter could not walk on the water except *in* Jesus. He was not becoming a water walker, a professional who for ever afterwards would say, "Roll up and see the water walked," and then preach to them afterwards. As far as I know, he never did this again – and this was a private occasion, not for public demonstration. It was to prove one point: Peter wanted to know if that was Jesus, because if it was, Peter could do something that otherwise he couldn't do. If it wasn't Jesus he would have gone straight under. It was his way of proving that it was Jesus. That is how you prove that Jesus is there—by launching out and finding that you didn't sink and you didn't go under.

There were two men in the north of England who were drowned trying to walk on water to prove this point to the public. I think the coroner recorded death by misadventure. That is very sad. It shows how foolish some people can be in taking the scripture to illogical conclusions. But I have no doubt that when this is part of the kingdom it can occur.

Now for the last miracle of Peter I will mention here. Peter wasn't directly involved with the miracle of the feeding of the five thousand. Andrew was the one mentioned. He brought the little boy. Peter was one of those who, along with eleven other men, had an empty picnic basket – they had eaten the lot, privately, out of sight of the crowd. They only had empty baskets left. Perhaps that's why they made excuses and said, "Lord, you would have to buy two hundred pennyworth of bread to feed all this lot" – and a penny was a penny in those days! Peter was one of the twelve who gathered up a whole basketful of fragments for himself afterwards. Twelve baskets full! It is as if the Lord said: you should have given your food, but I am going to give you a basketful of food from what is left over.

Peter sat munching this basketful of fragments, thinking the whole thing through. The next day Jesus preached to the crowd again, and this time he preached the kind of sermon that people don't like. He gave them a few home truths about themselves, and he said, "You came back today because you had a loaf of bread yesterday, right? It's all you're interested in. You're not interested in the next world, only in this one. You're not interested in spiritual bread, you're only interested in physical." Now that's not the way for a tactful preacher to begin a sermon, but that is how Jesus began. Then he went on to some things which were so difficult that they were puzzled by what he meant. He said, "I can give you life forever. I came here from heaven and if you eat my flesh and drink my blood you can live forever too, in heaven."

That day, Jesus' congregation went from five thousand down to twelve people. That's a big drop. If you don't give people what they want, unless they are sincere in seeking the Lord, they soon drop off. These people were not really interested in Jesus. They were interested in themselves and their stomachs; the material blessings of this world, not the spiritual blessings of the next – and Jesus told them so.

Jesus sadly watched them all go, and he saw that crowd disappear. Jesus was not the kind of preacher who would rather keep them. He would rather see them go than have them under false pretences, coming for the wrong reasons. He said to the twelve: "Do you want to leave too?" Then Peter came out with the most wonderful statement: "We have no choice. We're going along with you because you've got the words of eternal life." Hallelujah for this. Here is a man who has seen miracle after miracle after miracle and he says, "You've got the message."

The crowd wanted the miracles, the sensational Jesus; Peter wanted the spiritual. The crowd wanted material blessings in this world; Peter wanted the blessings in the next. Peter said that they had no alternative. There was no-one else who speaks about eternal life.

The tragedy of our own credulous day is that people are more interested in the sensational than the spiritual, the miracles rather than the message. You can fill your Sunday newspapers with miracles and the sensational and people will buy and read it, but if you try and give them the words of eternal life it is a different matter. A crowd goes down to the few who really mean business and who see that Jesus is the only person to turn to. Who else can you go to? There isn't a politician who talks of eternal life. There isn't a scientist who talks of eternal life. There isn't an entertainer who can offer you eternal life. There's no-one else to go to if eternal life is what you want.

What is eternal life? Two things. First of all, life in unimaginable *quantity*. It is life that goes on through death and goes on and on through the centuries, on and on forever. Some people say they don't want eternal life, they don't want to live forever. Fred Hoyle the astronomer said: "I want to live for 300 years but then I think I'd be fed up with life and I don't want to live any longer than that." But you see it depends on how much life is to you as to how much you want of it. If you have nothing to live for, you don't want any more life; if you have a little to live for, you want a little of it. If you have a lot to live for, you want a lot of it. The more love there is in your life, the more you want to live, and the more you can't bear to think of dying.

That's why eternal life is not just life in quantity, it's life in *quality*. It is the good life in every sense of the word "good". It is the real life in every sense of the word "real". It is life of such quality that you couldn't bear it to have a finite quantity. It's life that is so good that you can't bear the thought of it coming to an end. Jesus said, "I can give you that kind of life that has such a quality about it that you will want an infinite quantity of it."

Jesus replied: one of you is a devil but I can count on eleven of you. Those eleven started the church.

I don't think there is a miracle you can find in the Gospels that isn't happening today – yet the big thing is not the miracle but the message. The miracles are signs pointing to the message, they are God's confirming of the word with signs following. The important thing is that miracles don't give you everlasting life. They usually just help you through a crisis in this life. *It is the message that gives you eternal life*. It is not the works of Jesus—he may heal your body but your body still has to die. He may provide money that you need badly, and unexpectedly he provides it, but that only keeps you going so long.

Lord, to whom can we go? You are the only one and you know this world in which we live is full of millions of people trying to find life, trying to find life of a better quality, and the tragedy is that if they found a life of better quality they would still have to leave it if they found it outside of Christ. But *in* Christ is eternal life – life of such a good quality that we don't want it ever to end, and it never will. Lord, we are going with you all the way.

4

WHO DO YOU SAY THAT I AM?

Read Matthew 16:13ff

For most of his earthly life, Jesus lived incognito. His assumed name was "Jesus" and people simply knew him by that name and his address – "Jesus of Nazareth", or they knew him by his foster father whom they thought was his real father: Joseph. But for over thirty years people really had no idea who he was. For two and a half years, Simon Peter lived with Jesus and didn't know who he was. He never asked directly, and Jesus never volunteered the information, and so for a time there was a kind of conspiracy of silence.

The only people who knew who Jesus really was were the demons, the evil spirits who possessed various people and who said to Jesus, "I know who you are," and they shrieked this out. Jesus always commanded them to be quiet; he was travelling incognito. Before our Lord could get on with his main work his disciples had to know who he was, but they had to know without him telling them. This was absolutely vital to their education. The knowledge had to come from inside them, not outside them. So for two and a half years he bided his time, judging the exact moment when he should see whether they had discovered the truth. Not only did he choose the exact time when he put this question to them, "Who do you say that I am?" but he chose the exact place.

You should always read your Gospels with a map in your other hand, tracing the journeys. It is not for nothing that Jesus travelled around so much. For example, you find that the Sea of Galilee in his day was divided into three coastlines, and three separate rulers controlled that little lakeshore. So whenever he got into a boat to cross to the other side, he was deliberately moving from one ruler's sphere to another to escape for some reason. This time he had judged the moment had come to ask them the critical question. He took them far to the north, to the very border of the land of Israel, to the furthest town. It was then called Caesarea of Philippi, named after the Roman Caesar and the local prince, Philip, one of the four sons of Herod who was given that patch of the holy land by the Roman authorities, though he was a Gentile.

There is something unique about that place. Let me paint a picture of it. You are at the foot of a four thousand foot high mountain, and at the foot it doesn't slope gently down—it comes almost like a cliff in reddish rock. From the foot of this cliff, through no visible opening, a river appears – through a crack which must be under the water surface, and it is a crack that comes right down from the top of the mountain, for the water consists of melted snow coming down inside the mountain. It is a river that has no beginning or end, the Jordan River, and it meanders two hundred miles. If you go by boat down the river or sixty miles as the crow flies to the Dead Sea, there it finishes. It is the strangest river in the world. You wouldn't be surprised if I tell you that from time immemorial this place has been regarded as a religious centre, a shrine for pilgrimage.

At first, because it was such an unusual natural phenomenon, it became a centre of the fertility cult—that foul religion of which you can find traces in most parts of the world. They worshipped a male and a female god. The male was called Ba'al and the female was called Astarte. It was nature worship. So this place was named Ba'alius. Later, the Greeks took over the location. There is a cave in the cliff and they said the god of nature was born there. They called the god of nature "Pan" so they changed the name of the place from Ba'alius to Panius. The Arabs called it Banias.

Later still, the prince called Philip was given this place, and by this time the Roman Caesar had got so big-headed he began to claim that he was divine – that he was god not man. He was giving himself divine titles like "lord" and people were having to say "Caesar is lord." Now prince Philip was so grateful for being given this plot that he said, "I'm going to erect a new temple to the god Caesar." High above the source of the Jordan there stood in those days of our Lord a white marble temple dominating the scene, a temple to Caesar. So here, at this religious shrine, Jesus came with twelve men. There they stood, surrounded by statues of gods like Pan who had been thought to become men, and men like Caesar, thought to have become god. It seemed as if "god" and men were all mixed up at this place, and you didn't quite know where one began and the other ended.

Jesus said, "Now I have some questions to ask you." Question number one was: who do men say that I am? Do you see how gently he eased them into the challenge, how without telling them who he was, by the very place, he was beginning to shape their thoughts and, by asking them for the opinions of others he was getting them to share first? You may have found in a house group that when you discuss what other people think, it is much easier than discussing what you think.... Peter said: Nobody thinks you're an ordinary man. They all think there's something unusual about you. They can't quite figure out what but there's something different. You could not be at the age of thirty-three the man you are unless there's some extraordinary explanation. So they're trying to explain you....

Jesus is saying, "Well how do they explain me?

Then these Jewish men who could never have believed this answer said: some of them are saying that you are a reincarnation, that you couldn't be what you are today if you hadn't been someone else before, and you've come back after centuries maybe, but you've come back and you've come back with all the wisdom and knowledge of your previous experience; they can't quite figure you out, they know you came from somewhere and they're trying to figure out where.

So Jesus would say to those twelve men, "Oh, and who do they think I was in my previous existence?"

"Well some say Jeremiah and some say another of the prophets, and some say Elijah, and some even think it's John the Baptist but he didn't die until after you were born so that's a silly answer" – and so they would discuss it. It was a very interesting discussion until, with devastating directness, Jesus said, "Right let's finish with other people's opinions. Let's have your own. Who do you say?"

If Jesus had got the wrong answer to that question – it's one of the big "ifs" of history – I just cannot imagine what would have happened. He might have had to wander around with those disciples another two and a half years. It was the watershed of his ministry, for from this point he turned his face straight around, with his back to Mount Hermon, and he set his face to go to Jerusalem and to die, and six months later he was dead and buried.

Up to this point he wandered all over the place in the north and in the south and sometimes in Samaria in the middle, but from now on it is a straight line. From now on there is a directness and a purpose in his walking and there's a set in his face, and it was all made possible because he got the right answer to this crucial question. It was Peter who blurted it out. He no sooner thought a thing than he said it. Thank God for such people. It can be a means of rising to the heights. I am afraid, as we shall see, the same quality can drag you to the depths. If you open your mouth you do put your foot in it. Someone has said, "Better to keep your mouth shut and be thought a fool than open it and remove all possible doubt."

Eleven of those men were too scared to open their mouths. One of them at least had the courage to say it. That is why he became the spokesman of the early church; that is why he preached the first sermon on the day of Pentecost. God can use someone who is prepared to speak out, even if at times they say the wrong thing. Peter said it, and you have almost got to have Jewish blood in your veins for at least ten centuries to be able to get the flavour of what he said: "You are the Christ."

When you have been waiting for someone to come for a thousand years and you are able to say, "I believe you're the one we've been waiting for" – the very excitement of the moment doesn't get us Gentiles so excited. You are the Christ; you are the one we've been waiting for, for all these centuries. You're here; you've come.

Then he went on to say something else. You see, Jesus had been using cryptic, ambiguous titles of himself up to now. He always went near the truth but never quite stated it. For example, he called himself the Son of Man. Well that's a very ordinary phrase. It's used many, many times in the book of Ezekiel about Ezekiel and it means, simply, "Son of man." I am a son of man. You are a son of man or a daughter of man.

It is just a phrase that means somebody has been born of man, yet Jesus talked about "the" Son of Man, and tucked away in the book of Daniel (7:13) it says, "You will see the Son of Man coming in clouds of glory." It is just that one usage – everywhere else it means an ordinary man. Jesus used this very ordinary phrase with the one particular exception that could point the way to the truth. What a clever title to use. Rather than saying "I was born", Jesus said, "I came". "I came to seek and to save the lost." Now that is not a natural phrase. You don't talk like that, do you? Talking about your life, you don't say, "I came here," do you? You didn't come here from somewhere else. Do you notice the little phrase "I came..."?

Then there is that most ambiguous phrase of all: "I am". He was always using it with great stress. In the Greek it comes through clearly. He put it in sentences: "I am the bread of life", "I am the light of the world", which left it ambiguous. People could be excused for thinking it was just saying things about himself rather strongly. But the name "I am" is God's name, and it was hidden there. It was as if he was giving them the truth but hiding it all the time, so that only those who had ears to hear would hear it, and that was why he spoke in parables. They were such nice stories but only if you listened very carefully did you get the message. So for two and a half years he had been taking them to the brink of truth then bringing them back again by using ambiguous titles; by hinting all the time he had been giving them pointers, but not one clear one.

They had observed him and they had noticed that he never lost an argument, even from the age of twelve. They noticed that there was no situation beyond his control, even a storm. They had noticed over two and a half years that there wasn't a single flaw in his character. They had noticed that he was more intimate with God than anyone they had ever met. They had noticed that he preached with a firsthand authority, which was not dependent on the knowledge of the book. All these things were adding up, and Peter, in a blinding flash of light, saw the truth and came out with it – and now the moment of truth had arrived. You're the Christ. You're not the Son of Man only. You've been using that phrase haven't you, to hide the truth? Now I see it.

Jesus, in Matthew, says to them, "Who do men say the Son of Man is?" Peter's reply means: you're the Son of the living God; you're not a reincarnation, you're an incarnation; you've had a previous existence, but not on earth – in heaven. Jesus, if I may paraphrase, says, "Peter you're absolutely right. Peter you're just son of Jonah, aren't you? Simon, son of Jonah, you're right. I've been waiting for that answer for so long." Now let me underline two things. First, that no man told it to Peter, including Jesus. Nobody had instructed him, nobody showed him in a book. Nobody had written it on a blackboard. Nobody had said to him, "Peter, that's the Christ, the Son of the living God." It was inside knowledge rather than outside. He came to it inside his own heart.

Secondly, I want you to know that it was *inspiration* rather than intuition. It was not Peter's own discovery, and Jesus said, "I'm just so thrilled, God has spoken to you."

As a preacher I seek to instruct in the Word of God – from *outside* – but what a thrill it is when someone tells me afterwards, at the door, that God spoke in their heart; and that the *instruction* was matched with *inspiration*. It seems to come from inside. Someone comes and says, "You know when you said so and so, that was just what I needed, and it was God's word for me."

Now I have a fairly good memory after a sermon and I know when someone has said this that those words attributed to me I have never said but God was speaking inside your heart in such a real way you were convinced you heard it from the pulpit. It was not me, it was God. Isn't it exciting when God reveals to the human heart things that no instructor can pass on? So with Peter, it wasn't *instruction* nor was it even *intuition*, it was *direct inspiration*. Peter's chest must have been swelling. His head must have been a bit too, because he came such a cropper in a moment. He was just so thrilled to have given the right answer, chalk it up, you know? That's one up to me. I came out with it. Look at all those other eleven, they kept their mouths shut. I said it.... But the fall was not to come for a moment. Peter was learning the first of three lessons, which I'm going to pass on to you, which everyone needs to learn. Lesson number one: *We need to be prepared to confess Christ in front of others.* No matter what they might think, to confess Christ and to say, "I know who he is." He's not just a great teacher; he's not just the great reformer. He's been called so many things in his time. He's not just the carpenter from Nazareth. He's not just the master. *He is the Christ, the Son of the living God. We ought to be ready to say so in front of other people.*

Well now, Peter blurted it out first. Now he was told the second thing that he needed to know. For the very first time Jesus uses the word "church". It is no use talking about the church until you have talked about the Christ – no use trying to build people into the church until they have confessed the Christ. That is the order. You cannot build a church on people who have not confessed the Christ. These things are very carefully ordered and Jesus had been waiting two and a half years to tell them about the church and he had not mentioned it once so far. In all the Sermon on the Mount there was no mention of the church. In all his teaching so far there was not a single mention of the church, but now for the first time Jesus says: I have got something to build on; now I can build my church.

Do you notice that he will *build* his church? I can't build the church; you can't build the church. It is only as people have revealed to them from the Father who Christ is, and come to a living faith, that the church can be built – and it is Jesus who builds it. I could preach myself blue in the face trying to build up a church, trying to make Christians. I can't do it. All I can do is give the Word and pray that God the Holy Spirit will so speak to you in your heart that you say to Jesus, "You are the Christ, the Son of the living God." Then we can build you into the church, for Christ has already done so. And so he starts talking about the church.

I want to tackle a thorny question which still divides professing Christians from one another, particularly Catholics and Protestants. If anything, the Catholics have made too much of this passage and the Protestants have made too little, and I believe the truth lies between the two. Catholics have said, "This is the moment at which Christ appointed the first pope," and Peter became the first pope of the Christian church and there have been successors to Saint Peter ever since.

The church can only unite under such a pope. I have been to St Peter's, Vatican City, and seen that bronze statue of Peter with the toe worn away by pilgrims kissing it. I believe that has made too much of Peter, and Peter himself would not wish it. But, on the other hand, Protestants have made too little. We have tried to wriggle through this text, saying that the rock on which Jesus was to build was Peter's faith – only his faith, not Peter himself, and that the church is built on a faith like Peter's. I don't think that gives the place to Peter that he deserves to have, for Peter was not the first pope but he was the first pastor. He was the rock on which Jesus built the church. There is a subtle play on words here. You know that Peter's name was originally Simon, which means a reed, and Jesus said, "I'm going to change it to Petros", which means a rock. But there is a specific meaning to it, and I will come back to that in a moment. Now if I can give you the two words Jesus uses, he says: "You are *Petros*, and on this *petra* I will build my church."

Now if he was saying straight, "You are Peter and I'm

going to build my church on Peter," he would have used the same word "Petros", but he didn't. He is using a masculine word the first time and a feminine word the second. That certainly doesn't mean he was intending to have a lady pope. What does it mean? Peter was married, remember. What does it mean? Well, the masculine word for rock, which is *petros*, means a piece of rock that has been separated from its original strata – a lump of rock. In your rockery at home you have lots of "petroses". But if you go to the Lake District or Devon, Dartmoor, you will there see *petra* which is the rock in its original position, all joined up in a formation as strata. Now are you beginning to see the subtle thought behind Jesus' words here?

He's saying, "Peter you're the first lump of rock cut from the strata that I can use to build." But the rock on which I'm going to build is the whole thing, not just you. Can you see that? He is saying, "You're the first bit of rock I've got." Any stone-built house – and most of the houses in the Middle East are stone from the limestone hills of Judea – is a lump of rock chipped from the rock and put in place, and then another lump is chipped and put into place, and so it is built up.

Years later, Peter would have been horrified at being called pope. He called himself a fellow elder with all the elders of the churches to whom he wrote. But he also said, "You are living stones being built up into the house of God, a dwelling place for God, a holy place for God, living stones," and it is all there. Peter was the first "living stone". The church began to be built that day, the first rock hewn out of that stratum of rock, the first lump of faith that Jesus could build on. Therefore Jesus decided to make him the first pastor, and to build the church, and in Acts 1 to 13, Peter dominates every page. He was the beginning of the church so don't let us rob him of his place.

There are two important things that Jesus says about this church. The first is that the gates of Hades will not prevail against it. That could mean one of two things. I am going to leave you to choose between them. First, I wish we could get away from this mixture of Hades and hell. They are two quite separate words in scripture.

Our Lord used the word "Hades" here, not "Gehenna". Gehenna is the word for hell. "Hades" was a neutral word, meaning simply the world of those who had died, the world of spirits separated from their bodies. What he is saying, I believe, is this: that when members of the church die and their spirits depart to the other world, they do not cease to be members of the church. The gates of Hades closed on everyone else. They don't on Christians. The church is the only society on earth that never loses a member by death. As to the ancient people of God, Israel, as soon as a Jew died they lost him to the people of God, but not the church. The church goes right on, and the gates of Hades can't close its gates against the church – cannot separate us. Think of someone you have known and loved in Christ. Think of them at this moment. They are part of the church, and the gates between us and them are wide open. Christ links us to them. We enjoy the communion of saints – church militant, church triumphant, one church all together.

There are those, however, who take the word Hades in a more sinister way and assume that the term corresponds to the gates of a Jewish city where sat the leaders of that city – those who controlled the city; those who controlled the gates. The more sinister thing comes because death is not a natural event. Death is the implement, the weapon of Satan and his forces against us. If this is the meaning, Christ is saying, "Whatever the underworld of evil powers tries to do against the church, they will not prevail." Whichever way you take it, whether in its neutral or in its sinister meaning,

Hallelujah! – the gates of Hades are helpless when it comes to the church.

The other thing that Jesus says is a little more puzzling. If "the gates of Hades" is a puzzling phrase, than "the keys of the kingdom" are more puzzling still. Keys are used not just to open, as many Protestants have tended to take this phrase, but also to lock and to close. I want to feel my way very carefully into this phrase, which is a very important one. It concerns the discipline of the church.

You have probably seen a symbol of two keys. There are many jokes about Peter guarding the pearly gates and opening up to people arriving. Let me point out first that these keys are to be used on earth, not in heaven. Therefore, Peter only used them while he was on earth. He is not using them now. They are for binding and loosing on earth, so they are not the keys of heaven. They are the keys given to God's church on earth to open up to people or to close to people, to bind or to loose. Secondly, I want you to notice that these keys were not just offered to Peter, they are mentioned in two other places – in Matthew 18 and John 20. On one of these occasions they are offered to all the twelve disciples, and on the other occasion they are offered to all believers.

Therefore I believe these keys are not Peter's prerogative. They are only his as the first living stone. They belong to the Christian church on earth. We have the keys of the kingdom. It is a solemn thought. What kind of keys are these? They are the keys of preventing someone reaching heaven or the keys of allowing them to do so. I think we have to take terribly seriously that the church has this power of discipline – not an independent authority that we can exercise apart from the Lord, but only in the Spirit and in the Lord we have the power to shut heaven from people and the power to open it.

There are times when that power has to be exercised, both negative and positive. Peter did not use these keys until after the day of Pentecost, and woe betide the church that uses these keys without the Holy Spirit. That is why, in John 20, Jesus breathed on them and said, "Receive the Holy Spirit. Whatever you bind on earth will be bound in heaven. Whatever you loose on earth will be loosed in heaven" – in connection with the gift of the Holy Spirit, and by the power of the Holy Spirit this is what I believe it means. It means that the church does have the power as Christ's body to open or shut heaven to other people.

Now our normal duty is to use those keys to open as often as we can, but there come times when they must be used to shut. God will guide in those times. There is a serious side to the discipline of the church, which is mentioned again and again in the New Testament which, alas, modern, comfortable, affluent churches tend not to take seriously. The matter of discipline is complicated today, in that if one church exercised the keys to shut, somebody could get in their car and go three hundred yards down the road and find a church that would use the keys to open – that is a problem. But let me mention some instances. Paul says to Corinth, "Deliver this man to Satan." Look at how Peter exercised this. Do you remember when Simon the magician tried to buy through money the power to confer the Holy Spirit through laying on of hands, and Peter looked at him and said, "To hell with you and your money"? That is a literal translation. Or think of Ananias and Sapphira, two church members in the early church who said they had given so much to the church but they had not given that much, and it was a lie to the church. How did Peter deal with that? He said, "You will die," and the husband died, then the wife came in and Peter told her she would join her husband. There is Peter exercising the keys. He is exercising very serious discipline, and Christ is saying: "You will be exercising a discipline that will extend to heaven, that will apply as much in heaven as on earth," but it can only be done in the Spirit. As I say, one of the tragedies of church history is where the church has got away from the Lord, and out of the Spirit, and has tried to use the power of the keys. When that happens the church becomes a tyrant, the Inquisition follows, and awful abuses occur. But because the abuses have occurred we must not nevertheless run away from the power of those keys that we have.

That we have the keys of the kingdom in our grasp as the body of Christ is a solemn responsibility, so it is a serious thing to belong to the church.

Peter must have been so overawed by this, and then the whole situation went wrong. For Jesus began to speak of the third thing that he could now talk about, something he hadn't mentioned until now in any clear way. Now that the Christ was known, now that the church was revealed, now the third thing could come along: the cross. It says, "From that time he began to tell them that he must go to Jerusalem and suffer many things at the hands of the elders and the teachers and the priests and to die, be killed, and the third day rise again." Peter didn't catch the last phrase. He was so shocked by all that went before it that he never caught the phrase "the resurrection".

When the resurrection occurred, Peter was just as surprised as anyone. But he just could not bear the thought of Jesus suffering and dying. Do you see what Peter is saying? I tried to write down a sort of paraphrase of Peter's thoughts. These were some of the things I wrote down: Jesus, you've got entirely the wrong idea; Don't you understand the role of the Messiah? Now if I were the son of the living God I wouldn't do that. Do you see what he's saying? Jesus turned around to Simon Peter and changed his name yet again – to Satan.

Did you know Satan could talk through people? He can, and he can talk through your best friend. Someone close to you, who loves you dearly. Satan can use a human mouth.

Just so that you take this seriously, can I tell you what Satan does with some of the tapes of my talks? A minister in Brighton said, "We've got a woman in our church. She's just come to the Lord. It's very exciting. She's really been wonderfully converted, her son has been converted and her husband is very interested, and the whole family is studying the Bible together. They've started taking tapes from your church. They've started taking the tapes from the book of Revelation." Now there are two books that Satan hates – Genesis and Revelation. If he can persuade you that Genesis is all myth and Revelation is all fantasy, he's happy. He'll keep you out of those two books if he can because those two books describe his devices and his downfall, and they tell you everything you need to know about Satan.

When I gave those talks, we had some disturbances in church during the fourteen weeks we went through the book of Revelation, but in one of them I said, and it came out on the tape, "Satan is going to hate the next bit of this sermon. He will hate it." Now they were listening to this tape, and at that point my voice was jammed on the tape by a loud voice in a foreign language – shrieking. They could just make out my voice in the background. This demonic language had been put onto the tape.

For the next five minutes they couldn't hear a word I said. They sent for the minister. He came. He said, "Play it through to me." When they played it the next time that five minutes was totally wiped off the tape, and there wasn't any sound on it whatever. I told this to another minister the same day. He said, "Well that's funny, we've been having those tapes and we wondered why there were the blanks on them." If you don't believe that Satan can speak and can interfere with the revelation of God, I hope that will make you realise how seriously we must take him.

"Get behind me, Satan," said Jesus to Peter his best friend.

Then he said a very funny thing to Peter. He said, "You've become a rock of stumbling to me." Instead of a rock that I can use to build, you have become a rock I'm going to fall over. Oh Peter, what sort of a rock are you going to be to me? Satan is making you sit there in my path and stop me heading for Jerusalem. You are going to be a rock in my path and I'll fall over you.

What kind of a rock is that? Do you realise we are all living stones if we are Christians, and we are either stones whom Jesus can build up into his church or stones he is going to trip over. Which are we? "Get behind me, Satan." You're talking like men, not like God. You see, if men were going to be the Son of the living God, man would say, "Let's have all the glory and the majesty and the power. Let's have a revolution and impose it by force." But God said no, I'll do it by suffering and humiliation. Not a revolution but a redemption. God has his own way of doing things. Satan is always logical, but it is based always on wrong premises.

Peter must have felt very crushed and broken at this point. Pride goes before a fall, and it was to be another six months or more before Peter was full of the Holy Spirit and could be trusted to open his mouth and say the right thing, for the Holy Spirit is the only one who can cure this kind of problem of a talkative person who brings out the wrong and the right things, and is inspired one minute by God the Father and the next minute by Satan – and it can happen.

So Jesus said something more. He laid bare the real reason why Peter came out with that outburst, "Perish the thought Jesus. I'm not going to let that happen to you. It mustn't happen to you." Why did Peter say that? because he was so fond of Jesus that he couldn't bear to think of Jesus suffering? –No, the reason why Peter said that comes out in the next verse. Peter was afraid that if Jesus went to the cross he would have to as well—that's why.

So the next word that Jesus said was to all of his disciples. He virtually said this, "I'm going to Jerusalem to die and if you want to keep on following me, you'll have to take up your cross too. You'll have to deny self, take up your cross, and follow me." From now on that's the cost. Until now you've followed me around Galilee, healing, preaching—it's been wonderful but from now on it's the road of the cross. It is the Via Dolorosa from now on – following me will involve that. Peter, that's why you said this, isn't it? You can't bear the thought of a cross for yourself. You are still so worried about saving your own life, aren't you Peter? You're still worried about hanging on to this existence. Deep down, most of our instincts go back to the instinct of self-preservation in some form or another. It is the deepest instinct of all to hang on to our existence – to hang on to my life as it is and not to be willing to let my life go, and Jesus said, "It's a cross, not a crown. I'm the Christ but I'm a suffering Christ—that's why I told you not to tell anyone. They want a Christ with a crown, but I'm a Christ with a cross." So that's the third thing: the Christ, the church, the cross. He's saying, "Peter, how far are you prepared to go with me?"

I just conclude these thoughts about this great confession with three very simple questions. It is not whether you begin the Christian life but how far are you prepared to go? That is the decisive factor in the quality of your Christian life. Here are my three questions. One, are you prepared to confess the Christ in front of other people? That's the first thing that Peter was called on to do in this situation. He did it courageously, bravely, came right out with it, and he said it. Are you prepared to do that?

Secondly, are you prepared to be built into the church with all the discipline that involves, with all the responsibility that involves, with all the commitment that involves? There are an increasing number of people today who are prepared to confess the Christ but not prepared to be totally identified with the church, for you cannot be committed to the church unless you are committed to a local church. It is the only way to be committed to the church, for the church is a nebulous thing unless it is expressed locally in the body of Christ locally.

How far are *you* prepared to go with Christ? Are you prepared to confess him publicly as the Son of the living God? Are you prepared to commit yourself to a church of authority and discipline, a church that the gates of Hades can't prevail against? Well that's still not as far as Jesus wants you to go. He says thirdly, "Are you prepared to take up your cross, to let your life go?" Maybe in martyrdom or not, for Christians are being killed for their faith in various parts of the world today.

I'm asking you right now: if the crunch comes tomorrow morning between Christ's life in you, and your life, which will go? That is what it means to take up the cross and deny self and follow him – until you can say: "I live, yet no longer I, but Christ lives in me." That's the cross. The cross is not comfortable, it's painful and it kills self dead. So how far are you prepared to go? Simon Peter thought he was prepared to go a long way, but he wasn't, as we shall see, later, when he swore that he didn't know Christ. He still was in the grip of Satan at that third point. He was prepared to confess the Christ. He was prepared to be built into the church and to have the church built on him but when it came to the cross, yet Satan still had that part of his life, and Jesus made it quite clear: "Peter, if you try to save your life you'll lose it, but if you lose it for me, you'll find it."

There may be a real clash between the life that Jesus wants to live in you and the life you want to live in him or outside of him. At this point the cross looms up and Jesus asks you whether you'll get on that cross and submit to the nails as he did and have self, in the form of ambition or affection or anything that cannot be sanctified by Christ, nailed to that cross and killed. Tell Jesus how far you are prepared to go as you follow him.

5

JESUS TRANSFIGURED

Read Luke 9:28–36 and 2 Peter 1:1–18

Thirty years later, in his second letter, Peter wrote about the Transfiguration. It must have made a tremendous impression.

Mount Hermon is in the north of Israel. It has been a popular place for skiing, but in photographs the skiers just look black against the against the glistening background of snow. But I think of the time when a man stood on that very spot and made the snow look dirty, drab and grey.

What we are studying now happened a week after that great moment when Peter said, "You are the Christ." Now you notice that Peter said it before he saw it, but he saw it after he said it, and this is the order of Christian understanding. You say a thing by faith first and you see it later; it has to be that way round. Jesus waits until you have said it by faith before he shows it to you. That is the way he teaches how to trust him and how to believe in him – so that I have never seen Jesus face to face, but I say now that I will do, and I'll look forward to doing so. But I know that having said it, I will see it. I have never seen heaven and I can't imagine how beautiful it is, but I say it now—I'm going there and I'm looking forward to exploring those pearly gates and golden streets. One day I will see it, but I'm prepared to say it now by faith.

Jesus never showed his disciples his glory until they had said, "We believe that you're the Christ, the Son of the living God." They said that by faith and he could now show it to them, and they could see it with their eyes. He chose this mountain, the only mountain in Israel that has a snowcap almost all the year around – often all year round. In fact, though it recedes in the summer, it's still there and you can see it towering away up in the sky.

There is one tradition that the Transfiguration, as we call it, took place on a little mountain near Nazareth called "Tabor". But in those days the only thing on top of that mountain was not snow, but a large Roman garrison, and it is highly unlikely that this took place in the middle of a Roman fort. Apart from anything else, we saw that they had been in the far north at Caesarea Philippi, at the foot of this Mount Hermon. So when it says, "He took them up into an exceeding high mountain," it must be that mountain.

Let's go up the mountain. It is a long climb and it will take all day. We go up with Jesus, with Peter, James, and John—none of the other disciples. This was going to be pretty special for just these three. So we go up with them, up the mountain, by imagination. If you have climbed Mount Hermon, the one thing you want to do at the top is to sit down and have a sleep, which is precisely what Peter, James, and John did. They sat down and they were very sleepy. As the sun went down and the last gleam of sunlight on the snow faded, they must have cuddled together; they must have pulled their sheepskin jackets close around them and they must have got very close together. They got dozy and they began to droop their heads.

I don't know which of them noticed it first, but one of them began to notice that it was getting brighter again. That is not very helpful when you are trying to get to sleep, is it? The light began to dazzle, and it got brighter and brighter. When they shook themselves awake and looked around, they saw that Jesus had changed. It must have been a weird, unnerving experience.

They had lived with Jesus for two and a half years and he had always looked the same, and suddenly they saw him totally different – literally, in a light in which they had never seen him before. His light was so great, shining from him, that Peter later told John Mark, who wrote it down, that you couldn't have got his clothes whiter with any "fuller" on earth. We would say, "With any detergent or soap powder." It couldn't have got it brighter. It was just so bright that you couldn't bear to look at him.

The brightness was not so much shining on him, as if there was a special light from heaven shining down upon him, the light was actually shining through him. This was not reflected light, but if you want the scientific term, it was "refracted light" coming through his clothes, making them transparent so that the clothes just looked almost as if they were not there, as if it was just a ball of light standing, and they could just make out his face in the light.

With half-closed, sleepy eyes, you can imagine the scene. They were peering at him. "What on earth is happening?" Then suddenly they realised that he was not alone. There had only been four of them climbing up the mountain, and they had gone higher and higher, above the snowline, but now there were six of them. As they looked, they realised that the other two had been dead and gone for many, many hundreds of years. There they were talking, chatting with Jesus.

Now that was the experience. There are many things it points to. It points to the past, it points to the present, and it point to the future. So let's look at those three things. First of all, it points to the past. It tells us that saints, when they die, do not cease to live. That is not a contradiction. God is the God of the living. God is the God of Abraham, Isaac, and Jacob. We don't say, "God *was* the God of Abraham, and Isaac, and Jacob." He *is* and he *is* the God of Moses and he *is* the God of Elijah because these men are all very much alive. They are more alive than we are this moment.

In this moment, the three realise that the saints of centuries ago are very much alive and are conscious, and able to communicate and talk. It is one of the things that tells us the other world is a wonderful world. You will be talking with the Lord in the other world. We shan't be unconscious, not knowing what's happening.

Moses and Elijah were there. How did they recognise them? Have you ever wondered that? They didn't walk around with labels on, as if they were at a church social — "Moses", "Elijah". They had never seen them before, they had only heard about them. They had never seen a photograph of them. I can only speculate here, but I believe that in the other world, there is instant, intuitive recognition, and that as soon as you get there you will know exactly who everybody is. You will look over and say, "Why, that's Simon Peter. So that's what he looks like." You will know. You see people die at different ages. Often people have asked, "Well how will we know? How will we recognise them? We will have changed. Will they have changed?" Well, yes they will. How will we know? We'll just know.

If one of your relatives goes to Australia for ten years and then comes back to visit you, have you noticed how very quickly you can pick up the threads again? Even though they may have changed out of all recognition. Or someone you went to school with – it isn't long before you are right back in communication, is it? If that can happen as quickly as that on earth, it can happen instantaneously in glory, where we shall know even as we are known. So whatever the appearance of people, we will have no difficulty in knowing who they are.

But there are many more things than this. This shows the continuity of Old and New Testaments. It shows that Moses and Elijah belong together. What an insight into the past this gave, but it also gave an insight into the present. Now remember that three times already Jesus had tried to tell Peter and the others that he was going to die, that he was going to have to leave this world, that he was going to suffer and be killed by evil men. Each time they would refuse to listen and said: we can't accept it; we just can't believe it. Each time, he had come up against a brick wall. Do you know, if you are going to die, you have got to be able to share it with someone?

I remember hearing a tragic case of a hospital ward mostly full of terminal cases. There was the usual conspiracy of silence about all of them. The doctors and nurses weren't telling the truth; the relatives weren't telling the truth. There was a cleaner who went through that ward, scrubbing the floor, and each of the patients would talk to her and say, "You know, they won't tell me, but I'm going to die. I must talk to someone. Can I tell you?" With simple, practical, honest to God realities, she just helped them and talked to them and allowed them to get it out. Wasn't that incredible? I have very serious doubts about hiding the truth from dying people. I have seen some wonderful final days and months when people have been told the truth and it has been shared with them. They need to talk. The agony was already beginning and Jesus had to share it. He kept saying, "Peter, James, and John I've got to die; I've got to suffer." Peter would just say, "Never; you're not going to go that way. I just won't have it." Jesus had to say, "Get behind me, Satan."

So Jesus had to go back into the Old Testament to find someone who understood. He had to bring Moses and Elijah back into this world to have someone to talk it over with.

It says they discussed his departure. He was able at least to talk it over with Moses and Elijah and they understood. Both of them had had unusual deaths, but neither of them had suffered as he was going to suffer. But they understood that God plans your death as well as your life. They both understood that, because God had planned their death. So when Jesus wanted to talk it over with someone, his own disciples couldn't do it. As it were, he took them up the mountain to teach them the lesson that there were some people he could talk to about reality, and that he could talk about his departure at the age of thirty-three.

Furthermore, not only does it say they discussed his departure, but the word used is intriguing. It says they discussed his "exodus" which he was about to accomplish in Jerusalem. Marvellous man, Moses would be, to discuss exoduses with, wouldn't he? Moses would say, "Well, this is how my exodus worked." Jesus would say, "Well now, we are going to have another one – now it is going to be mine. Just as you put blood on the doorposts, the blood of the lamb, so that the angel of death passed over, this time I am going to use my own blood for my exodus." They talked it over. I would have given anything for a tape recording of that conversation, wouldn't you? To hear those two spiritual giants and the Son of God discuss his death and talk about the cross. So it was a great insight into the present too. Peter, James and John were being taught a profound lesson.

It was also an insight into the future. They were catching a little glimpse of Jesus as he would be when they saw him in heaven in glory. You see, when Jesus came to earth, he switched the light off, and he was no brighter normally than any other human being. The result was that for eighteen years, as he worked in the carpenter's shop, nobody had any idea that he was any other than a human being. "Is not this the carpenter's son, Joseph's boy?" They never guessed. For two and a half years he had never shown them his glory, never shown them how bright and radiant was his personality, but now the veil was drawn aside and they were on the edge of another world, they were on the edge of eternity. They saw his glory, just a glimpse, maybe for half an hour and it was gone. But they knew then what Jesus really looked like.

The Jesus that you and I see will be that Jesus in glory. The first time I see Jesus, I will see him exactly as he was on the top of that Mount of Transfiguration, not as he was as he walked the dusty lanes. I will not even see him as he was after his resurrection. I shall see him as Paul saw him on the Damascus road, brighter than the midday sun. I shall see him as Peter, James and John saw him on the top of the high mountain that day. Thirty years later, Peter says: "We saw his majesty on the sacred mountain." Sixty years later, John wrote: "We beheld his glory, glory as of the only begotten Son of the Father."

If you saw Jesus now against a white wall, the wall would look dirty and dark. You ought to be thankful you can't see his glory at this moment – you would be blinded. You will need a new body with new eyes to cope with it.

They saw him that night and he was dazzling. Somebody has said of Peter that he was so full of humanity he was spilling it all over the place. I'm afraid he was. He was frightened, and some people, when they are frightened, go dumb whilst others when they are frightened talk too much. Peter was of the second kind. Peter again just opened his mouth and put his foot right in it. Oh Peter, why don't you keep your big mouth shut until you are filled with the Holy Spirit? Then you can open it wide, but as long as fear makes you speak, as long as ignorance makes you speak, you say the wrong thing.

Look now at what Peter said: Master, this is just great. Let's keep it; let's stay up here forever. It's alright. I know it's cold, but we'll build a shelter for you to spend the night. We'll build a shelter for Moses and Elijah; we'll keep them too. This is marvellous. Let's just the six of us settle down up here. That's what he was saying, and of course, he was just so frightened he didn't really know what to say. How human that is – to want to capture a noble experience, to want to keep on the mountaintop. You and I are so guilty of this. We have a great experience of the Lord; we want to stay with it. We want to keep it; we want to capture it. "Oh, let's just stay right here. This is marvellous, let's live a mountain top experience."

A speaker was talking about giving testimonies. He pointed out that your experience may go up and down if you trace it on a chart – as "valleys" and "mountaintops". If you are asked to give your testimony, what do you do? You might draw an imaginary line about ten percent down from the top, and then you take all the peaks and you string them together, and you give your testimony. You may give a totally false impression of what your Christian life has really been like. You just give the high points because those are the ones you want to keep, but an honest testimony goes down into the valley too. It talks about the difficulties, the dangers and the troubles we have seen.

But Peter was speaking for all of us when he said: Let's stay up here. Let's settle down on the mountaintop. Let's stop thinking about a hill called "Calvary". Let's look at this sacred mountain, let's stay right up here, above that lot down there. Let's just be as near to heaven as this. Let's enjoy the communion of saints. This is heaven on earth. Of course it was, but it was not to be.

There may have been many ideas in Peter's mind. He may have been thinking of erecting three shrines – that would be a typical religious response. Whatever was in his mind, he had the honesty to say to John Mark thirty years later, "I was afraid and I didn't know what I was saying." But he got not one word out of his Master, not one word out of Moses, not one word out of Elijah.

One little thing I noticed as I read this passage was that he made the suggestion when Moses and Elijah had turned away from Jesus and were walking away from the mountain and going back to glory. It was as if he couldn't bear the thought of them going. He was trying to grab them back. Stay, it's alright, I know it's cold down here, but look, I'll build you a shelter. Typical response of a man who is more used to doing things with his hands than his heart and his head – typical response to do some earthly, practical thing.

This was one of those moments when Peter should have been using his ears and not his mouth. Some of us lose a great deal because we are using our mouth too much and our ears too little in relationship to the Lord. We want to use our hands for the Lord as well as our mouths, but the Lord says, "Use your ears." We become "Marthas" and we are troubled about many things, because our hands and our mouths are busy doing and saying things. Mary is the wise one who sits at the Lord's feet and says, "I'll listen if you want to talk." I am sure that when Mary sat at his feet and Jesus talked to her, he talked about his death. That was why she anointed him beforehand for the burial. She understood.

Jesus didn't say a thing to Peter even though Peter made the suggestion to Jesus: Master, I'll build some shelters for those two before they leave, and for you. Suddenly, down came the clouds and the light went dim. The whole thing was spoiled. The glory was going. How often we miss the glory of the Lord because we spoke, because we didn't just remain quiet and listen.

The cloud came down and the three men disappeared. Jesus, Moses, and Elijah were in the cloud, and out of the cloud came a loud voice directed to Peter, containing a double rebuke. Rebuke number one: "This is my beloved Son." When the cloud filtered away again, there was only one man standing there and it was Jesus. Do you realise what a mistake Peter had made? A week earlier he had said, "You are the Christ, the Son of the living God." Now, a week later, he had gone back to calling him "Master". Mature Christians rarely use the title "Master". Some young Christians do, and I have heard unbelievers use the term of Jesus.

You see what Peter was doing. He was putting Jesus back on a level with Moses and Elijah, back among those three. "Let's build three shelters" – you're all the same; you're all great men of God."

But God blotted out Moses and Elijah and said, "This is my beloved Son" – not Moses, not Elijah. Peter, you are getting all confused, putting Jesus in the category of great men of God.

The second rebuke from God himself to Peter, the only time in Peter's whole life when God spoke out loud to him, direct, he said, "Listen to him." Fancy having God himself rebuke you! Peter needed to listen to what Jesus was telling him.

When the cloud disappeared there was Jesus only. The light had gone out and they didn't dare tell anybody for months what they had seen. It was too holy, too precious, too deep. But what did it mean for Peter? I can only begin to guess at some of the thoughts that must have gone through his mind. He would certainly be convinced now that there was a life after death. He had seen Moses and Elijah. He was absolutely convinced now of who Jesus was; he had seen his glory. He had heard what he had said but there is something more than that. The amazing thing is this: first, that you and I and Peter will see Jesus like that again. When he comes in his glory, with clouds of glory, we shall see him shining as the sun. We shall see his lovely face. The transfiguration is an experience that you are going to have. You will see it and you will be about the same height as Peter, James, and John were – only you will be above the Mount of Olives. You will be in the air and you will see him as he is. But there is something more: when I see him, I shall be like him, for I shall see him as he is. Do you realise that if you could see Simon Peter now, you would see him glorified too?

In 2 Corinthians 3, it describes an experience that Moses had when he went up into Mount Sinai. He talked with God face to face and he came back down. When he came back, the people looked at his face and it was shining – fluorescent. They were so frightened of him, in fact, he took a veil and put it on his face. He hung the veil there so that they shouldn't see him. Gradually the light faded, until a few days later, he was back to normal. Just as a luminous watch catches the light and reflects it in the darkness, he caught the glory of the Lord.

Arthur Blessitt (who carried a cross around), and a friend of his, were walking by a lakeside late one night. He looked out over the lake and he saw a figure walking on the water towards him. He thought, "That's Jesus." Then: "No, I'm seeing things." He didn't dare talk to his friend about what he had seen because he thought his friend would think he was mad. But he glanced at his friend's face and realised he had seen the same thing. They watched, and the figure of Jesus came walking over the water, towards them very near, then disappeared. The two friends walked home in absolute silence and separated and went to their little flats in Los Angeles. Arthur went into his own flat and his wife took one look at him and ran, screaming, into the bedroom, slammed the door and locked it and wouldn't let him in, not until the next morning. When he asked her next morning why this had happened, she said, "Well your face was all shining. It wasn't you." When he met his friend later that day, he discovered his friend's wife had reacted in exactly the same way.

From that same passage, 2 Corinthians 3, "Not only did Moses have this glory reflected, but we all, with unveiled face reflecting, as in a mirror, the glory of the Lord, are being transfigured into the same glory." Think of that: shining faces being transfigured before the world. One day the world will get the greatest shock ever. It will see Christians, men and women they have known, men and women with whom they have been on the same bus and train up to London, men and women with shining faces, the glory of the Lord shining through them.

Peter was getting a glimpse not only of the future of the Lord Jesus but of his own future as well. One day we shall be like him. For the words that God said in that cloud, "This is my beloved Son", he only said on one other occasion. He said that phrase on the occasion of our Lord's own baptism, "You are my beloved Son".

Our baptism begins the process of getting us white, and clean, brighter than any water, soap or detergent on earth could ever get us. It is a cleansing that begins with the blood of Jesus when we ask for forgiveness, but it is a cleansing that does not stop until we too share the same glory that Jesus had before the foundation of the world. We shall see him and we shall be like him, for we shall see him as he is. Simon Peter will be whiter than the snow that day, and so will you, by the grace of God.

6

TEMPERAMENT

Hypocrates was the first to label four basic temperaments of man as the sanguine, the choleric, the melancholic, and the phlegmatic. He named these after the various fluids of the body, which he thought were responsible for the way we behave, so that the sanguine probably has a bit too much blood around him and therefore, is fairly outgoing and alert and energetic. The choleric – he has a bit too much yellow bile, thought Hypocrates. This comes out in a rather domineering leadership. The melancholic has a little too much black bile moving around his body and therefore tends to look at the black side of things. The phlegmatic has too much phlegm and is a bit heavy going in most circles.

Well, the medical reasons for the four temperaments are just not valid, but his division of four temperaments, two of them extrovert or outgoing, the sanguine and the choleric, and two of them are rather introvert – the melancholic and the phlegmatic – have become very useful labels, ways of identifying your own personality and finding out, therefore, what your weaknesses and what strengths are likely to be.

Most Christians pass through two stages. Temperament plays a vital part in your Christian experience. You see, when you become a Christian many things do change, but your temperament doesn't, any more than the height of your body changes. Yet something can happen to your temperament.

The two stages every Christian passes through are labelled in 1 Corinthians the 'carnal' and the 'spiritual'. But I would define those two stages in terms of your temperament. In the carnal stage, when the flesh is uppermost in the Christian's life, usually at the beginning as he battles with his old habits and old affections, his temperament governs his Christian experience, but in the second stage, the spiritual – when the Spirit takes over from the flesh – then Christian experience governs your temperament, and you can usually mark the watershed. You certainly can in Simon Peter's life.

For the first three years of his Christian life, his temperament controlled his experience. This comes out again and again, but the watershed came on one memorable Sunday morning at nine o'clock in the morning when Peter was filled with the Spirit and spoke in tongues. The weaknesses went and were overcome, though not entirely. He had his lapses later, and there is one notable one in Galatians 2, where he had a stand up argument with Paul.

So far we have been seeing Peter with temperament controlling Christian experience. There are five characteristics which I am afraid were the undoing of Peter. We noted that he was impulsive. Peter wanted to jump out of the boat to try and walk on the water, and he jumped into the water to swim to the shore to meet Jesus. He pulls out a sword to chop off someone's ear! You find that one of the favourite words of Mark's Gospel is often applied to Peter, "And immediately, straightway...." This is Peter: immediate response; immediate reaction. You can't hold him back. When he gets an idea, out it comes. He either speaks it out or he does it. His hand and his mouth are always running away with him. This impulsiveness is there all the way through. It was an impulse that led Peter to run to the tomb on Easter Sunday morning.

Let us look at the second weakness of this temperament.

It is restive. It doesn't like sitting still, much preferring to be busy doing things with the hands. There is Peter on the Mount of Transfiguration, the holiest moment of his life, and he says, "Let's build three tabernacles". It is Peter who later can't even wait for Jesus to get to Galilee to meet them after the resurrection. He says, "Let's go fishing."

The third weakness is being talkative. Do you know that we have more words of Simon Peter recorded in the four Gospels than of any other disciple? Therefore we also have more replies to Peter than to any other disciple. Thank God for that, we have got some lovely parables because Peter opened his mouth. But we also have some of the severest rebukes that Jesus offered.

We are going to see three of these between Mount Hermon and Mount Calvary. During this period, Peter went through a very difficult patch, but one that was vital to his development, and preparation for his being filled with the Spirit. Peter was always opening his mouth—sometimes it is a great word, sometimes spontaneous: "Depart from me, a sinful man, O Lord." Sometimes it is an inspired word from the Father, "You are the Christ, the Son of the living God," Sometimes it is from Satan, "Never, Lord; you'll never go to the cross. Far be it from you, Lord." So he keeps coming out with these words all the way through. It's so quick.

At the transfiguration, when Peter saw Moses and Elijah about to leave Jesus and wanted to keep them, it says, "Then answered Peter and said, 'Let us build three tabernacles.'" Well, who asked him? The sanguine person answers questions nobody is asking. "Then answered Peter...." no one had talked to him. Always giving answers before he is asked the question! When Jesus says at the last supper, "You're all going to run away...." – "I won't." Like lightning comes the response. Talkative Peter! Peter who, when that temperament came under the control of the Holy Spirit, would be the spokesman of the church, the first preacher on the day of Pentecost.

God can use talkative people far more than he can use the silent saints. Once he's got that temperament under control, God can do wonders with a Simon Peter because he's willing to talk, willing to let it out. The trouble is that when your temperament is controlling your experience, then frankly you will often let out the wrong thing.

Fourthly, a weakness of this temperament is that it responds very quickly to circumstances and people around it. It is too easily influenced by environment – from outside rather than inside. So when Peter stepped out on the waves and looked at Jesus, he could walk on the waves – then he looked at the waves, and immediately his temperament sank. He was influenced by the circumstances.

Or when he was standing, warming his hands at a fire, and there were people around; he was in the wrong company and within minutes he was going back to his blasphemous language or that of a fisherman. He was swearing that he didn't know his best friend. But once that temperament is under the control of the Holy Spirit, he ceases to be responsive to the environment in a cowardly way, and responds in a courageous way, and now tackles a situation with boldness.

The temperament doesn't change, but you can see in a Christian where the temperament and spirit are that way round. The watershed was Pentecost for Peter, but the last three months leading up to Calvary were the crucial preparation for what had to happen later.

The final weakness is that this temperament is very emotive – it tends to feel a situation rather than think it. This kind of temperament can be very near to tears. Peter went out and wept bitterly. Only men of certain temperaments weep as readily as that, and for Peter emotion was near the surface.

With that introduction, let me now take you into three passages that all happened after that mountain peak of Mount Hermon. From there, the trail goes down and down and down to Calvary. Hundreds of feet down geographically and physically, but a million miles down spiritually. Peter had to be bruised.

Remember that the name "Simon" meant a reed, someone easily shaken in the wind – upright, maybe, but not strong. Peter was to become a rock. Before the reed could become the rock, the reed had to be bruised, not broken. One of the predictions of Isaiah 42 about the Christ, when he came was: "a bruised reed he will not break." You can almost say, "A bruised Simon he will not break," but there had to be a bruising.

Temperament does not submit to the Holy Spirit until that temperament has been bruised, humbled, humiliated. We see that in this three-month period when Peter began to do something that he had not done before to any great extent. Every time he spoke now, he spoke about himself personally. Everything Jesus said, he took personally. Now that is a great step forward for a sanguine temperament because the greatest weakness of this temperament is that it can be seen very easily in others – it is almost impossible to see it in yourself, and therefore you tend not to examine yourself too much. Typically, extroverts examine other people but not self, whereas introverts do so much digging around in their own soul, it will do them good just to forget themselves for a bit. Some people put the spiritual thermometer in too often, and keep looking. "How warm am I this week?" Throw the thermometer away and get busy in the service of the Lord, you who are always taking your own temperature – but some of you never do. Peter had tended not to apply things personally, but look at the difference now.

The first passage is where Jesus has been speaking a

parable, an intriguing one. Peter's normal reaction to a parable, which comes out earlier in the Gospels, was: "Explain this parable to us." For example, Jesus once said when he was criticised with his disciples for sitting down to a meal without washing hands: "Nothing going into a man's mouth can make him unclean. It's only the things that come out of his mouth that make him unclean."

On that occasion Peter said, "Explain the parable to us." Jesus said, "Well, any dirt that goes into your mouth just goes straight through and out with the excreta, but it is the dirt that come out of the heart that comes out of your mouth and that's what makes a man unclean. These Pharisees have got it all wrong. Getting clean in God's sight isn't a matter of washing your hands, but getting your heart right."

So Peter at that stage, was simply intellectually interested, Explain this parable. What did you mean by that? That was a bit of a cryptic remark, Lord. But now see what happens; now Jesus tells a parable about a man who has gone away to get married – gone to the wedding reception, and he is going to come back. His servants are in the house, waiting for him to return. Jesus says, "Blessed are the servants who are waiting and ready to open the door, immediately he comes with his bride."

Then another parable, "If the householder had known what time the burglar was coming, he would have sat up and watched and his house would not have been burgled." Now Peter does not say, "Explain this parable to us." He says, "Are you telling this parable against us or against everybody?" Are you getting at me or was it just a general sermon? Now can you see the beginnings of applying a thing to himself – just the beginnings? From: "explain this to us" to "are you getting at us?" Peter is beginning to feel the personal application.

We are going to see this become clearer through these last

few months. Jesus is teaching: am I getting at you? —well, let me tell you another parable and you can work it out from there. Often Jesus didn't give a straight answer to a question, but gave the kind of answer that made the questioner think more fully about the application to himself. Jesus gave another, similar story. A man went away from his household and left a manager in charge of his servants, and he left the manager to see that the servants got the food. But while the master was away, the manager said, "Oh, he may be gone a long time. I won't bother." He got slack and abused his position. He didn't feed the servants and, said Jesus, he will get caught out when the master returns.

Do you see what he is teaching? Peter, do you want to know if that general parable applied to you? Well I apply it to you as manager. As manager in my household, I have made you the first pastor of the church and I want to find you looking after my servants when I come. A very personal rebuke. In fact, there's a very serious thing Jesus says, and you can work out the theological implications of this at your leisure: "The master coming back and finding the manager not looking after the servants will give him a lot with the unbelievers." That's a pretty stern word for Peter.

Peter, you see, the rock, the foundation of the church, is feeling a bit big for his boots and he is thinking he is above parables getting at him, but Jesus is saying that greater privilege brings greater responsibility. He finishes that parable or that answer to Peter by saying, "If you've been given much, much is required of you, Peter. The fact that you are manager doesn't make you exempt from my teaching; it means that all the more is expected." So Peter got the message the first time.

Let's move on to the second. This time it's in Matthew 18. Again, feeling it personally, Peter says, "Lord, how many times do I have to forgive my brother? Seven?" As much as to say, "That's about the outside limit for me and that's very generous." It was, by current Jewish standards. Let me just put it in the context. Remember that, just a few weeks before, Jesus had said to Peter, "I give you the keys to lock and unlock. Whatever you bind on earth will be bound in heaven. Whatever you loose on earth will be loosed in heaven." Peter is now saying, "How often do I have to use the keys with my brother?" I wonder if he had had a bad day with Andrew, or whether he is referring to his fellow disciples as "brother". One of the problems with following Jesus is that you can't follow Jesus alone; you have to go along with the others who are following him. For every one of these twelve men who had followed Jesus, they had to live with eleven other men and they were just so different. There were collaborators and terrorists in the same bunch. There were people who worked with their hands and people who worked with their heads. You know, I cringe when people say churches must be just one social group or another and all those who work with their hands should be at the mission hall down the road. It is just so unchristian—to follow Christ is to follow with all the others and learn to get on with them.

Jesus has recognised that if you put a bunch of different people together they are going to tread on each other's toes. They are going to offend each other, hurt each other. Indeed, if you are not close enough to hurt your fellow Christians, you are not close enough to them. When two people marry, they get close enough to hurt each other. In Christ, brethren should be close enough to hurt each other.

Jesus assumed they would – he had no delusions about human nature – so he said, "When your brother hurts you, when he offends you in some way, you must not talk to anyone else. You must go straight to him first before you go to anyone else." How much worry would have been saved if we had always followed that! But supposing he doesn't listen and say sorry. Then take two or three fellow Christians with you and talk to him as a group. If he still won't listen to you, tell it to the church and let the church speak to this brother. If he still won't listen, put him out of fellowship. Let him be to you as a Gentile.

Then comes the question from Peter: "How long do you have to go on forgiving? Seven times?" If he had gone to a Jewish rabbi of his day, do you know what the answer would have been? Three—the Jewish rabbis taught that that's all that God could expect of human nature. If your brother offends you, if your fellow Christian, or fellow believer, or fellow member of the people of God does something to you, the Jewish rabbi would say, "Three times; that's as much as you can do. Then you can let him have it."

Now Peter thought: I am sure Jesus will have a higher standard than the rabbis. He usually does, so we'll double up. We'll say two threes and add one in, and that makes a perfect number anyway—seven. Seven times, Lord? That's very generous. You know, that's really pushing me hard. Jesus said, "No, seventy-seven." I know your old version says "Seventy times seven", but "seventy-seven" is probably more accurate. Does that mean I can count them up and on the seventy-eighth really let him have it? Jesus read Peter's heart like a book and told him a story. There was a man who owed one million pounds. He went to his creditor and he said, "I can't ever pay it." His creditor said, "Alright. I'll forgive your debt." Then he went to a friend who owed him five pounds, and said, "When are you going to pay me that five pounds you owe me?" He said, "Peter, when the first creditor heard about that, he said, 'You pay your million pounds to the last penny or you go to prison." If you're not prepared to pass on the mercy that I give you, then you won't get it.

In fact, what is wrong with asking the question, "How many times shall I forgive my brother?" Because you are envisaging a limit, because you are drawing a line, because your heart is not a heart of mercy, because a heart of mercy will go on and on. In that little story there is a very profound truth and that is: how many times would you like God to forgive you? Seventy-seven? Do you realise that if you have only sinned once a day, either a sin of commission or a sin of omission, something that you should have done that you hadn't done, or something that you should not have done that you have, if you have sinned just once a day for the last thirty years of your life, you have already ten thousand sins to deal with, and God has every one of them recorded—just one a day!

If you expect to receive more than seventy-seven from God, then you must give more than seventy-seven, for it is a fundamental truth that mercy is like electricity – it cannot flow until the circuit is completed. However much I reach out one hand to God and say, "Mercy, God, have mercy on me, a sinner," if I do not stretch out a hand of mercy to those who have wronged me and complete the circuit, the mercy cannot flow. It is not so much a bargain; it's a challenge to our hearts. That's why in "The Lord's Prayer" Jesus said, "When you pray, say, 'Forgive us our trespasses as we forgive....'" We complete the circuit, Lord, so it can flow. We don't *deserve* God's forgiveness by forgiving others, we just make it possible.

So what Peter was told meant beyond counting. Don't be a calculating forgiver, God isn't. If God were, then frankly, if we had only seventy-seven to play with, I would think that every one of us is heading straight for hell, wouldn't you? Dare we ask for more from God than we are prepared to pass on? Yes, Peter, you are thinking about yourself, but you are still thinking about yourself the wrong way. You've got a calculation there that is not of God.

Why did Christ say "Seventy-seven"? There is only one

other passage in the Bible that uses that number and it is an intriguing one. You've got to go way back to Genesis 4 to find it. There it talks about Cain killing Abel. Then Cain went out, away from the presence of the Lord, and he lived with a mark on his forehead that kept people away from him. He had sons, and one of his descendants was a man called Lemach and Lemach was a bright lad, a very inventive lad and he first began to use metal for tools.

Then he discovered – as every discovery of man has gone over the centuries – that metal can be used for a weapon. He produced the first weapons of mass destruction, and do you know what he said? He boasted that if someone does something to me, I can now be avenged seventy-seven times, I've got the ultimate weapon. From Lemach comes this argument that we have heard in our day too: "Get the ultimate weapon and you've got the deterrent. You can be avenged and people will be scared to touch you."

You see, from the very beginning of the word, there is a spirit of revenge: seventy-seven times. It is as if our Lord consciously went back to that and said, "A spirit of mercy seventy-seven times." That's to be the spirit of my followers. Let me add, just to get the record straight and to temper what I've said, that it is impossible to forgive people until they ask for it, and we need to know that. Forgiveness is not overlooking something, but facing it and then forgetting it. We cannot forgive someone until they have said, "Sorry." That's why Jesus said, "If your brother offends you," he didn't say, "Forget it." If he's done wrong towards you, don't ignore it, go and tell him. Go and face it, and then forgive it.

It is very important that forgiveness is not overlooking. Forgiveness is not forgetting. Forgiveness is, first, facing and then forgetting. It is important that that is what forgiveness means. It is too easy to overlook, to let someone off—that's not forgiveness. Parents, if you let your children off all the time, you will reap a very sad harvest because your children will never know true forgiveness, never mind discipline. They will just know indulgence on your part. No, true forgiveness is something that's costly, and part of that cost is to go and face a person with what has been done, and then to forgive seventy-seven times until you have lost count.

Now for the third occasion when Peter talked about himself. They had met a rich young man. He had plenty of money. He had everything money could buy and nothing that he couldn't. Of course, as John D. Rockefeller once said, "The poorest man I know is that man who has nothing but money," and this is a profound truth. This young man had all the money he could ask for, but the one thing he didn't have was life. The tragedy is that so many people think that money brings life, but it doesn't. This young man came to Jesus and said, "Look, I want life. How do I get life?" Jesus said, "Well the first step is to get rid of your money because that's preventing you from having life, and the second step is to come with me, for to be with me is life."

Faced with that stark choice, the young man's face fell and he walked away sadly, and Jesus let him go. You can walk away and never come back to hear the preaching of the gospel, and you can live the rest of your life without Christ, and Christ will let you go. He doesn't force anybody to make the choice that means life. He will allow them to make the choice that means death.

This young man was too fond of his money and just couldn't let that go. When faced with the choice of either/or, how he would have loved to have both; how he would have loved to say, "Well I'll give you a tenth of it and I'll join the corporate giving scheme and all the rest." But no, Jesus said: Get rid of this thing in your life. It's holding you back. He doesn't say that to everybody, but to those to whom that's a barrier, he says, "Let it go." Your barrier may be something quite different but he says let it go and then come and follow me. You can't have both.

Peter listened to this and his heart was rather swelling with pride. He thought, "Well there's that poor young man. He didn't make the right choice, but two and a half years ago I did." He turned to Jesus and said: Jesus, you know we left everything and followed you. You know, that's one up to me. I am afraid Peter, though applying things to himself, is still applying them in the wrong way. Jesus says: Peter, you didn't lose a thing. No one ever does, of course. He said, "People may lose their families, their homes, their lands, they may lose all this. But even in this world, they will get a hundred times back." Is that not true?

You may have lost the friendship of some of your physical relatives, maybe even brothers and sisters, but how big a family did you get in return? Before you became a Christian, there were some homes that you had access to. How many homes have you access to now? I just know, as a Christian, I can go anywhere in the world and there are homes that I can go into and call my own. You don't lose anything by coming to Christ. Mind you, the sheer honesty of Christ! He says, "No one has left houses, lands, family, anything, doesn't get a hundredfold in this world with persecution." Now what honesty there is there: with persecution.

I know it is tough. I know there are tensions. I know there are problems. Jesus never promised anything else, but he was saying: Peter, you haven't really lost anything, have you? You have gained a hundredfold. I know it's tempered a little because there's persecution with it, but you gained a hundredfold. You have got a bigger family now than you ever had before you left your own. You got more homes that are available to you than you ever had before you left your home. This is true. Then he said, "And in the world to come. What will you have there? You'll be sitting on thrones there,

Peter. There are twelve thrones and you are going to govern the Jewish part of heaven. You are going to reign over the tribes of Israel. You will be sitting on a throne, Peter. You say you left everything? For a throne." So in this world and in the next, you don't lose by leaving everything to follow Christ. Nobody has ever lost. They can never get the Lord in their debt. You try and get the Lord to owe you something and you are in for a delightful shock. You just can't make it.

So Peter is still not getting the right messages. He is thinking of himself, but he is still the reed, not the rock. Peter – you have not got to be broken, but you have got to be bruised.

In one dreadful night, within the space of about six hours, Peter was so bruised that he could lift up his head. It started with a foot washing and he just couldn't take it. It went on through a prediction of betrayal and, like the others, he was now very worried. He said, "Lord, is it I?" It went on to the point where a mere slip of a girl had him so scared for his life that he swore that he had never known Jesus. That night, Peter made the first positive step. He got to know himself as he really was.

The ancient Greeks realised that the first step of wisdom was to know yourself. If you go to Athens, climb the hill and see the Parthenon, you will find engraved on it the words "Know thyself" in Greek. They felt this was the beginning of all true knowledge, and it is. I want to make this statement, which you may question, but the more I think of it, the more I believe it to be true. You cannot know the Lord until you have got to know yourself. Until you see yourself as you really are, you cannot bring your real needs to him and you cannot know how he really meets them. As long as you live in a delusion about yourself, you are in delusions about him also. It was when the prodigal son got down to the pig trough that it says, "He came to..." Who? The Lord? No.

His father? No. To himself. That was the beginning.

I remember a man with a good job – a chief accountant, in good neighbour schemes, respected by all, wonderful, nice person, regarded highly by all his neighbours and all who knew him, but he came to a church of which I was pastor over a period of about two years. He said, "You know, every Sunday, the Lord took one brick off the wall of my self-respect until one night the wall had gone." In front of his three grown-up sons, he walked out to the front like a little child and became a Christian.

That has got to happen I'm afraid, or temperament will control your Christian experience. Your Christian experience should be controlling your temperament. The bruising of the reed must take place. You need to discover what your temperament is to be shown yourself as you really are. You need to discover your real weaknesses. You need to be thinking about yourself, but not in the wrong way – in a factual, realistic assessment of your need. Whether you are brought to the point of tears, as Peter was, or whether you just come soberly to a realisation that you are a sinner needing a saviour, without the Holy Spirit your temperament will always have the upper hand – whichever it is, it doesn't matter – it is at that point that the reed is in a position to become the rock.

7

JESUS SERVES

Read John 13:5–15

The Bible has no superstition in it whatever. Christians are set free from superstition, among many other things. So I am glad John chapter 13 is about the thirteen who sat down at that table for the Last Supper.

We are looking at these great events through the eyes of Peter. We are not just going through the events, we are trying to get inside Peter's skin, trying to understand how he felt, and what was going on in his mind and heart on that last evening. It started in a rather funny way, which made Peter think that something was up – he didn't quite know what. It had been a hectic week, and something of an anticlimax. Jesus had at last looked as if he was going to do what everybody wanted him to do, and claim the throne and become king, lead a rebellion, get the Romans out of there, and set himself up. In which case, of course, he would be looking for a new cabinet, a new government – in which case Peter and John thought they were well in the running for top posts.

Indeed on that very night they were arguing as to who of the twelve was the greatest, and Jesus knew it. Mind you, the promise of that Sunday morning had not been fulfilled. After a clash in the temple with the moneychangers, and the whole thing just fizzled out like a damp squib – came to nothing. The next day they just had a bit of debate and that was it. By the Tuesday evening, Peter, John, and the rest were wondering whether it had been badly stage-managed. They were beginning to feel that Jesus had had the ball at his feet and he had missed it, the whole thing was fizzling out. But they still had hopes. Why? Because the Passover was about to start on the Thursday. Two and half million people had gathered in that city. It was the best opportunity of the whole year to do what they believed Jesus would do. They believed that Sunday was in a sense just like a little commando raid before the big invasion, and was just a little tryout to see how the public feeling ran. So they were expecting big things, they were expecting the kingdom to be restored, and they were expecting positions in it.

So, that night, Jesus said, "I want to have an evening meal with you." Then he said something rather strange. He said, "Peter and John, come over here a moment. Look," he said, "I don't want anybody to know about tonight. I've been making some secret arrangements. Don't tell the other disciples, but the two of you go into town and look out for a man carrying a pitcher of water." The humour of that doesn't hit us in the West but if you have ever seen a man carrying a pitcher of water in the Middle East, well you've seen something. It is a very rare sight. Carrying a pitcher was something a man would normally never do – his wife would do that. They found the man and they made the meal ready, but Peter began to wonder why the secrecy – why the kind of cloak and dagger stuff? Is something happening? Is there a danger? What is it? So already there was a little bit of tension building up before they sat down that night.

What Peter did not know, but what Jesus knew perfectly well, is that everything was going exactly according to plan. Jesus had deliberately challenged both the political and the religious leaders by riding in on an ass that Sunday morning. He knew that was all that he needed to do to set the wheels in motion. He knew that already they were plotting for his death and that they must get it through before the Passover began. He knew that he had only a few more days of life.

So he just pottered around the temple answering questions, knowing all the time God's foreordained plan, which he had set in motion – he was the master of events, totally. It was all happening. He knew, too, that one of his own closest friends had already arranged to sell him for hard cash to the authorities. He wanted this one last night with his disciples. He still had just one or two things he must say to them to prepare them for what was coming. He wanted desperately to have a farewell meal. He was the one whose heart was troubled that night, and he should have been receiving that comfort of those who were around him. They should have been comforting him; he was about to die. Instead he had to spend the whole evening saying, "Let not your hearts be troubled," comforting them and preparing them for all that lay ahead. So that's the setting and we now enter the room.

Since it had all been secretly arranged, nobody knew about it but the man who owned the room, and therefore there were no servants laid on, so when they went into the room the first thing they saw they ignored because it was a bowl of water and a towel. Since there was no servant there, nobody used it. You see it's a hot climate in the Middle East. Your feet get hot and sticky and the roads were not tarmac in those days. Even as late as September I walked down from the Mount of Olives to Gethsemane, and it is a rough, stony, dusty road. My feet were in sandals and they were filthy by the time I got to the bottom. I looked down at my feet and I thought of this very chapter.

Now normally in the hierarchy of servants the very lowest was the man who washed feet. The next one above loosed the sandals. Everybody had their place. It is interesting that John the Baptist was a very humble man, but not quite at the bottom. He said, "I'm not worthy to unloose his sandals."

In other words, "I'm not worthy to be the second lowest," which makes it all the more startling that Jesus just went one lower than John the Baptist. It's one thing to untie someone's shoes; it's another to wash what's inside them, taking the lowest position. So they all ignored it, sat down, and tried to hide their feet. They lay down. They reclined in those days, so they reclined with head in towards the table, feet out, but you can almost see them sort of just shuffling and pulling down their robes over their feet.

Why did they not wash each other's feet? The answer is, they were far too busy doing something else, which they regarded as more important. What were they doing? The answer is very simple: they were trying to grab the best seat. In the East you can tell a person's social position by where they sit. Protocol at a meal is vital, and since this was coming up to the kingdom and since they had been discussing who was the greatest, and since this was a real issue, whoever wanted to be 'Prime Minister' must get close to Jesus.

Peter and John were scrambling. John got there first and he got nearest; Peter came second and was next nearest. The scripture tells us this, and they were so busy grabbing seats that they couldn't wash feet. So Jesus just sat down with them and he read them like a book. He just looked at them, and then quietly he stood up, stripped to his underwear, walked over to the bowl, and picked it up. I put it like that so you can feel the shock which they all felt. I am quoting the Bible, incidentally. That's what he did. He was later that night to be stripped in the same way again and dressed up like a king in mockery, but first time he was stripped that night he did it himself voluntarily for service, and then he started.

Peter's thoughts and feelings were in a total turmoil.

His ideas of protocol were going to the winds. The whole thing was just so topsy-turvy. These who were later to turn the world upside down had first to be turned upside down themselves and this was happening right now. You see, they had regarded Jesus as above them and foot washing below them – beneath their dignity – and now, suddenly, the whole picture is reversed. You see here we have divine protocol, which is just the opposite usually of human protocol. This was the lesson that Jesus was going to teach. He could hardly have chosen a better way to teach the lesson for it was seen before it was said. It spoke to their eyes before it spoke to their ears, but Peter's thoughts were in a turmoil.

First he was so thoroughly embarrassed that he hadn't thought of doing it. Most of us, I'm afraid, have good intentions just too late, and realise afterwards what we might have done. He was also feeling, "Now this is just wrong way around. I want a Lord whom I can look up to, not look down on. The whole thing is just wrong." As Jesus got nearer to Peter, Peter as usual was the spokesman for all of them. The others were thinking it but he spoke it. Now that doesn't make him worse than the others. In fact, it could mean that he's better. But if you'll forgive the pun, I don't think Peter was just the spokesman, he was also the spoke of the disciples, and always putting it in. When it came to Peter, Jesus couldn't get any further. Peter said: Never. Never. You're not going to wash my feet, are you?

Yet, at the same time, shame and embarrassment that he is in this situation, that he could have avoided it, that he could have washed Jesus' feet. That would have been in keeping with all that he felt was right, but why didn't he think of it? Because he was grabbing the seat and John got there first. Why didn't Peter say, "Lord let me wash your feet," right at the beginning as soon as they got there? It would have been a privilege and an honour. Anybody would have been glad to do it and it fitted in with protocol.

Jesus then had to say something to Peter, which every one of us has to hear and learn, and which is one of the hardest lessons to learn. Jesus said, "Unless you let me wash you, we have nothing to share, Peter. You have no part with me," or literally, "You have no partnership with me. We cannot go on together. This is the end, Peter, if I cannot wash you." After three years this would wipe it all out; it would end the relationship.

Now the important lesson is this: it is not what you do for the Lord but what the Lord does for you that establishes the relationship. But the trouble is that we can give and keep our pride; we can't receive and keep our pride—that's the problem. I have had men and women come to me and say, "Look, if there's anything I can do in the church, tell me. If there's anything I can do for other people, I want to serve others." Yet these people never seem to get into service. They never seem to get the opportunity. The doors close and they are frustrated.

I know why it is. The simple thing is the Lord is just waiting for them to ask, "Will someone serve me? I'm in need." You see, the relationship often begins when you prepare to be served, not when you are prepared to serve – that can be patronising. "It's more blessed to give than to receive" – and it is a good deal easier too. But to receive help, to have someone else do something for you that you could have done for yourself, you have got to swallow pride with a big lump in your throat, and it has got to go.

That is how you became a Christian. You can neither begin the Christian life nor continue it until you have learned this lesson: that Christianity consists in letting the Lord cleanse you. It doesn't consist in what you do for him – that could be patronising. You can keep your pride and say, "Look at all I've done for him," and that's the snag with that attitude. All he wants to do is get us clean, and he says, "Will you let me do it for you?" It is true of our relationships with people that there can't be a real relationship until you are willing to receive as well as to give to someone, until it's a two-way relationship of mutual help. It is most certainly true of your relationship to God; it can't even begin until you come to God humbled.

Self-sufficient people don't get anywhere in relationships – that's why Peter reacted. "It's all wrong. I'll do it for you if you like." That would be dignified, but, "No, not for me." "Unless I wash you, you have no partnership with me." Relationship with the Lord is a covenant, not a contract. It is on his terms – there is no bargaining – and his terms are: "Let me wash you." Those are his sole terms.

Having been told that, Peter, still firmly in the saddle, is still determined to dictate the terms, and he reacts in a typically human way with the grand gesture. It has still got to be different from all the other twelve. Do you notice? Well now, you've washed the others' feet. Lord, if that's the way it is, I want to be the closest of all of them – so wash my head, wash my hands, and wash my feet—everything, Lord. I want to be totally yours. It is such pious sentiment, and the Lord has to unravel the motives behind this apparent expression of devotion. It might have impressed some of the others deeply with Peter's devotional life, but the Lord was not impressed. Peter was still telling Jesus what he should do. They would all have had to bathe before the Passover. "Peter you had a bath before you came. Your hands and your face, they don't need washing. It's just your feet that are dirty but not all of you are clean." Not "all of you" (singular) to Peter, but "all of you" (plural), the disciples. "You are clean Peter. You've just picked up a bit of dirt between Bethany and here and that's all I want to deal with."

Oh God, give us grace to be realistic. Neither so to hold

back that we say, "You'll never wash my feet," nor to come out with these grand gestures of devotion, but simply to look squarely and honestly at the dirt we have picked up and then get that dealt with by the Lord – that's what he wants. Peter is going from one extreme to the other: "Never, nothing" and then "everything" all at once.

So Peter is now subdued and submissive. I want now to look at the next little bit because Jesus now says, "Peter, do you understand? All of you, do you understand what I've done?" which tells me that there is far more to this foot washing business than just getting dirt off someone's feet. "Do you understand?" Well, if it is simply a physical act of getting someone clean, everybody understands that. Somebody had to do it and somebody did. What is there to understand? It shows us there is something much more, and there at least three levels at which we may look at this story.

The first is simply the straight physical level: they had a need, Jesus met it. The second level at which you can look at this story is to see in it a quite profound, symbolic, spiritual meaning because Jesus said, "You are not all clean," and now we are out of the physical realm; he is speaking spiritually. He is teaching them: What I'm doing is a picture of something spiritual that I want to do, that I can't do with one of you. I'm doing it with the rest of you. I want you to see that my main purpose in coming was to get you clean. I'm not going to manage it with all of you but I'm going to get some of you clean.

So there's a deep symbolic spiritual meaning in this act. It is therefore, in a sense, a sacrament if it is an outward, visible act with an inward and spiritual grace or meaning behind it. But there is a third level, and this is the main one—the moral level, meaning: This is not just an act of meeting your need. It is a moral act which is an example to you. It is a pattern; it is a model. It is a quite profound principle that I have shared with you. I've taught you a very deep lesson. Have you got the message?

That deep lesson was that love and power need each other. Love without power is sympathy; power without love is selfishness. Love with power is service, and we need both. The amazing thing is that Jesus, knowing that the Father had put all things under his power, then put himself under other people to serve them. That is what power does when there is love in it.

If I may coin a phrase, which might make it memorable for you: Christians are called not to lord it *over* but to lord it under. Now that may seem a very strange phrase to you, but Jesus was teaching them: you call me Lord and rightly, now this is the kind of lordship I exercise; I lord it not over but under. He used the phrase "lord it over". He said, "You must not be as the Gentiles and lord it over people." So remember this phrase. He is saying the lesson is: Lord it under people. There is a dignity in true royalty.

A rather silly little story will just illustrate this. King George V came to my home area in the northeast and there was a big banquet in the city of Durham for the Durham miners. King George was sitting next to the leader of the Durham miners. The tables were spread to be fit for a king, with silver laid out. In front of each guest there was a little glass bowl, a finger bowl full of water, so that when the fruit came around the guest could dip their fingers in the bowl and keep them clean. The miner's leader, sitting next to the king, with a loud gurgling sound, drank it. Some at the table looked horrified, a few further away sniggered. But the king immediately picked up his finger bowl and drank it. That is royal protocol, it was magnificent gesture. It is a tiny little story but it is an illustration of true royalty.

Jesus is saying, and he says in Luke's version of the same event: Look, I have thrones waiting for you. There are twelve thrones in heaven for you. You will rule over the twelve tribes of Israel. You are heading for a throne, but if you want to prepare for that throne there, it is through humble service here. There couldn't be a better preparation for a throne than to go and do a menial task for others.

As late as James II, the king or queen of England every Maundy Thursday went to the poorest quarters of London and washed dirty feet. Even after James II it was carried on by the Lord High Almoner until about 1731. The Pope does it, and groups of Baptists in the USA do it. It brings you down at someone's feet, and they are not the most beautiful part of someone else. They are only beautiful if they bring good tidings to Zion, otherwise there is no attraction. It is the lowest part – that picks up the most dirt physically. Jesus is saying that is how you prepare for a throne. You lord it under people until you are ready to reign – a very deep lesson. I think Peter got the message. Certainly later he shows signs that he did.

The night darkens at this point, both outside and inside. We are now going to see the first of the disciples lost to Jesus. It is a horrible moment. Jesus goes back to something he has said. He has already made this mysterious remark: "You're not all clean." Now he gives a broader hint. He says, "I've told you that you'll be blessed if you do what I've said, but not all of you will be blessed." He keeps saying this in the next few sentences, "Not all of you". Until they are beginning to get worried, "What's he meaning? We have been with him for three years; we'll see it through."

Then it says that Jesus began to be very troubled. The word is pretty mild in the English but in the Greek it means he began to be overcome with his emotions. Then he said, "One of you is going to betray me." The shock came like a douche of cold water to Peter's heart. "One of you." Now it is interesting that all the others said, "Lord, is it I?" They knew they were each perfectly capable of doing this dastardly deed, but Peter did not say that. Peter said, "Who is it?" Since he was not near enough to Jesus to speak directly, he whispered to John next door, "Ask him who it is." John said to Jesus, "Who is it?" Peter's waiting, listening. Jesus said, "I'm going to give a piece of bread to someone in a minute or two. I'll give it to the man." He dipped the bread in the soup and gave it. It is a normal gesture for a host in the Middle East to dip the bread and to taste a bit of soup, and give it to a guest. So it passed, maybe unnoticed by the rest, but John saw it. And he gave it to Judas Iscariot, which means that Judas grabbed a place too – he was near enough. It was all over in a few minutes, so quickly that nobody quite realised what had happened.

Had Peter realised, Judas would not have left the room alive. We know that Peter had a sword hidden somewhere. He used it a few hours later, though Peter, a fisherman, wasn't any good with a sword anyway – we see he aimed at a man's head and only cut off his ear. But even so he was restrained from murder by the sheer speed of events, and Judas had gone. Note the language describing this, when Judas took the bread at that table: Satan entered into him.

That can happen to someone taking communion. At the very table taking bread from the Lord, Satan can enter into you. If you have been listening to Satan, if you have been dabbling, if you have been being prompted by him, and indeed we are told already that Satan had already prompted Judas. But now it says, "Satan possessed him," and that's the order. If you listen to Satan's prompting it will not be long before he takes possession. This thing doesn't happen in a moment; it doesn't happen suddenly. Nothing happens suddenly, everything has a lead up to it, and Judas would not have done what he did if he had not been leading up to it. He followed the promptings before the possession came, but as soon as he took the bread he was possessed.

Indeed, 1 Corinthians 11 says be careful how you take the bread at communion. You can eat and drink damnation to yourself. That's what happened to Judas at the Last Supper. He went out, and as the door just opened and closed, they saw outside it was black as black, and nothing could be more symbolic, "And it was night." Judas never saw the daylight again. Before the dawn came the following morning he had hanged himself. He had made even a bad job of that. The rope snapped and he fell headlong and he finished up, it says, "with his bowels gushing on the ground." It happened in the hours of darkness that night; it was a terrible end.

I will come back to it shortly because that was someone who walked with Jesus for three years. It was someone who preached for Jesus. It was someone who cast out demons and healed in the name of Jesus. It was someone who had been all that – a classic case of Hebrews 6. Peter missed it, but no doubt he was thinking about it. We know the cast of his mind, it comes out in his next remark – even if everybody else would betray him, he wouldn't.

There are some little touches of scripture, almost the incidentals, which you may never notice. Consider Judas's name. He had two other names. One was "Iscariot", which means that he came from Keriot, or Kerioth, in the southern part of Israel, "Judas of Kerioth," but his other name was Judas bar Simon. He is of this very name. I have told you it means "a reed", somebody easily swayed, and Judas was a "Simon" too. Judas was a reed, and Judas was easily swayed. Peter is saying – well at least I'm not a reed, I'm not a Simon. Jesus turned to Peter at this very point and he said, "Simon, Simon."

Now can you imagine the hurt that must have come when Jesus went back to that old name? When they had first met, Jesus had said, "You will be 'Peter.'" A few months before the events of which we are speaking, up on the top of Mount Hermon, Jesus had said to Peter, "You are Peter." Not just, "You will be", but, "You now are, and on this rock I will build my church." Now, just a few months later, we can imagine unspoken things: Simon, you share that name with Judas; you are a reed, and Judas is a broken reed. Simon, you may be glad and be relieved it wasn't you that's going to betray me, but Satan's been trying to get you and I've been fighting for your soul. You are only with me today because I've prayed for you, Simon—do you realise that? That you would be doing exactly what Judas is doing if I hadn't prayed for you. You see, up until this mountain Peter still did not take Satan seriously, and Peter was a battlefield between the Saviour and Satan. The two had been praying about him. Satan had been praying to God about Peter, and Jesus had been praying about Peter. Because Jesus says, "Satan has asked to have you." Who had he asked? The answer is there's only one to ask and that's God Almighty.

Satan cannot do a thing unless God gives him permission – remember that. That is why you can't be tempted above what you can bear, because God controls temptation. That is why in the Lord's Prayer you need to pray, "Lead us not into temptation" – because God finally decides how much power Satan has over you. It is a sobering thought, and Satan has to have permission from heaven's throne to inflict Job with suffering. "Satan has asked for you, Peter, and I have asked to keep you." Now when those two are asking for a soul, who is going to win? There is no question about it, the prayer of Jesus is mighty over Satan. It means, frankly, that Jesus had stopped praying for Judas. There could be no more terrible thing that could happen to you or to me than that Jesus should stop praying for us, because then Satan is free to prey.

So Simon, don't be too proud of yourself. You are still

Simon basically. We haven't got you through to be a rock yet. Satan has wanted you, I've prayed for you. When you have returned to me, you will be able to strengthen the others....

Returned? What is that supposed to mean? I'm not going to leave you, says Peter, I'll never leave you. I don't need to return; I'm going to stay with you. I will go to prison and even to death for you. He honestly believed it, that's the saddest part. You see the person we deceive most often – most of us – is ourselves. "If we say we have no sin, we deceive ourselves...." You rarely deceive anyone else, but you deceive yourself. You can think that you are so great and so strong, that you would go all the way with Jesus. Peter said, "Return to you? I'm never leaving," and his very next words were, "I'll go to prison and death." Would he?

Why, a little servant girl would have Peter tied in knots before the night was out. Jesus knew it, and he said, "Simon, before dawn, before the cock crows tomorrow morning, three times you will have disowned me. You will have said you don't know me." That shut Peter up for the rest of the Last Supper, you find. They still had an hour or two together, but that really put Peter in his place.

I find those words of Jesus tremendously encouraging, "Before the cock crows you will deny me thrice." Why encouraging? Because Jesus knew the worst about Peter and he knew it before it happened, and he still loved him. The reed may be bruised but the prophecy about the suffering servant in Isaiah 42 (who is the coming Messiah) is, "He will not break a bruised reed." Simon means "reed" and Peter means "rock" and Jesus says, "When you have returned to me you'll strengthen your brethren." The gospel of the second chance is there, isn't it?

There are few believers and disciples who know the grace of God so clearly as those who have let Christ down since they followed him, and come back. They know more of the grace, more of the love. They are fit to lead others then because they cannot lord it over people after that; they can only lord it under then. The fact is you can't be sure of yourself and sure of the Lord at the same time. The two are incompatible, and this is why most men in middle age find it so difficult to admit our need of the Lord – we are so self sufficient. The more sure you are of yourself, the less sure of the Lord you will be.

"I will go to prison and I will die. The others may leave you but I won't. You can wash none of me or all of me, but I'll tell you what you can do" – so sure.... Within three hours Peter would be crouched in a back alley, somewhere in the back streets of Jerusalem, sobbing his heart out, bruised until the sap was flowing. That would be the beginning of Peter the rock. Isn't it strange that you have to be broken to be mended; that you have to be humbled to be exalted; that before you can sit on a throne the Lord has to put you under everybody else? Because only then can you sit on a throne with the right expression on your face and the right attitude in your heart.

Are you a Judas or a Peter? They both had the same opportunities. Outwardly at any rate, they both followed the Lord. Judas was even the treasurer, looking after the distribution of money to the poor. They had both preached and healed, yet one went right through and one didn't. Why? Peter nearly lost the relationship when he said, "You shall never wash me." He nearly lost it but he didn't. It was when Judas looked at Satan too much, when he allowed Satan to prompt him, he was undermining the Lord's authority in his heart. Judas didn't argue about washing feet. Judas let Jesus wash his feet. At least Peter expressed what he thought. The sheer hypocrisy of Judas that night in receiving the bread comes clearly through, but it was due to the fact that he dabbled with Satan.

117

Peter survived because in the last analysis he knew that Jesus knew the truth. Peter would come to discover the whole truth about himself; the truth set him free from himself, and then he was to be restored: "Simon, son of Jonas, do you love me? Feed my sheep." He would become the first pastor of the church.

8

THE FLESH IS WEAK

Matthew 26:31–58 and 69–end

If you'll forgive the pun, for Peter to become a rock he had to get to rock bottom. This has to happen to everyone, maybe not in such a spectacular crisis sort of way, but every one of us has to come to the end of ourselves before the Lord can make of us what he wills. It may come in as dramatic a way as it came to Simon Peter on that last night of our Lord's earthly life. It needed to for his temperament because, as I have told you about the sanguine temperament, one of the most difficult things for that sort of person is self-knowledge, to see themselves as they really are. They almost have to come to such a tragedy as this to come to themselves, but like the prodigal son, when you come to yourself you are on the way up because you can't get any lower.

You need to get to the point where Paul himself, with quite a different temperament, came to in Romans 7, where he says, "I know that in me, that is in my flesh, dwells no good thing." You really haven't discovered yourself truly until you can say honestly, "I now know that in me, that is in my flesh, dwells no good thing." That is not an exaggeration, it is the sober truth. If there is anything good in my life, it is due to the influence of God's Holy Spirit in me. Whether I am a believer or an unbeliever, and but for the grace of God that would not be there, in me as I am by myself, in my flesh, as I am by nature, if I did everything that came naturally, then frankly there would be no good thing. It really takes a long time for some people to get to that point. It took Peter three years.

Christ, you see, can't do anything with those who are somebodies. He can only work with nobodies. That's why he chose the Jews. Not because they were special, or because they had anything that nobody else had, he chose the Jews because of what they didn't have. Because they were nobodies, a bunch of slaves with no future, no resources, and he made them what they were. If you look at the twelve disciples and say, "Why did he choose those twelve?" You could look in the wrong direction. You could look at each of the disciples and say, "Now what qualities were there in that man that he wanted?" That's the wrong way to look. If you want to know why he chose those twelve, look at Jesus, not at the disciples, and you will discover that he's the sort of person who wants to take very ordinary people who have nothing, who are nobodies, and make them something. That's why he confounds the wisdom of the world, by taking the nobodies of this world and just making them such spiritual giants that all the somebodies are confused and bewildered.

So Peter had to come to this understanding that he was nobody. It began with that remark at the Last Supper: Jesus said, "Before the cock crows you will deny me, disown me three times. You will say you don't even know me three times." Peter virtually called Jesus a liar and said, "I don't believe it. If I have to die with you I'll go all the way," and with a sidelong glance at the others, the others might run away but not Peter, not your rock.

How cheeky, how impudent, to say to the one who had just said, "I am the truth," "You don't speak it. You don't know me well enough." Here is a Peter who is still a little sure of himself; who still feels that he can with his own natural resources go all the way with Jesus, and that has to be broken – and broken it will be before a few hours have passed. Now when Peter disowns the Lord three times, that doesn't happen overnight. It doesn't happen out of the blue. It doesn't just happen without steps leading up to it. Such a denial, when you curse and swear, and on oath say you don't know Jesus, that is to use an example of truth to cover a lie because the point of taking an oath is to reinforce the fact that you are speaking the truth.

Peter was going to use an oath, normally used to reinforce truth, to cover a lie. That doesn't happen just like that, there is a lead in. We are going to follow the steps by which Peter went down and down. The denial was the fruit of everything that had happened before that. So often when we finally crash in the crisis and say, "Well what on earth made me do that then?" It is because already the weakening has taken place and we are in a position to do it.

Now the first step I believe took place in Gethsemane where Peter fell asleep. I don't think he would have denied the Lord later if he hadn't fallen asleep earlier. It's all part of the same picture. It all leads on, one thing from the other. This was perhaps the most difficult period in the life of Jesus over the whole thirty-three years. He never had a more difficult period than those few hours, probably about a couple of hours in the little garden of Gethsemane on the slope of the Mount of Olives down in the valley of Kidron. It was difficult because it was the very last chance he had to run away from the cross. The only person keeping him on that course that would lead to Calvary was Jesus himself.

He desperately needed reinforcement, he desperately needed help and encouragement. He wanted to have people with him as he faced the crisis, as you do when you are going through an ordeal, when you have got an almighty decision, a difficult one to face. When you have to face something which you know is necessary, but which you don't want to face and your whole being cries out, "Run away from it." Isn't it a help if you can have a few people around you just saying, "No you've got to see this through. We'll pray you through." Maybe you have heard that you have got to have some major operation. Maybe you have heard you have got to close your business. What a help it is when you are facing a major crisis to have a group of people who say, "We are going to pray you through. We'll see you through."

So Jesus, facing this final crisis, knowing it was now or never, he could run away in the darkness now, he could even run back to heaven now if he wished. He could avoid the cross right now, the last chance, and so he says, "Peter, James, and John will you see me through the next hour or two? Will you pray? Will you stay on guard here? Will you watch and pray? Watch for men coming and pray for me. Be alert. I want to know as soon as those men come for me. So will you watch? Will you pray? Will you back me up and will you see me through?"

There is a medical condition when the blood vessels near the skin can burst with sheer emotional and mental pressure and drops of blood do appear on the forehead. This is what happened, and it is such a rare condition that it gives you some idea of the stress and strain that Jesus was holding himself in that garden until they came to arrest him. Everything in him wanted to run away, everything in him wanted to get away under cover of darkness, but he held himself there. "Peter watch and pray. Just keep me going. Help me through this."

Now alas, we know that they did not do so. Jesus always intercedes for us, but here is the one occasion that he asked them to intercede for him and they missed it. It's tragic really. We know that angels came and ministered to him. It's as if earth failed and men let him down. So God had to send angels, and angels came and ministered to him. But there's a very important thing here: angels even are no substitute for human support at a time like this. The very real humanity of Jesus comes through – that he missed the disciples' support even though he had angels helping him, even though God was listening to him, he desperately needed human support. I think it's cruel to say to someone that the ministry of God and even the angels is enough for them and they don't need human help. This is not true to our humanity. We need human help to see us through crises. It is not enough to leave a person alone with God. God has given us people to pray and we need them. So you may be needed to see someone through a crisis, and it is cruel to say, "Well, just trust the Lord. He'll see you through. Goodbye." Peter, James, and John let him down and he desperately wanted that human support. He came back to them and he said, "Peter," no he didn't, he didn't say "Peter," he said, "Simon." Oh there's that name coming back in again, "the reed," Simon the weak. "Simon, could you not stay awake for one hour? The spirit is willing but the flesh is weak."

Let me say very frankly that when I taught on this passage, as usual I went up after lunch to prepare for the evening and really go through it, and get right into what I wanted to share. I was just so dog-tired I was drooping and drooping. Finally I made the fatal mistake, I put my head down and I was out like a light. At four o'clock (I knew it was, I looked at my watch) I was trying to open my eyes and I just couldn't get them open until about a quarter to five. I just struggled and struggled, and I thought, "Well, I'm getting into the story tonight all right. The spirit is willing, I want to get ready for tonight but the flesh is just so weak."

You see, until you've come to yourself you don't take the flesh seriously enough. You don't realise what a weak creature you are. You see, we are not just spiritual beings, we are fleshly beings as well. In some countries when a man murders another, the punishment is that his victim's corpse is strapped to his back, chained to his back, and he's got to walk around with it for the rest of his life, that rotten stinking thing on his back. It is a pretty rough punishment but it certainly fits the crime. In a sense, every Christian feels like that. There is the corpse of your old life hanging on your back. You killed it; you buried it in baptism. But there it is, seemingly hanging around all the time and you walk around with it.

The Christian is torn between spirit and flesh. Read Romans 7, it is the description of a Christian in torment. Paul was honest enough to say, "The good I would I do not, and the evil I would not that I do." Spirit and flesh were in conflict, and they always are. "They lust against one another," says Galatians 5. You can never go both ways. You either walk in the Spirit or walk in the flesh. The two are there so that what H.G. Wells said of Mr. Polly is true of every Christian: "He was not so much a human being as a civil war," and this is the tension. "Peter, the spirit is willing but the flesh is weak." Peter, all that you say, you say in ignorance of the weakness of the flesh.

Now let's realise that the flesh is not just the physical body. It includes that, that is part of the flesh, but the word "flesh" in Scripture means everything you are by nature. It includes your brain as well as your body, and all the patterns of that brain were computed during your days outside of Christ. It includes all your natural affections and ambitions. It includes everything you are by nature. There was a pop song many years ago, which summed up the word "flesh" perfectly: doing what comes naturally. You haven't got to the point where God can really use you until you have fully realised the weakness of the flesh, until you've got to rock bottom and realise – in me, in my flesh, in my natural being, that if I did what came naturally there would be no good thing in my life. Then you can start on the upward road – having been emptied of your self-confidence, you are ready to be filled with the Spirit and go on with God.

So, Peter, the spirit is willing but the flesh is very, very weak. Do you understand this yet Peter? No he doesn't. He rubs his eyes, mutters an apology for going to sleep, and suddenly it's too late. There's a rabble, there's noise, there's Judas, there are soldiers, and there are swords. It's happening and Peter jumps up, and now I'm afraid he does the second thing in his flesh. You see, the denial was the final act of a series of fleshly acts, of natural things, which he did naturally. It is natural to go to sleep when you are tired, perfectly natural. All he did was do what comes naturally, but Jesus had said, "Watch and pray". The devil gets hold of you when you do what comes naturally. The devil gets hold of you not through your spirit but through the weakness of your nature, of the flesh.

So the second thing he did. What is our instinctive nature? What do we do naturally when we are threatened? We defend ourselves. It is the natural thing to do. If you are in a position to fight, you fight. If someone is coming for you, you get ready, it is natural. Instinct, preserve number one, self-preservation, is the deepest natural instinct in the human being. There is Peter, and he has a sword. It has been there for some time and Jesus had said at the Last Supper a rather unusual thing. He had said: things are getting difficult; times are coming when you will have to provide your own food; you won't be able to live by faith any longer; you won't be able to go out and just believe that the Lord will provide. You will have to take your own food with you because nobody will give you any. You will need to sell your shirt and buy a sword.

Now that was a figure of speech. Quite clearly in the context you can see that Jesus was using a figure of speech. But as soon as he said it, Peter said, "I've got one. I've got one. It's all right, I've anticipated your need. That shows how clever I am and I knew you'd be saying that sooner or later so I went out and got one." Jesus response to that is, "That's enough." That's a literal translation of what he said. Now Peter, you're just not getting the message are you? Still Peter deciding.

So now Peter still has that sword, and when he finds himself surrounded, the other disciples said, "Lord, should we fight?" Now when Peter said, "I'll die with you," he meant just this: we will go down together fighting; you can count on me. He did not reckon on the way that Jesus was going to die. He thought that Jesus, if he died, would die with his back to the wall and a sword in his hand. If it was going to be a fight to the finish, Peter would fight to the finish – and he would have done. He meant it, he would die with Jesus.

He pulled out that sword, at overwhelming odds at that point, and he would have died for Jesus then, but it was Peter's way to die, that's the problem. It's still the flesh dictating: we'll go down fighting, Jesus. If they spill our blood we'll go down together, but I'm a fighter. So, though quite clearly he was more used to handling nets, he took a mighty swipe with the sword, missed, and got an ear for his trouble, and that's all. The humour of the situation comes through. Peter couldn't even handle a sword properly by nature. Sixty years later, John wrote this up. It shows that John had some inside information on the court of those days, but it also shows how vividly you can remember details, because John said it was the man's right ear and his name was Malchus and he was the high priest's personal aide. Intriguing. It is these little details that give the ring of truth to the accounts of scripture. What committee would think of including "the right ear". It is these little details that show that it is an eyewitness account. Immediately, Peter has acted in the flesh. Impulsive, true to his sanguine temperament, he does things before he thinks. The other disciples asked Jesus, "Should we fight?" But Peter wasn't even asking. He knew what was best. After all he had the sword and he was going to use it.

At that point, Jesus rebuked Peter. Do you realise that Peter came within an inch of spoiling God's purpose? Do you realise that if others joined in with swords they would have killed each other and Jesus would have been lying dead in his own blood in the garden of Gethsemane? There would have been no sacrifice for sin, no atoning death. Already five times there had been attempts to assassinate Jesus, and every time Jesus had evaded them by hiding or running away. When they tried to stone him he escaped from the crowd. When they tried to throw him off the cliff at Nazareth he walked through the crowd. Every time he had refused to face death and he got out of the situation. You see, it was not God's will that he die by stoning or being pushed off a cliff; it had to be on a cross. Peter nearly started a fight that would have killed Jesus before he got to the cross.

Can't you see how Satan used somebody who is acting in flesh? Satan had tried to destroy Jesus before he got to the cross. He had tried to persuade him to throw himself off a pinnacle of the temple. Had Jesus done so he would have dashed himself to pieces on the stones below because the promise was quoted out of context and it wouldn't have worked. So Satan was now trying yet again to kill Jesus before he got to the cross, and Peter was the instrument. So Jesus picked up the ear, pushed it back against the bleeding head of the man and it knitted together. Now you can think what you like about that but every miracle that happened in the Bible is still happening today for Jesus is the same yesterday, today, and forever. I don't have any problem with the miracle. I am profoundly disturbed, challenged, and humbled by the fact that Jesus did this for a man who had come to arrest him. He could so easily have said, "Serves him right." He could so easily have left the thing undone, left the man scarred for life, as he dared to come against the Son of God with staves and clubs, but that was not the way of Jesus. In the Sermon on the Mount, three years earlier, Jesus had said, "If anybody hits you on one cheek, turn the other cheek." After three years Peter had not got the message. He still acted in the flesh – pulled out a sword and struck. But Jesus practised what he preached. This was the last night of Peter's natural life when he was still the fleshly reed Simon.

Can you see that the denial was all of a piece with everything that had happened up to that point? He simply did what comes naturally. He went to sleep naturally, he pulled a sword naturally. Now he was finding himself alone, on the spot and in danger himself. So what did he do? He denied his Lord naturally. It was the natural, fleshly thing to do. It wasn't a sudden unexpected change of behaviour, it was just a continuation of what had been happening all that night through – natural. Have you ever noticed how often Peter uses the word "never"? It is a dangerous word to use. "He will never wash my feet." A few minutes later Jesus is washing them. "I will never disown you," and a few hours later he is disowning him.

Peter had himself all summed up, as to things he would do and the things he wouldn't do. "I will never do this. I will always do that" – and he couldn't have been more wrong.

You may have discovered a fatal thing to say to the Lord is, "I will never go to so and so." The word "never" is a fleshly word. "I could never pray in public"; "I could never witness"; "I could never preach." Don't you believe it!

Jesus said, "I must go and be crucified, suffer many things

at the hands of wicked men."

"Never," said Peter. But he did. The word "never" has a way of looking very silly in the presence of our Lord.

Now we come to the final climax of this fleshy evening. Peter did follow. John did as well, as far as we know. And he got right inside the house of the high priest. He had connections at court. Peter stayed in the courtyard – you couldn't see the other disciples for dust. What a night of running that was. There was one young man in the garden of Gethsemane, a man who heard Jesus pray, who wrote it all down afterwards, and his name was John Mark. He had seen them slip out in the darkness, he had got out of bed, and he hadn't much on so he slipped just a bedsheet around himself and followed them to the garden. He only just got away. They tried to seize him and he escaped by getting out of the sheet, and he ran off naked into the night. But that young man later wrote down what Jesus said when the others were all asleep (see the Gospel according to Mark).

But Peter did follow, and got inside the courtyard. Why did Peter deny knowing Jesus? Try to get into Peter's mind. It was not just his temperament, though his temperament was the sort that was so easily influenced by people around him. This kind of temperament is one thing with one group and one thing with another, hates to be different and hates to be the odd one out. It is scared stiff of being the only one who is different. But I believe there was more – that at this point Peter had stopped trusting the wisdom of Jesus.

Peter had said, "I'll die with you," but thinking: surely the Lord would put up a fight; I didn't mean I'll commit suicide with you – I'm not going to throw my life away, that's a senseless, useless thing to do, it's against reason; if you are going to throw away your life, I'm not going to. That's how his mind was beginning to operate. So he wanted to be involved as an observer, but uncommitted. He wanted to be near enough to see if Jesus would fight, in which case he would come and die with him. But he also wanted to see if Jesus was just going to mess up the whole situation, give in and not raise a finger, in which case Peter wanted to be in the courtyard, near the back door, and get out quickly. I am sure that's how he felt. "He went into the courtyard that he might observe the outcome." Can you see what's happening? He's saying: Jesus, I trust you. I thought you would manage the situation better than this. I thought at least you would try to avoid death. But if you are just going to go straight to your death like that, well then I'm sorry my promise doesn't hold. I promised to die with you – backs against the wall – but not to throw away life like this. The natural instinct of self-preservation is arguing in Peter's mind.

Then it has to be a little girl who says, "Peter you were one of them." Now what is the point of throwing your life away because of a little girl? It's not a big enough issue. That doesn't make sense – to let a little girl betray you – so Peter told a white lie so that he, as he thought, could stay on there and observe. My grandfather, years ago, was preaching in Manchester and he used the phrase in the pulpit "a white lie" and somebody from the gallery of the Oxford Hall in Manchester shouted out, "Nay lad, they're all black uns," and this is perfectly true. The little white lie leads to the bigger white lie and sooner or later to the black one. The first little step of compromise and you are finished. The first decision is the most difficult and the most important. The rest will be easy after that, and if you make the right decision on the first occasion the rest will come easier. If you make the wrong decision then the wrong decision will come easier. It may have been a little girl, and Peter may have naturally said, "What's the point of throwing your life away when it's just a little girl who has made a remark? This isn't the big issue. This isn't the real point to fight yet." That's how we talk ourselves out of doing the right thing, but mark my words, it is when we do the right thing in the little circumstance that we will be able to do the right thing in the big one.

From time to time someone says to me: "Supposing I had to face the possibility of becoming a Christian martyr, I don't think I could." My answer is always the same: if you are faithful to the Lord in little things now, he will give you the grace to be a martyr when the big time comes. But if you flunked it in the little situation with the servant girl, well when the forces of the land are against you, you won't be able to face them. This was true of Peter. The little white lie became a black one, and the black one became cursing and swearing. Mind you, he had been a fisherman, and he had plenty of vocabulary at his disposal, and he used it. Here's the old swearing fisherman coming back. "I don't know him. I don't know what you're talking about." – But you've got the Galilean accent; you're a northerner, so was he.

Cursing comes naturally especially to this temperament which speaks before it thinks, and therefore has to fill in with a lot of words. Yet for three years Peter has been with Jesus.

At that point, Jesus was led through from the court, across the courtyard, to the cells for the night. If it is the place where now stands the church of St. Peter in Gallicantu, you can still see the very courtyard. Across that courtyard Jesus was led, and he just looked at Peter. That look broke Peter's heart. I wonder what it said. I have seen many pictures by artists who have tried to portray the look Jesus gave, but I am not satisfied with any of them. I just don't know what that look said. Did it say, "Peter, who was right?" Did it say, "Peter, so I am all alone, am I not?" Did it say, "Peter, I still love you in spite of it all?" I don't know what it said, but I know that it broke Peter's heart and that he went out and just sobbed and heaved, and it was night. The same black, cold night. Now Peter was stumbling through the back alleys of Jerusalem, sobbing. What was it all about? What was happening?

The nearest experience I can bring from my own personal experience to match this sight of Peter heaving, quivering, sobbing, is from the animal world. I remember when we were breaking in a horse. If ever you have done that, you will know the point that comes. You are struggling with every natural instinct of the horse to be free, to go where it wills, to throw things off its back. You struggle, and you may have to spend hours at the end of that rope holding that horse while it tears around you. You go on until there comes a moment, and you know when it comes, when the horse is broken in. You see the horse standing—it will be quivering, sweating, shaking, heaving, but it is standing still. Then you take a bridle and a saddle, you slip them on, and it stands there, and you have won.

As I look at Simon Peter with his shoulder shuddering in the back alleys of Jerusalem, I see Simon broken in. I see him ready for the bridle, to go where the Lord wants him to go. I see him ready for the saddle, for the Lord to ride. I see *Peter* now, the beginning of the rock. He has got to rock bottom but that is where you find the rock. I see hope.

The glorious thing is that Peter must have told all this to someone else or we would never known. It is in all four Gospels and since, alas, human nature remembers us for the bad things we have done rather than the good things, you know about Peter's denial probably more than anything else about him. But he talked about it, he shared it. Why? Because it was not the end of the story, it was the beginning. It was not a despair that led him to do what Judas did and hang himself. It was a broken reed lying flat on the ground that night, but it was becoming the rock.

9

THE RESURRECTION

Read 1 Corinthians 15:1–28

Here is a portion of that passage:

> For what I received I passed on to you as a first
> importance that Christ died for our sins according to the
> scriptures. That he was buried and that he was raised
> on the third day according to the Scriptures and that he
> appeared to Peter and then to the twelve and after that
> he appeared to more than five hundred of the brothers
> at the same time.

We are going to look at the evidence for the resurrection,
at the experience they had of the resurrection, and then the
significance of the resurrection and the meaning behind
these stirring events.

If you could have seen the disciples on that first Easter
Saturday, you would have seen a group of broken men whose
little world had ended, whose dreams had been shattered,
and whose life had come to an end – men who couldn't even
face going back to their ordinary jobs, stunned, bewildered,
hopeless, having lost all their self-respect. Their morale was
at the lowest ebb because their leader had been assassinated,
another member of the small group had committed suicide,

they were now down to eleven. It was enough to break the heart of anyone. Behind locked doors, cowering, afraid, hardly daring to look at each other, you see the truth is that when Christ died, Christianity died.

If Christ had died and that were the end of the story there would have been no church. The universe would become a vast cemetery of lost values and dead dreams, for the hopes of the disciples were pinned on this man in a way they had never been pinned to anyone else. They couldn't go back and pick up the threads of their old jobs and their home life and face it again. In fact, Jesus had spoiled them for anything else and I have seen this tragedy lived out in people today. Once you have seen Jesus, once you have known him, once you have tasted of the powers of the age to come, you can never be the same again. You have been spoiled for everything else and you can never go back to where you were before. You can try, and how miserable and hard you become! You can't live again the life that finished when you met Jesus. You can never get him out of your mind. So many things will remind you of him – the sound of singing out of a church door, a sunset, a chance meeting with an old Sunday school friend.... So many things can come back, and they can remind you of the life you knew with Jesus.

When the tomb was sealed, the disciples' hopes and dreams were sealed within that tomb – dead. It is against that background that the day of the resurrection shines. In a sense, you have to go through the darkness to the light – as you have to go through the conviction of sin before you can find the Saviour. You have got to be brought down low before you can be lifted up. It is against the background of the broken disciples that the resurrection shines in all the glory of the Lord.

Let us look first at the *evidence* for the resurrection. I mean now the circumstantial evidence, which is not the best kind of evidence in a court of law. These are the kinds of evidence that look at the things that point towards a conclusion but do not prove it. The indications, which for those who interpret them rightly can reveal the truth, are part of a cumulative case, and four pieces of evidence are very telling. Each one of them in themselves could be explained another way, but all four together are very powerful.

Firstly, when they went to the tomb on Easter Sunday morning the garden was deserted. Do you realise how startling that evidence is? Do you realise that for a soldier under those circumstances to guard a tomb and to run away from his sentry duty in those days would mean certain court martial and probably death?

The garden was empty within just hours of the soldiers having been put in it. Something extraordinary happened in that place. There must have been something greater to cause a greater fear in those soldiers than the fear of court martial and execution. You have got to find that "something" if you deny the truth of the resurrection. You have to explain the evidence of the deserted garden.

Secondly, there is the evidence of the rolled stone — imagine a huge round stone weighing a ton and a quarter. See the men heaving it into place and sealing it. Within twelve hours the stone is lying flat and the seals are broken. You have to explain that if you are not prepared to accept the truth of the resurrection. The women could certainly not have done it, and it was done before they got there. The record states that none of the men got there first. Then who did it?

The Bible states simply that an angel – one angel – came, pushed a ton and a quarter over and sat on it. But of course the angels are far superior to human beings in physical strength. If you don't believe that interpretation then what's yours? Any better? The third indirect or circumstantial evidence is the empty tomb. That's something no-one has ever been able to explain away. It is basic evidence. No-one ever challenged this. They tried to explain where the body had gone, but nobody ever said the tomb wasn't empty. It could never have been mistaken for another. There was only one tomb in that place. It was a private tomb in someone's back garden, not a cemetery. So no-one has ever been able to say, "It was a mistake, they went to the wrong tomb in the half-light of early morning." If they had, then the authorities would have found the right tomb very quickly. If you do not accept that Jesus rose from the dead, you must find a better explanation.

The fourth piece of circumstantial evidence is the folded grave clothes. When they buried a body in those days they did not put it in a shroud. They had a forty-foot long bandage of linen and they wrapped it round and round the body as they sprinkled spices in – almost mummifying the body, but they left the shoulders and the face bare, and then they took another small bandage and wrapped the head in a turban.

When they got to that tomb and looked in, they found the grave clothes wrapped around but collapsed, and the turban, still wrapped in the shape of a head, was lying by itself. When John saw that he realised that no human hand had touched those grave clothes. Now that is the evidence and no-one has ever been able to deny the way the grave clothes were laid. No-one ever was able to prove that those who said "That's what they found" did not find that. It was open for anyone to go and look during the rest of that day or the next few weeks.

Those four circumstantial things were enough to make John, the author of the fourth Gospel, believe that Jesus was not there. But all these bits of circumstantial evidence point to the absence of Christ from the grave – that's all, his absence, and that is not enough. They do not say anything about his presence. It would not be enough in a court of law to clinch a case with final conviction. More than circumstantial evidence is needed. I rang up a solicitor and said, "Can I talk with you about the evidence for the resurrection? Would you put it in legal terms to me how this would be presented in a court of law? What you would call this kind of evidence?"

He told me the best kind of evidence in a court is not circumstantial but eyewitness—that is the finest evidence. Not the evidence of things but the evidence of people – of people who were there and who saw what happened, and who had firsthand eyewitness testimony. Then he reminded me of something I had already pondered deeply, which is that when you get good eyewitness testimony there will always be apparent discrepancies between the witnesses, which on further examination turn out to be not inconsistencies but evidence that they are good eyewitnesses.

To put it negatively, if you sat in a court of law and ten people all swore that they would tell the truth the whole truth and nothing but the truth, and then brought out the identical story, word for word, any judge worth his salt would dismiss the case. But this kind of apparent discrepancies are, some of them, in the resurrection narratives. One of the Gospels says, "There was an angel inside the tomb dressed in white who said, 'He's not here, why do you look in the cemetery for someone who's alive?'" Then another Gospel, describing the same event, says, "There were two angels, one at the head and one at the foot at where the body had lain." Not a contradiction – you will find exactly that kind of discrepancy in good eyewitnesses. If there were two cars in the crash, one witness would have noticed one of them, another witness would have noticed both, and both are testifying, and that kind of discrepancy is profoundly convincing. It shows they had not agreed on the story. It shows they are talking of that which they had seen. I can list about fifteen such seeming "discrepancies" in the Gospel narrative which, on closer examination, prove to not be contradictions but proof – to be evidence that this is the very best kind of eyewitness testimony. So we move from the circumstantial to the eyewitness. This is the best kind of evidence – those who have said, "I have experienced his presence."

The first witness in the box is Mary. She was not in a pre-conditioned state to believe that he had risen from the dead. In fact, it is a remarkable indication of the truth of her evidence that she admitted later that when she met Jesus she did not recognise him. If she had been cooking up a story she would not have put this touch in: I thought it was the cemetery keeper, the gardener; I thought it was a man who looked after that garden – and that rings true. But it was Mary who heard just one word, "Mary" – and she is an eyewitness. The story is told with such restraint and delicacy that no-one can accuse her of playing of the situation.

Then Peter – I wish we knew this hidden story in his life. It has never been recorded. Where did it happen? When did it happen? Some time between morning and evening on that first Easter day, some time in some place, Peter looked up and there he was. Before any of the other apostles, already Peter is standing out as the leader, and Christ approaches him first. The Lord appeared as the apostle said, later that night, "The Lord appeared to Simon" – notice that word "Simon". By now you will know the significance of that – the Lord has appeared to Simon "the reed." But appear he did, and Peter joins the rank of witnesses.

Later that evening they were sitting having their supper. They were hungry, they needed to eat. They had probably not had a square meal since the day Jesus died. They had been so down, but that night, with the sense of growing excitement, with the rumours spreading around, with Peter's knowledge of Jesus by personal experience, they decided to have a good meal, and they went out and got their food, and they came back and they sat down, and there they were. Suddenly, the well-remembered voice said, "Peace be unto you." Now again the story rings true. It says, "They couldn't believe it." Not, "They were cooking up a story," but they couldn't believe it. They hadn't been able to believe it for sorrow up to now, yet now they couldn't believe it for sheer joy. Until Jesus said, "What are you having for supper, lads? Give me some fish." They sat down and they stared dumbstruck while they saw their supper disappear. That is real evidence, when you see your supper go.

They were convinced that night, and so it went on. We could go on filling this witness box with eyewitnesses. What do you imagine would happen in a court in this country if you could produce nearly five hundred people who were able to give the kind of direct eyewitness testimony that would ring true? Do you think they might accept that the case was proven? I don't know of a single case ever in a court of law that could call on five hundred witnesses to the truth of a personal event. I stand to be corrected, but I don't think it has ever been done. If you could get ten to give such testimony you would think you have the strongest case you needed. But it went up to five hundred, and as Paul, writing some thirty years later about that five hundred said, "Most of them are still alive, you can check." This was the confidence of the early disciples—they invited people to check. They were so sure of the truth that they laid themselves wide open to be shot down if the evidence was weak, but nobody ever was able to do it.

So the evidence passed to the *experience*, and this is what must happen to everyone. You will not be convinced that Jesus rose from the dead until the evidence has become an experience – until you have met the risen Lord.

I remember a young man who came to see me once and we went through the evidence. He was interested and I gave him a book to read. He went through it. It was Frank Morrison's little book *Who Moved the Stone*, which is a very convincing book written by a young law student who set out to prove that Jesus didn't rise from the dead, realising that if he could prove it, Christianity would collapse. He says in the Introduction, after writing part of the book, "I have to stop and write a totally different book." The young man to whom I gave the book talked, and then he went away. He returned to me a week later and said, "Do you know, I was walking down the High Street in Slough. I met Jesus." Slough is not the most romantic place. I wouldn't have said it was a place for mystical experiences! But he has known Jesus ever since. The High Street in Slough! You don't need a religious sanctuary. You don't need the right atmosphere, not when it's truth. If it wasn't truth we would need to build up, wouldn't we? We would need to condition folk. But with the truth, all you need do is state it, and say, "Check up for yourself, try it."

But even that is not the deepest meaning of the resurrection. I want to move on to the *significance*. Why did it happen? That is a far more important question. We can't go through it all here, but I want to begin by pointing out that in fact the life which Jesus lived after his resurrection was in several material respects very different from the life he had lived before he died. It was not simply a case of coming back to life. If it had been as other cases have been – you have heard about the "kiss of life", massaging the heart and all the rest of it – those are "resuscitation". I would not call them resurrection. When a person comes back after resuscitation he comes back to live exactly the life he had lived before. He will go on getting older and he will die again, and he will go through it all again, and the life he lives afterwards will be the same.

But resurrection leads to a different life and that is a

very important point we have to grasp. Now there are many indications that Jesus was in some way different. It was the same Jesus, and yet different. The same voice, the same gestures, the same memories, the same kind of conversation, the same patience, the same wisdom in handling people, the same gentleness, it's the same Jesus all right, and yet there are differences. For one thing, quite a number of those who knew him best failed to recognise him. Mary was one. Cleopas and his wife on the road to Emmaus were another two. They failed to recognise him, there must have been something a little different. Then there was the fact that he now told them, in a very different way, not to touch him.

Now it isn't that they couldn't touch him – in fact he did invite Thomas to do so – but when Mary in the garden saw him she got hold of his ankles and she held on. He said, and I give you the literal translation: "Stop clinging to me, Mary. I haven't yet ascended to my Father and your Father" – as if the relationship with Mary has got to be different from now on. You could touch me before, but now I don't want you to. It wasn't that he wasn't touchable, that he wasn't real. He was. She got hold of him. But in some way he's saying, "Mary, it's got to be different now." She must have been very puzzled. Then, thirdly, there was the fact that he only appeared to chosen people. He never appeared to Pilate, he never appeared to Annas and Caiaphas; he never appeared to Herod. They would have been very convinced if he had but he didn't.

He didn't move in the same circles, and one person he had absolutely nothing to do with after his resurrection was Satan. There is not a single temptation recorded after his resurrection. There couldn't be. It was a different life, a life beyond the reach of Satan. The fourth difference was this: a thing he had not done before he died, but which now he did frequently, was to keep disappearing. They just sat down with a meal and he broke bread, and suddenly there they are looking at a pile of crumbs on the table and he has gone. He kept doing this until, frankly, they felt a little insecure.

Thomas was the one who really felt it first. He was out wandering the streets that first Easter day evening so he missed the Lord, and when he came back they said, "We have seen the Lord".

He said, "Unless I see the nailmarks in his hands and put my finger where the nails were, and put my hand into the wound in his side, I will not believe it."

A week later he happened to be there, and Jesus said: Thomas, I heard you. Come and do it.

You heard me? Were you here last Sunday when I couldn't see you?

It gave them a sense of insecurity, and then gradually, over six weeks, the insecurity changed to security, as they knew now that you don't have to see Jesus to know that he is in the room with you.

As long as they were dependent on seeing him with their earthly eyes, he was tied down to that one place. Christ was weaning them from a dependence on physical senses. As soon as they had learnt to trust him without seeing, he could return to heaven and send his Spirit throughout the world, and that is what he was working towards. It was a different relationship. Prior to that it was a physical relationship, now it was to be a relationship of faith, so it was different.

What was the meaning of this difference? It means four things, each of them more profound than the last. If you only remember one of them, that is enough, but if you remember all four that should be a great blessing to you. **First it means a new body that will not grow old, get diseased and die.** Frankly, I am not terribly thrilled with the kind of spiritual future that some people think about – floating around as spirits. Thank God my future is as real as the resurrection.

When I conduct a funeral and the coffin has been lowered into the grave, we repeat those marvellous words: "Who will fashion a new body like his glorious body." Then you put a body in the earth, and I must say I still prefer burial to cremation for this reason. It is like planting in the earth, and when you plant something you expect to see something from it. But whether it is from dust or ashes doesn't make any difference to God. Don't get worried, God is able to bring from dust or ash, it doesn't matter, but he is going to bring a new body. I don't believe in spirits floating on forever without any tangible expression. The resurrection means for me a new body. "Handle me and see"; "Give me some fish to eat." A ghost doesn't have flesh and bones. Jesus was trying to tell them, persuade them, convince them, that our future is not the future of a ghost. Hallelujah for that! Who wants to be a ghost? I want to be a whole person.

The second thing that the resurrection means is a new life, a higher plane of existence. If you think that being a Christian is imitating Christ, you are absolutely right, but that does not mean imitating his life before he died, it means the life after he rose. Christians are not to live the life he lived before – they are to live his *risen* life. That you can't imitate, of course. You can only do it as he lives it in you. "I live, yet no longer I but Christ lives in me." We are to live this new life; we live it now. What is baptism but saying my old life is buried, it's washed away. I am now living a risen life. We rise from the waters. We don't just bury as he was buried. You are buried with him in baptism. As he was raised, you are raised. What to do? To live a risen life, to live in the power of the resurrection, to live the kind of life he lived on earth after his resurrection, which was a life that Satan had nothing to do with.

Thirdly, it means a new humanity. As Adam began our race, and as I am a descendant of that Adam and you are too, there is now a new race that has begun by a second Adam – Christ – and he is the firstborn of it, the beginning of a whole new humanity. There are two races of people on earth. They are not black and white, not on the outside. They are on the inside, in God's sight. The two races on earth are those who are *in* Adam and those who are *in* Christ – and all in Adam will die, and all in Christ shall be made alive. Even though people look much the same on the outside, and even though they may get on the same train to go up to London on a Monday morning, even though they mingle together so closely, yet when God looks down he can see two humanities – the old one and the new one. The resurrection means a new mankind, a new human race, and *in* Christ you belong to the new race.

Finally, it means a new universe. The most amazing thing about the resurrection is that in it we see the very first inkling of what God is going to do to the entire material universe. He is going to dissolve it, burn it up with fire, and then he is going to create a new heaven, a new planet earth, new space, a whole new universe – after all, if we have got new bodies we will have to have somewhere to live.

How do you know that God can do that with material things? How do we know that he can take planet earth and evaporate it and build a new earth? I tell you how we know – because he has already started doing it. They laid a cold corpse in a tomb. That corpse evaporated into nothing. That is why the clothes collapsed – because there was nothing left inside them. The body that they laid in the tomb didn't come out of the tomb, it disappeared, and Jesus came with a new body. It was the first part of the material universe to evaporate and be recreated. I ask you this simple question, which you may never have asked yourself: where did Jesus get his clothes from in the resurrection? Do you think he had to go around looking for a shop? No. It was all part of the new creation. We are told that in heaven God has clothes ready for us – it is part of the material new creation. So even the clothes which Jesus wore after his resurrection were proof that God is able to create new material things.

So the old disappeared and evaporated, and the resurrection is the beginning of the new creation. It is the first part of the material universe that God has re-created, and in that lies the promise, the earnest, the first instalment of an entirely new creation. That is why I want you to get a big view of the resurrection, and realise that it is the beginning of a gigantic re-creation programme. New life, new bodies, new planets. That is what God is doing, and he began it on the morning of the resurrection.

No wonder we Christians get excited! You would have to have a heart of stone not to get excited, wouldn't you? When you consider it all, it is almost beyond the imagination, but it is not beyond faith, and by faith we accept all this to be true.

The greatest news of all is this: you can start all this right now. You don't need to wait until after you die. You can begin to have eternal life *now*.

Note
I have said little or nothing about Peter in this chapter, simply because we have no record of his encounter with the risen Jesus on that first Easter Sunday. But we can conjecture part of their conversation from an extraordinary claim in his first epistle or letter. Maybe Peter had asked: 'Where on earth have you been?' Jesus must have told him he had been in the world of departed spirits (Hades, not heaven or hell) and had been preaching the gospel, not to all the dead, but to the many who had been drowned in the flood in Noah's time, premature victims of the only such universal judgement (see 1 Peter 3:18 – 4:6). But all that I have said about the evidence and experience of the resurrection was true of Peter, who was so convinced of its reality.

10

MEETING JESUS IN GALILEE

Read John 21:1–25

When delivering a series of talks on Simon Peter, I received an anonymous letter which began: "*Dear Sir, I have never heard a more mean-mouthed hypocritical nauseating load of mythological rubbish....*" It continues in much same way: "*Nobody dead or alive can disappear into thin air, and no person can produce fish by a wave of the hand or turn water into wine, etc., you must be raving mad.*"

Well, I would rather be this kind of mad! It feels good. I would love to introduce this person, had he given his name and address, to a friend of mine in the North, a converted bookmaker. He is now with the Lord in glory, but somebody who was saying the same thing to him said, "How can you believe that somebody could turn water into wine?"

"Well," he said, "he's turned beer into furniture in my house."

Which points to the fact that, to Christians at any rate, the more wonderful things that the Lord does are not just with material things but with people – the change he can make in human nature. Who said human nature cannot be changed? It is far more wonderful to mould human nature than it is to manipulate nature, and the Lord was good at both. Now there is an element of truth in the statement that you can't

147

change human nature. I never cease to marvel at this, that a person who comes to Christ changes, yet doesn't change. Peter remained Peter to his dying day. Paul remained Paul. Paul never became Peter; Peter never became Paul. Yet both were changed. How the Lord can change us, and yet keep our identity and personalities.

What exactly happens to our temperament when we come to Christ? We are not given a new temperament, a new personality. The same temperament goes right through into our Christian life, but it is gloriously transformed.

We are going to see this in this chapter. Peter and John, after they became Christians, were the same temperament basically as before. God doesn't want a lot of robots in heaven, he wants people each with their own individual personality – so he doesn't want you to cease to be you, but he does want to change you.

Is this a paradox? Yes, it is. It seems to be absurd and yet it is really true. Peter's temperament remained the same but the difference is that in the first part of his life, right up to our Lord's death, he was what is called a "carnal Christian", which means someone whose temperament controls his Christian experience, whereas after our Lord's resurrection we see a different Peter. We see someone with the same personality but now his temperament is controlled by his Christian experience. He is now what we call a "spiritual" Christian, and after the day of Pentecost the Holy Spirit really gets going with Peter. All the facets of his temperament are still there, but now they are at the perfect disposal of the Lord himself.

Now they are not a handicap, now they don't lead him to saying and doing things impetuously that are wrong. Now he is the first one to jump up and speak on Pentecost, as he has been the first to open his mouth for many months, but for the first time he doesn't put his foot in it, and that's the difference. So we are looking at a man who is transformed. From the resurrection onwards the change begins, and you can notice it. Peter is still the impetuous one, still the one who is first into a situation, but now Peter is being put first not by his own self-will, not by his own impetuosity, but by the Lord himself. It is quite obvious that Simon Peter was the most important Christian in the early church. Just as with the Virgin Mary, Roman Catholics have made far too much of her and Protestants have made too little of her, so with Simon Peter, Roman Catholics have made far too much of him in calling him the first Pope, but we have made far too little of him in just treating him as one of the disciples.

He was in fact the first rock on which the church was built. He was the first living stone to be built into the foundations of the church of Christ. He was the first pastor if he wasn't the first Pope. In fact, you could almost say he was the prime minister in the early church, in the normal sense of both those words – spelling them with a small "p" and a small "m." So let's give Peter his due and let's see how he became first.

You notice, for example, that when the women went to the tomb it was an angel who gave Peter a special place. The angel said, "Why seek the living among the dead? He's risen; he's not here. He will go and meet you in Galilee. You'll see him there as he told you. So go and tell the disciples and Peter" – and there it is, Peter is now singled out, not because of his own impetuosity but because the angel singles him out, and presumably the angel was told this message by the Lord.

The next thing we find is that Peter and John were the first men at the empty tomb. When the women get back and report the message, you couldn't see Peter and John for dust. They ran across Jerusalem, through the streets, up the hill to get into that cemetery and find out what happened. John was a better runner than Peter and got there first, but John stooped down and looked into the tomb to see what had happened.

It was Peter – notice the impetuosity still, but it took him further than John – Peter not only stooped down and looked in, he ran straight in. He was the first man into that tomb.

Once again there is a primacy of Peter coming through, but of course Peter could act first, John could think first. John thought more than Peter did. Peter wondered what on earth had happened. John looked at those grave clothes rolled up and he just knew that no man had touched that grave. So John got the message, Peter didn't. Peter wandered off. I don't know where he went but I do know that one of the greatest untold stories in the Bible occurred that morning. I wish I knew where, I wish I knew when. I wish I knew what was said, but some time that morning Jesus met Simon Peter, and Simon Peter was the first man to meet Jesus after his resurrection.

Why did Jesus choose Peter first? He had been the first to confess faith in Christ. "You are the Christ, the Son of the living God."

"Upon this rock I'll build this church."

So it was natural that Jesus should appear to Peter first. But so sacred an interview, so deep was it to Peter, that he never shared it. You presumably know that Simon Peter shared his memories with a young man called John Mark, and John Mark wrote them down in the Mark's Gospel. What we know of Peter comes direct from Peter's own lips. We know of the denial from Peter himself, but this was one story he never told. Are there not in your life some experiences too sacred to share, some things too deep? They are between you and the Lord; you couldn't talk about them.

I do know from what was said later that Jesus never once mentioned to Simon Peter his denial. He appeared to Peter, and later that night, when the two from Emmaus ran back fifteen miles up the hill and got to Jerusalem, told the apostles "He's alive", they said, "We know. He's appeared to Peter so we know." Oh, I wish we had that story. I would love to be able to preach on it! Peter, the man whose world had just dropped out three days before – "Go and tell Peter," and he met Peter. Now all these things happened on Easter Sunday.

A funny thought struck me: "I wonder if they were intended to happen." I have the feeling that Jesus didn't intend to meet the apostles in Jerusalem because the message at the grave in the morning was, "Go and tell his disciples to get straight off to Galilee and they will see me there."

But that night they are still not heading off for Galilee, they are still in a locked room in Jerusalem. It is as if Jesus had to meet them halfway, as if he knew they just weren't going to set off to Galilee, that they just wouldn't accept the message – and as if Jesus had to appear in Jerusalem two or three times to convince them that when he said he would see them in Galilee, he would. I have the feeling that these were an extra bonus to help them along. How like the Lord if it was, but he specifically gave the message, "Get straight off to Galilee and I'll meet you there." I can understand why Jesus wanted to get them back to where it all began; to get them away from the atmosphere of tension, strain, hatred and hostility in Jerusalem, and get them up to Galilee.

If you have been to the Holy Land I think you will understand. Jerusalem is fascinating but it is busy and crowded, smelly and claustrophobic, and even more so when you feel that everybody is against you. But when you get to Galilee, it is like a jewel set in the hills – that lovely little lake thirteen miles by eight miles wide, deep blue-green – and brown hills. You know why he wanted to meet them there. Let's get away from all that's happened here, let's get back there to where it all began. Let's get back to simplicities. Why? Because our Lord Jesus was going to have them start all over again. They had all let him down. Peter had denied him, so it would be back to the beginning. In fact, they were to go back to their fishing, and Jesus was to stand on the seashore and say again, "Follow me."

Now we need to balance what we read in Hebrews and what we read in John. Hebrews has some very serious things to say about those who commit apostasy, those who, having tasted of the powers of the age to come, turn their back on Christ and go away. Hebrews says there is no possibility for repentance for people who deliberately do this. They crucified the Lord afresh, they have killed their only Saviour again, and they can do no more. We need to remember that serious word. But on the other hand, let's draw tremendous comfort from the fact that those who deny Christ and those who run away from him out of sheer cowardice, he's prepared to take right back to the beginning again and say, "Follow me." Many of us would not be in the church now if the Lord hadn't taken us back to the beginning of our Christian life and said, "Let's start again; let's wipe the slate clean. Let's go back to the beginning. Now, follow me." When he does it like that, you are more determined to follow him than you ever were before, The sheer grace of giving you a second chance!

Let's go up to Galilee with Peter and John. The chapter starts in the hours of darkness but it finishes in a blaze of sunlight. The chapter starts with a backward look. It finishes with a forward look. Peter and six others were back in the original place they came from. This was home for every one of the twelve apostles except Judas. Judas Iscariot was the only one from the south, the rest were all from the north. They had that northern accent and they went back to the north. There they were in familiar surroundings; they felt more secure. After Jerusalem, Galilee was wonderful. This was where it all began; this was where the memories of the crowds and the miracles flooded back into their minds.

When they got back into their old situation, they tended to

go back to their old life, and Peter said, "Let's go fishing." People have debated why he said this. Some have thought it was Peter's temperament again – impetuous Peter, he had to do something with his hands, you know: we can't sit around all day waiting for him to appear, he came to us while we were on the sea formerly, he can walk on water; let's go fishing, let's be busy.... There's something about Peter's temperament that likes to be busy. But I don't think that's the real reason. Did he need the money? Well they had learnt that the Lord had provided their money, so I don't think that was it. Was it to get away from people because people would be talking, and it would be a little embarrassing to try and explain all that had happened? But I don't think that would be it. Was it the pull of the old life when there is the boat there and the nets? You put a tractor within three yards of me and I want to get back on the seat and go ploughing, I just love to. Was it the pull of the old life or could it have been most deeply that Peter, after his denial, thought that Jesus would never have him back as a fisher of men, so he had better become a fisher of fish again? I have the feeling that was it. In spite of the meeting with the resurrected Lord, I know that Jesus had not yet wiped out the memory of the denial. He had not squared the account on that one. I think deep in Peter's heart was: I had better pick up my old trade; I am glad that I met Jesus but he will never have me as an apostle, not now. I had better pick up the threads of a useful life – I'm going fishing.

The others said the same. The seven of them set out that night and it was a complete failure. Night is the best time to fish in Galilee. The fish will rise, they seek the moon, and if there isn't a moon the fishermen will take an oil lamp and hang it over the boat, and the fish will come to that. Still to this day you can see the little wooden boats and little lights dotted about where the fishing boats are trying to attract the fish. It is a most romantic scene, a marvellous place to be at four in the morning. The fishermen are there, but this night they caught nothing and that is highly unusual. Galilee is very well-stocked. Sometimes they get a better catch than other times, but they always get something and this time nothing. I wonder if Peter was thinking his old skill had gone, that the three years had wasted his gifts for fishing.

It is breakfast time now, first light of day, morning mists, someone on the shore about a hundred yards away. A voice carries well over water at that time in the morning. You hear the fishermen calling to each other, and this voice said, "Lads, you haven't caught anything, have you?" The very word "lads" tells us something very important. For those disciples were still in their late teens or early twenties at the latest. They were young men. Christianity didn't begin with old people. It began with young men in their very prime. Jesus began with young men. I hope that helps them to feel part of the story. What the Lord can do with a bunch of lads!

He knew, as he knows everything about you. He knows your failure; he knows when you are depressed. It wasn't a very tactful remark to make to fishermen. Have you ever tried it on a fisherman? Haven't caught anything, have you?

The next most tactless thing you can do to a fishermen is to give him advice. The biggest miracle on this morning was that they took it. You try advising a fisherman where to cast. It's just not done, and this man on the shore: "Try the other side of your boat." Now that's only ten feet away at most. How ridiculous! But do you know what he's saying? You get used to throwing the net out of a certain side of the boat. You get into a tradition. You get into a rut. It's the way you've always done it. It's the way it has to be done. There's a lesson coming up now, do I need to underline it?

"But we've always done it this way." Well, just try doing it the other way! You see, that way may suit the fishermen but the other way will suit the fish. Do you get the message? Because that's where they are. I remember a dear brother who faithfully ran an open-air meeting regularly at a street corner. He went out faithfully every night, and he preached the gospel faithfully. There was only one snag: he was about an hour late. The crowds were there an hour earlier, but that open-air meeting had been held at that hour year in and year out, and he was going to see it through, but the fish weren't there. If he just gone an hour earlier they would all have been there on their way home. How bound we are by the way we have done things.

Throw your net the other way. Do something different. Because it was the command of the Lord, and because it suited the fish, they did it and they caught many. Which do you think was the bigger miracle? That the Lord had kept the fish away all night, or sent them all there as soon as day came? People have debated whether there was a miracle here. From the bank of the Sea of Galilee you can certainly see the fish, which do gather in groups in the water because off Capernaum there are hot springs coming up through the waters. It is a most unusual experience swimming there. You swim along – cold, hot; cold, hot – and very soon when we have taken a busload of people there, and they have gone in swimming, we have seen that they have gathered in groups. You can certainly see them from the shore, but from the shore you can see better through the water than you can looking down from a boat. H. B. Morton, in his book *In Search of the Master* describes how an Arab called Abdul used to stand on the bank and tell the people where to cast the net. Is this simply a matter of someone doing that? No, I don't think so. I think it was more than that. John saw that it was more than that because John realised that it was quite uncanny that you can cast your net from a boat all night and catch not one, and cast the net six feet away at the other side and catch a hundred and fifty-three. There's something supernatural about that, something a bit eerie, and John realised the truth – that's no ordinary man telling us where to cast the net, that's the Lord, that's Jesus.

Peter's temperament – he just pulled off his clothes and jumped into the water. What a way to prepare! John was a better businessman: he stayed and pulled the net, and the other six were thinking of both. Having toiled all night, they wanted something to show for it.

How human it is, how people react in an immediate situation according to their temperament. Ah, but you see Peter wanted to get to the Lord. Fish – you could get the fish another time – but he wanted to get hold of the Lord, and the Lord will honour anybody like that.

They counted the fish later. You would be amazed at all the commentators have to say about 153. They go to town! Those who like working out numbers have a great time. Somebody realised that one plus two, plus three, plus four, plus five, plus six, plus seven, plus eight, plus nine, plus ten, plus eleven, plus twelve, thirteen, fourteen, fifteen, sixteen, and seventeen adds up to a hundred and fifty-three. Well, what do you know? They therefore said there must be some significance in seventeen. Ten commandments plus the perfect number seven. I hope they found it edifying! I expect you know that the Hebrews didn't have figures for numbers, only letters. If you take Simon Jonah, which was his surname, and turn it into figures, it adds up to 153, which is really interesting but neither here nor there. Some people have said it means a hundred Gentiles, fifty Jews, and three of the Trinity. Well, that's not bad. Somebody else worked out that there are 153 different species of fish to be found in the Middle East! I will tell you the meaning of 153. There is a profound and deep meaning in that number and here it is: that is an awful lot of fish, and that's all it means. That is more than they usually caught in one catch, in one cast you might get a dozen, you might get twenty, but to get 153 large ones, that's worth counting. In fact, that's all it means.

It underlines this truth: that the Lord wants us to *catch* fish. A fisherman returned and his wife said, "Did you catch any?" "No, but I've influenced a good few." Now that is not our job. We may influence many people as we go through life, but we are called to catch fish – not just to influence but to catch. He was saying to Simon Peter: I can still help you to catch. I can still make you a fisherman. I can still do this for you.

Do you remember that in Luke 5 the same thing happened? They cast the net and they caught a great load of fish. But do you notice the one difference between the incident in Luke 5 and that recorded in John 21? The one difference is that in Luke 5 the nets broke but in John 21 the net held. You know the difference has been made by the death and resurrection of Jesus. It is after the death and resurrection that you can cope. In other words, now not only will there be a big catch, but now you will cope with it.

Just seven weeks later, Peter was to catch 3,000 people and the net didn't break. A church of 120 members was able to cope with 3,000 visitors or enquirers! One Christian had 25 people to help to grow up – 25 orphans, now with a new heavenly Father – to look after. Oh, the net didn't break, they coped, and within a few months they had 5,000 to look after. That is the church, and so the miracle happened.

Now remember Peter was pretty wet, and remember it was early morning. When they got to the shore and found Jesus, there he was. It says, "This was the third time he manifested himself to them." That word "manifested" is important. It means prove physically that he was alive – not just proof to their sight but to every other sense. They could smell the breakfast cooking, they could touch him, they could see him, and they could taste the breakfast. Every one of their five senses. That is why Acts 1 says, "He appeared alive and gave them many proofs that he was alive." To those who accuse me of mythological nonsense by talking about the resurrection I want to say: he gave them proofs, *physical proofs*. This was not a hallucination; this was not a ghost appearing.

Have you ever noticed that people rarely, if ever, see ghosts at breakfast time? It is not the time of day for having hallucinations. It is not the time of day for manifestations of spirits—broad daylight, the sun beating down, breakfast time. You are at your least mystical at breakfast time. I want to praise the Lord that he didn't just appear at night to the disciples in a locked up room when they were all under tension anyway, but in the broad light of day when they could look at him – and he built a fire. Where had he got the charcoal? He got fish on it. Where had he got the fish? He had been fishing too. It's so utterly real and so practical. My faith isn't based on night hallucinations; it's based on proofs in the daylight.

Christianity stands up to the day. It is in the night that wrong things happen. It is in the darkness that wrong things happen. In one tragic case connected with exorcism they ignored one little fundamental rule, and that is: don't fight the powers of darkness on their own ground, fight them in broad daylight. Too many Christians have been caught by trying to deal with someone all through the night, and the Lord doesn't want us to work with such things through the night. The day is given to man to work, and we are children of the day. We should live in the light. Christianity is a thing of the light and of the daylight. It is not a thing that you've got to get people in the night and in the darkness to do.

It was early morning, the sun was there, and the breakfast was set. Peter, soaked to the skin, came and he held his hands over the charcoal fire. There are only two occasions in the whole of the Bible when a charcoal fire is mentioned. One was the night before Jesus died when Peter warmed himself at a charcoal fire, and the other is in John 21 in this early morning breakfast scene. Peter holds out his hands, and suddenly it is all there. Suddenly he can't get it out of his mind – the last time he held his hands over a charcoal fire he was swearing and blaspheming and cursing, and telling a little girl that he didn't know Jesus. Suddenly, as he held his hands out, he realised that his conscience was carrying a burden that he just couldn't carry, and Jesus saw it and realised it.

Jesus, in a kind of catharsis of therapeutic healing, took him through the three denials by asking him three questions to get rid of the guilt of each denial, to get the splinter of denial out of his conscience, that it might not go on causing pain. Over the charcoal fire, Jesus looked at Peter again. Oh isn't it marvellous? You couldn't have invented a more moving story; fiction is nothing compared with fact, is it? The scene is set. "Simon..." – Oh, why didn't he call him Peter? Because he's not Peter yet? "Simon, Simon, do you love me more than these?" More than these what? More than these boats, nets, fish? No, I think it means more personal than that—more than these other six. You said you loved me more than them all. You said that if they all ran away, you wouldn't. Do you love me more than these do?

Now there is something comes out in the Greek. The interplay of words is important. We lump all these words together under the one English word "love" and we destroy so much of the meaning of the Bible in doing so. We are very short on words in the English language. I'll try and use the nearest equivalent so you'll get the message. Jesus says, "Simon, son of Jonah, do you really care for me?" Simon replied, "Lord I'm very fond of you." Or to put it in

one word instead of a phrase: "Simon, do you love me?"
"Lord, I like you."

At last Simon is honest. At last, Simon is realistic about
himself. At last Simon is not prepared to say anything beyond
what is true. Gone is the man who said, "I'll die with you."
Gone is the man who'll say, "I'll go to prison with you" and
who didn't." In his place is a man who says, "I like you.
I'm fond of you, but how could I say I care after what I've
done?" So they went on eating breakfast, and after a bite
or two of fish, Jesus turned to Simon again, "Simon do you
love me?" Not, "More than these" this time, just a straight
question: "Do you love me?"

"Lord I'm very fond of you. I like you."

"Feed my sheep."

They went on eating,

Then, third time over the charcoal fire, "Simon are you
fond of me?" The third time Peter was so upset because Jesus
came down to his level. He was so grieved at the third time
Jesus asked him in his own terms. "Are you fond of me?
Do you like me?"

Lord, you know everything. You know how far I can go.
You know how far I can't go. You know the limits now.
You know I'm fond of you. That's as far as I'm going to go.
I won't say any more than is true.

"Simon, feed my sheep."

In that moment not only was the denial cancelled, but the
big fisherman became the big pastor. Changed occupation – a
fishermen became a shepherd. It is such a change of calling,
but Jesus took him where he was. Jesus is not asking for
great things. He is simply saying: will you come to me and
be honest and let me use you as you are? Will you say no
more than you mean?

Jesus is teaching: Don't say it if you don't mean it. But if
you mean what you say then I can use you. He is looking for

real people. That's all, honest people who will not say things they don't mean, but who have so thought of themselves soberly – not more highly than they ought to think – but can thank God for the grace given to them for the gifts that have been given, and say soberly, "Yes, Lord, this is true of me." The Lord says: now I can use you. It is a moving conversation.

So the shepherd became the pastor and Peter was the first pastor ever of the church. "Take care of my little lambs." You can only give responsibility to real people. The final thing to look at here is that Jesus went on to say something else. Peter had said, "Lord you know all things about my past," but the Lord knew all things about his future too.

Jesus was saying: "Peter I'm going to tell you something now. The real problem up to now has been self-will. Right up to now you've dressed yourself, you've decided where you want to go, and you've gone there. Peter, you've been deciding. When I tried to wash your feet you decided how much I would wash. When I told you I was going to the cross, you decided I wasn't. It's self-will, Peter. All your life you've been like this. You're a young man who does what he wants to. You've chosen, you've decided what clothes to wear. You've decided what you're going to do today. But from now on it's going to be different. When you come to the end of the road someone else will dress you up and you'll be taken to a place you don't want to go. Your limbs will be stretched out."

Peter got the message. He was being told that he would be crucified as Jesus had been – mocked, and put in a purple robe and carried where he didn't want to go and then had his limbs stretched. Peter would do the same. But you know this time it's not Peter saying, "I'll die for you." It's Jesus saying, "You'll die for me." Self-will has been replaced by a submission to the Lord. Peter hasn't become a nonentity, he hasn't ceased to be the lovable, impetuous Peter, but now it is under control and now it's under the Lord and now the Lord is saying, "You feed my sheep. You die this way."

The marvellous thing is Peter accepted it calmly, quietly, as the truth, and the truth is that years later he did precisely that, with only one difference. When he came to be nailed to a cross he requested that he be turned upside down and nailed head down, because he didn't feel worthy to be the same way up as Jesus. That is Peter now. He quietly accepts it. Oh what a change! Still Peter, but a much nicer Peter, and a Peter whom God could use now.

But suddenly there's a little bit of the old Peter comes in. "Well, Lord, what about John here?"

Jesus said, "I will make my own plans for John. If I want him to stay on this earth until I come back again, that's my business. It's not your business Peter. What is that to you?"

Hebrews 1:2 appeals to us, "Let us strip off every handicap and the sin that clings to us and let us run with patience the course that is set for us." How important that word is. We are not called to run anybody else's race. We are called to run our course, and the course for Peter included crucifixion. For John, Jesus was hinting that it wouldn't, and in fact, out of the twelve apostles, John was the only one to die of old age. But Peter, that's none of your business. My plan for John is: follow me. And with that, Jesus rose from the breakfast and he walked back along the shore, along the same piece of shore that he had walked three years earlier, when he said, "Follow me." Now Peter got up and followed, and John got up and followed, and they began again. But this time it was to end not in miserable failure and denial, it was to end in heaven with a church that no man could number. It was to end with multitudes, millions accepting the word of Peter and John that Jesus is the Son of God.

11

PASTOR PETER AND BALANCE

Read Acts 1:1–26

One of the things that may happen when you follow Christ is that he will change your job. He did with Simon Peter, changing him from being a fisherman to being a shepherd.

The change took time. Even after the resurrection he still was harking back to the fishing and still saying, "Let's go fishing." He was still essentially in his outlook of fisherman. But Jesus got him on the seashore of Galilee that morning and he said, "Feed my sheep. I want you to be a shepherd," and so he switched jobs. One memorable day, a friend of mine who was a farm manager in the northeast of England said to me, "David, I think you'll finish in the pulpit and not behind a plough." The Lord did change my job at that point but it is still a job – and a job to be done for his glory.

So Simon Peter had his job changed and we can now call him Pastor Peter. The Roman Catholics have made far too much of Peter by calling him the first pope, but Protestants have made far too little of Peter by treating him as one of the other apostles. From now on he is the pastor of the church. He is the one first mentioned in Acts 1 where all the eleven remaining apostles are listed. Peter comes first. He is the pastor, and Jesus appointed him as such. We are going to ask: how did he do his job as a pastor? We are not looking at him now as a fisherman, a disciple. We are looking at him as a pastor. We start with Acts 1, which may seem dull and probably 75% of a pastor's job is quite dull. It is a strange mixture, a pastor's life: the heavenly and the humdrum, the miraculous and the mundane. Anybody who thinks it's sort of living from mountain peak to another should study the life of Pastor Peter. Acts 1 is as important to the history of the church as Acts 2, but most of us treat it as if Acts began with chapter two. I have even heard it said that the church began on the day of Pentecost. It did nothing of the kind. There was a church in Acts 1 and it had a pastor and it was doing all the right things that a church should do.

True, a new dimension came into that church's life in Acts 2, but in Acts 1 we have a picture of a good pastor doing his job. It is rather humdrum and very ordinary. There are no fireworks in Acts 1, nothing that gets you all excited, but Acts 1 is the prelude to Pentecost. Acts 1 laid the foundation for Acts 2. The Spirit came in Acts 2 because Peter had been doing the ordinary job of a pastor in Acts 1. It is so important to realise this, and this is going to be the main message as it comes out. When the wind blows, how vital it is that the ship be shipshape, and has the sail set and the ropes handy, and that everything is ready to catch the power when it comes — that's part of pastoring. So Acts 1 is getting things shipshape, not very exciting. There is a church meeting, business to be discussed, appointments to be made. I meet Christians who say, "Oh, church meetings — a waste of time, you just discuss business. I want to go to inspirational meetings where I'm lifted and the Spirit blows," etc. Have you ever heard anybody like that? You won't meet them at the church meeting. You will find them at the big events, moving around from one to another. They cannot cope with the mundane, the ordinary, the humdrum. I have noticed that as soon as you start sailing they hop on board very quickly. They haven't helped you get the ship ready though. Let us look at how they got the ship ready in Acts 1 – things that Peter kept in balance, and the more one experiences the work of the pastor, the more you understand that the key word is "balance". For example, both scripture and the Spirit are needed, then you get heat and light and that's pretty combustible.

Firstly, notice that Peter was a good pastor. In Acts 1 there are no miracles. There is a church meeting doing its business, and Peter is there as the pastor and he knows what he is doing. So the first balance is that between *intercession* and *instruction*. It is vital that a church has a balance in talking to the Lord and talking to each other. There should there be a ministry of intercession and a ministry of instruction, and both these dimensions are there in Acts 1. Here is a church that is being instructed and interceding. Prayer and preaching are the twin things that must always be there in a church that is going to be healthy, a church that God can bless. You will find before every revival, before every move of God's Spirit, these two dimensions have been present. There were 120 members of this church, and how many do you think they got to the prayer meeting? 120! That is the first challenging thing. There is a lesson for today. God would really move in power if a church with, say, 500 members had all 500 in the prayer meeting. Some obviously have to pray at home because they are elderly or sick, but if every available member is at the prayer meeting I set no limit to what God can do at that place. Prelude to Pentecost consists of a prayer meeting.

Notice who was there. The eleven apostles were there: Peter named first, James and John and so on, right through to Judas (not Judas Iscariot, the other one). Then notice that the women were there. Wherever did people get the idea that women couldn't pray in a Christian prayer meeting? They didn't get it from this book anyway. Mary the mother of Jesus was there. That was her place, in the congregation – in the prayer meeting, praying to Jesus. Then there are Jesus' own physical brothers. Do you know that, out of twelve apostles, five were cousins to Jesus? In the early church, all his brothers were there. What a magnificent tribute to the earthly life of Jesus – his nearest relatives who were there. Isn't that marvellous?

What a life he must have lived in his family. In the early days they thought he was crazy. They accused him of religious mania. At one stage they tried to lock him up. But now the brothers are in the prayer meeting. One of them, James, is going to become the second pastor of the Jerusalem church after Peter.

Prayer involves waiting, and there are two sorts of waiting. There are people who just sit and wait for something to happen. But there is another kind of waiting, which is not just waiting for something to happen but waiting on the Lord. This is not passive. The kind of waiting that happened between Calvary and Pentecost was not: Oh well, something will happen some day – God in his inscrutable wisdom will act in sovereign power according to his own will and his own time. It was: Lord, we are waiting on you to move. But with the prayer went preaching, and it was Peter who stood up. Have you ever noticed the postures in the Bible? They sat for prayer when they were praying together, they stood for preaching, and when they prayed privately they knelt. Interesting that it is the opposite of the Jewish synagogue where they used to stand to pray and sit to preach – that is just another way in which Christianity turned everything upside down. Why did they sit for prayer? I have the feeling they were influenced in this by the fact that their Lord and Saviour Jesus Christ had entered heaven and sat down at the right hand of God the Father ever to make intercession for us, and that his posture in intercession is seated talking to his Father. That may perhaps explain the tradition that we may have accepted without thinking of sitting for our prayer meetings and our public worship. But when you are praying in private it is a good thing to bow the knee as Paul says he did when he was in private: "I bow the knee before my Father in heaven...."

Notice this phrase "Peter stood up" because it occurs twice – once in Acts 1 and once in Acts 2. Peter was always getting on his feet to speak, but now when he stands up his mouth is not filled with his own ideas or opinions – God's Word comes out. All preachers who have any effect have surrendered their own opinions and ideas and stopped giving their own thoughts in the pulpit, and have steeped themselves in God's Word, then stand up and give something worth listening to. Quite frankly, if I gave you half an hour or more of my thoughts or opinions it would be a waste of your time. It is not my job to do that.

Peter stood up among the believers (in Acts 1) before he stood up among the unbelievers (in Acts 2). If you are ever going to open your mouth outside the church, you had better open it inside first. If you are ever going to learn to talk freely about the Lord to people who don't love him, then learn to talk freely about him among those who do love him – that is the best place to start, where people know him and are sympathetic and will welcome what you share. If you really can't share with the Lord's people conversation about the Lord, I guarantee you will never be a witness outside. So Acts 2 was not Peter's first sermon but his second.

The second balance which comes out in Peter's preaching is the balance between *exposition* and *application*. Two phrases stand out in his preaching in Acts 1: "It is written" and "It is necessary." Every preacher should have those two phrases in mind.

When Billy Graham first came to Britain as an unknown American evangelist, he came to my home town of Newcastle as a baseball player just out of his teens. He came with a new phrase which we had not heard preachers use in this country as he used it: "The Bible says...." People said it was mere repetition, brainwashing, but it wasn't. He was giving his own paraphrase of "It is written...." He was a man of one book. As John Wesley, who was very widely read, said, "I am a man of one book. I want to know only one thing: how to get heaven; how to land safe on that happy shore and the way is written in a book so I am a man of one book." *Every preacher must learn how to expound God's Word.*

Where did Peter get this habit of preaching the Bible? Until this point he has never done it before. I remember the day that a crisis came for me. When I began my ministry I had copied other preachers. I gave out a text and then I strung a few thoughts on it – sometimes connected with the text, but not always. Sometimes the text was a pretext, and I ignored the context most times, or I took a subject that came from my reading. Then there came a day when I consented to be a fool for the Lord and I said, "Lord, from now on I'm just going to expound your Word. I'll take whole chunks of it, but I'm going to try it." I tried it in the Royal Air Force with a bunch of young men and I knew I had found my vocation because they were just so hungry for the truth. They weren't interested in JDP's ideas, they wanted the Word, and I have never gone back on that. I pray God I never will. What made Peter come to this? I will tell you what made him come to it: between the resurrection and the Ascension, what did Jesus do with those eleven men? For the first time he gave them Bible studies. It says in the Gospels that Jesus took them through the law – that's the first five books of the Bible, the prophets, and the Psalms – and he gave them Bible studies. Between the resurrection and the Ascension, Jesus did more

Bible study than anything else. He opened the scriptures to them until their hearts burned.

When you have these scriptures opened to you, you just want to get on and share what you have learned; you want to go and teach others. Peter now had the appetite, so when he got up to preach he *expounded*, and in this case from the Psalms. Have you ever realised that the Psalms are a wonderful guide for church meetings? I am thrilled that the book of Psalms, which was not as widely read in my young days as now, is one of the most popular books in the Bible. Psalms are being set to new music, and more people are finding their own existential experience described in them.

When I started preaching, I received this good advice: "Whatever you do, never finish a sermon without telling people what to do about it." Exposition is no use without application. Application is no use without exposition. The double task of a pastor is to go back into the passage and expound it until it is real, then to come back from the passage into the present and apply it until it is relevant.

That was a bit of a lecture for preachers but I hope you are a preacher. You only need a congregation of one to be a preacher! Many years ago I often did have a congregation of one. She was 88 and a real Scandinavian, a big lady who lived in a little cottage by the seashore in the Shetland Islands, next door to a little church with a felt roof, right on the rocks. The sea used to wash the windows, and there was a little ship's bell on top. In gales when nobody could get through by ship or by boat or along the track by motorcycle, she would stand in the storm and ring that bell. I would arrive and she would say, "Nobody is here – but you're here and I'm here and the Lord's here, so let's get on with it." I used to preach, take the collection, play the harmonium, and do the lot! When Philip went down on the way to Gaza and met that one Ethiopian eunuch, "He preached unto him Jesus."

Exposition needs application. Don't just make the Bible real, make it relevant. Don't just get back into it but come back to today and say, "Now this is what we ought to do." "It is written" *and* "It is necessary." Why is this so important? because you will be judged more seriously if you have heard something and done nothing about it than if you had never heard about it at all.

Here is one example. Supposing you have realised intellectually, from the Bible, that baptism is not an optional extra but is vital for every believer who is going to follow the Lord. Supposing you have agreed with that and said to me, "Well, you persuaded me, and it's in the Bible." If you haven't been baptised, you will be judged for this. How important this is. That is why it is necessary – not just that it is written. The last one of the dangers is that we all become sermon-tasters and we enjoy the "It is written" part but we forget the "It is necessary" part. Peter never finished the sermon without telling them what to do. When he preached in Acts 2 he finished up: "Repent and be baptised every one of you and you will receive the forgiveness of sins and you will receive the gift of the Spirit too." But he told them what to do, it wasn't just, "It is written" but also: "It is necessary."

Another thing Peter got in balance was *subtraction and addition*. I was talking to some young men who went into ministry some years ago and one of them said to me, "You know, when I was just a member of the church I couldn't understand why the minister was always pressing us to consider removing a name from the membership roll. I thought, 'Why keep doing this?' Now I'm a pastor I understand, and here I am now trying to keep the membership roll down in size. I just didn't understand it until I became a pastor." In fact this is true, it is part of a pastor's job, alas, to bring to the notice of the church those who have disqualified themselves from being part of the fellowship and to face the facts and to deal with them accordingly. Pastor Peter did this in Acts 1. Consider that if there was one black sheep among the apostles it was a man called Judas Iscariot, who had betrayed his Lord with a kiss. Now we forget that Judas had healed people. He had been a preacher, a teacher and a healer in the name of Christ. He had been a successful disciple, he had gone out and come back and said, "Even demons are subject to us." Have you forgotten that? Do you know in Acts 1 Peter says he was a deacon among us and he was an elder among us? He uses both those words in the Greek, variously translated in the English. But he says, "Judas was an elder and a deacon among us but he is now out of it." (So Judas was the only person in the whole New Testament who carried the three descriptive titles of apostolos, episcopos and diaconos!) Now he was already hanged and dead but you see that little church would never have thought about Judas if the pastor had not brought the name forward. They wanted to forget him. They would have buried this and they would have wanted to leave him in the past, but Peter brought it up: "We must do the right thing about Judas, we must deal with the situation. We must face it and see that the work is continued and that somebody else is added in." That is one of the more difficult sides of a pastor's life but it has to be done. In many churches the church meeting would never face names in this category unless they were brought up at pastoral level, but it is part of the job, part of the humdrum work that has to be done. It is not very nice to face facts but we have to say, "God, who do you want to replace that person? How do you want that work to be carried on?" Pastor Peter had a tricky church meeting on his hands but he said: "I remind you of Judas. He was an elder and a deacon. Now what do we do about him?"

Peter balanced subtraction and addition. He made them face the fact that Judas was no longer of them, and asked them what they were going to do about it. He has been criticised for doing this and for choosing someone else to replace Judas. In fact, one preacher told me that he felt that Peter made a mistake – that Paul was the man to replace Judas, and that Paul was the man of God's choice, and that if only Peter hadn't rushed into things, God would have shown that Saul of Tarsus was the twelfth apostle.

But I don't believe that, I think it is wrong because Paul himself says in 1 Corinthians 15, "the twelve", recognising that he was not one of them. When you get to the new Jerusalem, you will find twelve names of apostles engraved around the base of a wall. You will not find Judas Iscariot and you will not find Paul, you will find Matthias. So Peter led them to face facts, to subtract one man from their thinking and to add another—not a very easy task, but a pastor has to hold the church to doing this and insist that they keep on doing it.

The next balance in Pastor Peter's life was between *discussion* and *submission*. In other words, how to conduct or handle a church meeting. I want to mention two extremes in a church meeting. On the one hand is the view that the decisions of a church are entirely within the hands of the members and that you have met in the church meeting to use your own judgment, your own understanding, to come to your own conclusion. Then there is the other extreme, which says, "Decisions are all in God's hands and there's no point in discussing them in a church meeting. Why waste time? Let the Lord direct directly." Neither of these is Pastor Peter's method. He knew that it is a combination. It is partly our discussion and partly the Lord's decision.

The Lord does not want us to surrender our judgment, our thinking, so Peter said, "Now we'll have to judge ourselves who is qualified for this position." It must be someone who has known Jesus all the three years of his ministry and right through the resurrection. Only then can he be a firsthand witness to replace Judas. Incidentally, do you notice there can never be any successor to the apostles after the last one has died? Judas Iscariot was the only apostle to be replaced. You see, after another generation had come and gone, nobody knew Jesus in the flesh over those three years. So there are no successors to the apostles today, but look how Peter handled the church meeting. He said, "Now look out men who are qualified," and they did so and they put their brains to work, and they discussed and they finally settled on two names – Barsabas and Matthias. Both were qualified in the judgment of the church. Now at this point Pastor Peter showed the wisdom of his pastoral sense. He did not ask who they preferred. He did not give them any chance at all for their personal prejudice to come in. He said, "Right, we've now used our judgment to decide who is qualified, now the decision must not be ours but his." The only way he knew to ensure that no human being decided was a way that we never need to use today. They cast lots. Why? To make sure that the Lord made the decision and they didn't. Why use lots? Surely that's a chancy business? Not when God is in the picture. That was how they did it throughout the Old Testament. A priest had a black and white stone inside a pouch and he put his hand in. One was called the Urim and the other called the Thummim and now – was it yes or no, Lord? He would put his hand in and ask the Lord to direct his hand to the black or white stone – black, no; white, yes. If God can do miracles, if God can control material objects, then casting lots and praying beforehand was a wonderful way of letting God decide.

Today we don't need to do that in a church meeting. Why not? Because we are living the right side of Acts 2. We can now say to members in a church meeting, "Here are three or four men who are right for this job, who are qualified, and whom in our judgment could do the job. Now you can clear your minds of your own likes and dislikes, your own prejudices. You have the Holy Spirit now to show you which of these is God's choice." That is why when choosing an elder we go to prayer then, and we say, "Now God, the choice is yours, not ours. We may like this man or prefer the other, but Lord, it's got to be your choice, your man. We don't want it to be our decision because we are fallible and we can be wrong."

Do you remember when the people of Israel wanted a king? They made the mistake that some churches do when they call preachers with a view. They looked for a tall, handsome man, and they said, "Ah, that's the man for us: Saul," and they never made a bigger mistake. When Samuel was looking for the next king of Israel he went to a family and there were fine, strapping lads who looked real leaders every one of them, but God said no.

Was there anybody else in the family? The father, Jesse, said, "Well there's a little lad, he's looking after the sheep." Samuel went out and looked for David and, when he saw this little lad, God said yes. Israel regretted ever choosing Saul and were they glad that God chose David.

It is terribly important that, when it comes to the final decision in a church meeting, the pastor says, "Now it must be God's choice, not ours." We can allow the Holy Spirit to overcome our prejudice, to remove our thinking. Of course, when he does, in theory you should have a unanimous decision, for the Spirit has only chosen one.

Now let us look at the final balance – that between *organisation* and *inspiration*. I nearly said "perspiration and inspiration" because I mean the same thing! So often these are set against each other. I know that structure can be a shackle, I know that you can become institutionalised, fossilised, and you can die through over-organisation. We can kill the church with committees. I thank God the word "committee" never appeared in the Bible and we don't therefore have to have committees because you can really keep minutes and waste hours in them.

I believe that the Holy Spirit can work best where the structure is strong. There will be fewer errors. I think that the Holy Spirit is moving all over the world today in many denominations. I don't know if you realise that the Holy Spirit is moving perhaps more among the Roman Catholics than among any other denomination today. I don't know what your reaction to that is, but he is. Pope John XXIII prayed earnestly with all the sincerity of his simple peasant nature. He said, "Lord, another Pentecost," and his prayer is being answered in the Roman Catholic Church. I tell you this: the Pentecostal movement among the Roman Catholics has had far less unbalance than in any other denomination. The reason is that the structure is strong. It is among the evangelicals that the Pentecostal movements have often produced extreme and fanatical groups who by their unbalance have brought the movement of the Holy Spirit into disrepute.

Therefore I believe that Acts 1 is as important as Acts 2. If you are going to pray for Acts 2 then get Acts 1 into your system. Have a strong structure with a right leadership and a good eldership. Get the leadership right and the organisation right. Get the thing shipshape and then the wind of the Spirit when it blows won't wreck the church but will in fact blow the church along.

So I believe in organisation. The members of my church were expected to be at the business meeting to go through the structure, the discussion and the appointments. There might be some who would get impatient with us and say, "It's not spiritual enough. It's not exciting enough, there's no tongues of flame there. There's no mighty rushing wind there." Go back to Acts 1! Pastor Peter said, "Let's put things right."

12

EXCITING THINGS HAPPENED

Read Acts 2:1–41

Most Christians have one point in their pilgrimage, one step on the road, to which everything seem to lead and from which everything then flows. The crisis comes to different Christians in different ways. It may be while they are going through a real crisis. It may be while they are with Christians at some event.

The watershed for Simon Peter came in Acts 2. It came on a day in the month of May in the year AD 29 at nine o'clock in the morning. Everything we have studied in the life of Peter has been leading up to this. There have been some wonderful experiences and some deep and difficult ones, but they have all been preparing him. This is the point at which his life divided into two, not into BC and AD. He had been with Christ for a long time, but something happened that morning to change Peter.

He was already a long way on the road. He had known Christ for three years. He was undoubtedly born again of God's Spirit, he had been through the cross and the resurrection and had understood both. The Holy Spirit had been with him and had used him for healing, for driving out demons. There had been many experiences. Above all, Peter had come to understand that Jesus Christ was Lord. All this was part of his experience already. Furthermore, he had been called to the pastorate of the first Christian church and he was already exercising a pastoral ministry: chairing church meetings, guiding the flock from the Word of God, leading them in prayer. He had all that, but he was praying for more.

I'm so glad that Simon Peter realised he hadn't got all there was. I have a horrible fear that if he had been counselled by some Christians today, they would have said: "Now don't go chasing experiences, Peter. Don't go looking for anything more. You got it all when you were converted. Just explore it more and surrender to it more." I'm so glad nobody counselled him like that. Mind you, frankly, if they had done, he would have laughed at them, saying, "Well, I'm going to listen to my Lord Jesus. Though I've got so much to thank him for, he told me to wait for more and I'm going to wait."

They waited – Peter with the eleven other apostles and 108 other people. Are my maths right? Yes, I think so: 120 altogether – women including Mary, mother of Jesus, many other women. Just ordinary folk, most of them uneducated, yet these were the nucleus of a church that was to grow until today it probably numbers over a billion people and is still growing. It will never stop growing until God calls a halt. It all started with these 120 people who knew that they hadn't got all that God had for them.

Happy is the Christian who is not content with their experience to date, but who knows that there's more and who wants that *more*, and who, without panicking and, without chasing around after will o' the wisps, believes that God will meet them in the time and place of his choosing and in the way that is best for them, but who goes on asking. Jesus said to those who belong him, "Go on asking. How much more will your heavenly Father give Holy Spirit to those who go on asking."

This is what led up to the watershed: they were all in one place with one accord. If God is to bless a group of people, they should be together physically. It is important. We are people in the flesh; we live in the body. I remember the late Dr Sangster being approached by a gushing lady member of the congregation after one rally at which he had preached. She said, "Oh Dr Sangster, it's so wonderful to meet you in the flesh."

He looked at her with a smile and said, "But I'm usually in the flesh."

The fact is, we usually are. We express our spirits through the flesh—we are bodies and spirits joined together as single souls. Therefore, it is important to meet each other physically, to be in one place. But we may have met physically yet not be together spiritually or mentally or emotionally. There also needs to be *one accord* as well as one *place* – not just a lot of bodies squeezed together in a building, but a lot of souls squeezed together.

There are many descriptions of what actually happened. Many phrases are used. It says, "They were baptised in Holy Spirit." Notice that I miss out the definite article. That is rather important. It said that they were "...filled with Holy Spirit". It says that Holy Spirit was "poured out upon...." There are many different verbs used. It is almost as if the experience was so rich they couldn't get it into one phrase or into one word. Frankly, I think Christians, who argue about the phraseology are obviously living outside the experience because they would say, "You can use almost any term you would like to describe it; it's so rich an experience you could use verb after verb after verb and still be describing the same thing." But alas, some of these terms have become controversial.

When I went to New Zealand, somebody, in a kindly way, took me aside at the beginning and said, "Whatever you do, don't used the word '*baptised* in the Holy Spirit' while you travel around New Zealand." So I sat down and thought: "baptise" – that is not an English word anyway, so I'll use an English equivalent instead. So I decided to use the word "drenched". It means the same thing. So everywhere I went, I said "drenched in Holy Spirit". To my astonishment, whenever I said this there were welcoming smiles and openness of people's faces. I thought: "Well, this is wonderful!"

Now if you have been to New Zealand, you know what I am going to say. In fact, I had hit on the one word that would open a New Zealander's heart. The place is more full of sheep than people. Everywhere you look there is wool running around, and when they dip them, they don't "dip" them. In England we "dip" them. They say, "We drench them." So I hit on just the one word. I don't care what word you use. Whether you use "baptised", "drenched", "filled", "poured out" doesn't matter. The important thing that matters is: has it happened?

There are two drenchings that every Christian needs and which are offered in the Scripture. I didn't say "two baptisms" but I could have done. One is a drenching in water. You know when you have been drenched in water. Now I don't mind if you say "I've been drenched", "I've been dipped", "I've been dunked." The important thing is it has happened and it is part of your living experience of Christ. I don't mind what word is used for the other drenching as long as it has happened. You know in your heart whether it has happened. If it happened when you were converted, hallelujah, you got it all at once. But if it didn't, why not? Wait and pray and say, "Lord, in your own time, in your own way, deal with me. But I'll meet with your people and I'll wait with them if that's your will," and this is what Simon Peter was doing.

There was so much already that he could have rested on. So many people could have said to him, "Peter, you've got everything now. You really are the pastor, and you're doing all this. You're rejoicing in the Lord, you know Jesus is alive, you've got a grasp of the scripture, what more...?" Peter just went on asking, as did the others. God, in his mercy, met them.

The question, and I want to underline this, is not whether you have received the Holy Spirit. If you are a Christian you have. "If any man have not 'the' Spirit of Christ, he is none of his." That is why it is so important that in all these contexts of drenched, filled, poured, the definite article is missing. Take my word for it. If you know Greek, you could check up on me. I wish I could go through an English Bible and cross out the word "the" in the English. It has confused the whole issue.

The question is not whether you received the Holy Spirit, but how much Holy Spirit you have received – how much you have of him, not whether you have him. If you are a Christian you have him, but how much of him do you have? Enough of him to drench you? Enough of him to fill you? Or to turn it another way around: how much does the Holy Spirit have of you? That is the other side of the question. It is a quantitative question, not a qualitative one. It is not asking whether you have the person of the Holy Spirit in your heart; of course you have. If you came to Christ, you have the Holy Spirit. It is asking how much power you are enjoying. You can have electricity laid on to your house and never switch it on or only switch on an odd light. You may never have flooded the house with light. You may have a water pipe laid on to your house and you may have washed your hands in the water and had a drink of the water, but may never have had a bath in it. Therefore, this is what they were waiting for.

Jesus has said plainly to Peter on the night before he died, "The Holy Spirit has been *with* you, but will be *in* you" This wasn't a new experience; it was a new quantity though. It was a new depth, it was a new dimension, and it was a new amount of power. This is what they were to wait for: "Wait in Jerusalem and you shall receive power."

You will be drenched in Holy Spirit and then you will be my witnesses. You will go out from there and you will reach to the outermost parts of the earth. They will know that I am alive because you have been drenched.... So that's what we are talking about. I'm so glad that it happened at nine o'clock in the morning. That's the very time they can't tell you that you are being weird and mysterious. Have you noticed that things that go "bump" usually do so in the night? There are all kinds of supernatural experiences which people have in the darkness. We are children of the day. The Lord told us to sleep at night. Anything can happen at night and in darkness when you're in a funny mood anyway. That's when our thoughts tend to be a bit chaotic and our feelings go all over the place. But nine o'clock in the morning, that's different. So it was in broad daylight, the first thing in the morning that God came. Oh what some miss by not coming to morning service! God loves to do things in broad daylight, when we are fresh and new and we're not under any suggestible influence. So here they were in a public place, there were no gimmicks, no atmosphere worked up. They were just in a public place, in a corner of the temple and God met them.

Of course, there were exciting things that happened. The first thing they heard was a sound of a gale, yet their clothes didn't blow. They heard it, yet they weren't blown around. The next thing they saw was a fireball that came rushing through and then separated into flames, and flames just went and touched each of their heads, but not a hair was singed. Both of these were symbols of power – wind and

fire, two of the elemental powers of our universe, symbols
of the power of God the Creator. They were telling those
people the power's near. But as long as it was a sound of
a rushing, mighty wind and flames of fire in their head, it
was *outside* them. The next step: the power came *in*. Now at
this point Peter experienced something which all the others
did likewise – Mary, mother of Jesus, the other apostles,
all the others – and which thousands of Christians are
experiencing today. Hallelujah! Why should it seem strange,
what happened next? It seems to be the most obvious, the
most logical, and at the same time the most beautiful thing
that could have happened. They were so full they overflowed
– that's all. Now where do people overflow? There is only
one place you overflow whether you are full of sadness or
full of anger or full of happiness. Where do you overflow?
Through your fingertips? No! Through your feet? No! Just
as at home, in my bath, there's a little hole underneath the
two taps that tells my wife when I am using too much hot
water because it's full to overflowing, there is a little hole that
God provided for the overflow. When you are overflowing
with joy, that's where you laugh. When you are overflowing
with anger, that is where you shout. You overflow and it's
out of the heart that the *mouth* speaks—that's the overflow.

Now can you think of anything that could demonstrate that
– that comes out of your mouth? Except speaking fluently
in a language you have never learned, I can't think of any
other way to do it.

It seems so obvious, so simple, and so logical that it just
happened. Out of their mouths came something they could
never have done in a month of Sundays. They were, after
all, uneducated fishermen and they had a broad northern
accent. How utterly obvious for God to say: Right. I'll take
over your mouth.

After all, there's one other reason why this should be the

best way of showing God's power – because the last thing in my body that I can control is my tongue. "If I can control that, I'm a perfect man," says the Bible. If you have never said the wrong thing, then you are perfect. You don't need to worry about anything else; you're perfect because that's the hardest thing to control and to tame. "A great big ship is turned with a little rudder," says James. A forest fire is started with one match, and our tongues are set on fire by hell. There isn't one of us who hasn't got regrets about things that we have said.

So if God wants to demonstrate that he has got all of us, and can control all of us, then the one point I would expect him to control – and show that he has got control of – would be the most difficult part of me to control. So the whole thing just fits together like that. Now that is not to say that wherever the Holy Spirit demonstrates power that will happen—this is only one of many things it could be, but I can understand why it was this on that day.

There is another reason why this happened to Peter: if we are to be released in speech toward the world, towards others, than we have got to be released in speech toward God first. If we are not free in worship, we will not be free in witness. If worship is a duty that we have to make ourselves do, then witness will be the same. But where worship is free, witness becomes free. Where worship is relaxed and natural, witness becomes relaxed and natural.

This gift of other languages was not given for missionary purposes. When Peter came to preach to the crowds he didn't use this gift. He didn't need to, they all understood one language anyway. This gift was given for these 120 to express themselves freely to God – long before the crowd arrived, long before there was an evangelistic situation. Within that prayer meeting, they were being released in the one area where most of us need so much help: to know what to say to God. Isn't it right that that's a real problem? We have to have books or words displayed to tell us what to praise. How long could we go on singing to God without that? How long can we go on praying before we get stuck?

So God, in his mercy, released them. They began to tell God how much they thought of him and how wonderful his works were, and they were praising him. In other words, Peter was learning this secret: that when you are released in praise, you will then be released in preaching, released in worship, released in witness. That is the way round it comes. The easier you find it to talk *to* God, the easier you will find it to talk *about* God.

So if you have been struggling to witness, if you have been trying hard to talk about the Lord to others, and finding it very difficult and unnatural and forced, may I ask you to tackle the problem, not as a direct problem of witnessing, but to ask, "How free am I towards God? Do I pray aloud to him when I'm on my own? Do I sing to him – not just the songs I've learned, but new songs?" Do you ever try that? Have you ever tried singing a new song to the Lord and just saying, "I love you," and singing it to him? Make up the tune as you go along, but he loves to hear that. How creative God's people become when they are released towards him in worship. They find new words and new music to express themselves towards him.

Now the people came and they were astonished. They all spoke one language, but they were also bilingual since they came from all parts of the then known world, and so, they were astonished. "Galileans? Uneducated northerners and they're speaking every language we know? Listen." And they were perplexed. You know one of the most challenging questions I ever heard asked was this, "How often would people, watching you leave church, accuse you of having been drinking?" What a question! We are just so jolly sober, aren't we? But John Wesley said, "Give me a hundred God-intoxicated men and we'll turn England upside down." "God intoxicated" – he was almost quoting verbatim Ephesians 5:18, "Don't be drunk with wine because in that there is debauchery, excess, wastefulness, but be filled with the Spirit, and sing and make melody in your heart."

There are two kinds of intoxication and everybody in between is miserable. So people said, "They're drunk." But since when did alcohol enable someone to speak fluently *in another language?*

So Peter got up to preach. Having been released in praise, now we have the preacher. What a sermon! Every preacher can learn from this sermon. An uneducated fisherman and it's a brilliant sermon. It has every mark of good preaching and no wonder there were so many conversions at the end. First, it was *topical*; right bang up to date. Look how he starts. He said, "The pubs aren't open yet." What a delightful introduction, it got the interest of the congregation and was humorous. It got inside their thoughts. He was beginning where people were. It's marvellous preaching. How on earth did Peter get this ability?

It is not only topical; it is *biblical*. Here was a man who could take his Bible and make it relevant to what was happening right then and show that things written centuries before are the clue to the meaning of existence now. It's not only biblical, but it's *historical* preaching. What a sweep of history he has. Within the first three minutes he's talking about the periods of God's purpose and the last days and that we have now entered into the final period of history. Oh, he's painting on a big canvas. He's also going to say that they are key to the whole of history – the events of our Lord Jesus Christ, his life, his death, his resurrection and his ascension. He is gearing it all to historical fact.

Our religion is based not on fiction or fancy but on fact.

That is what gives us such dogmatism, such certainty, because nobody can alter history. Nobody can put Jesus back in the tomb, not now. Nobody can un-crucify Christ. Our faith is built on history, the facts of Christ and the future facts that are yet to come, when the sun is turned to darkness and the moon to blood. That will happen. It is coming. As certain as Christ died on the cross and the sun went black that day, it is going to go black again. So with this sweep of history, Peter shows them the whole panorama of God's purpose.

Then this preaching is *theological*. You would think he had been to a theological seminary. After all, he had had three years of very good training and teaching, but look at the theology. In one sentence, he talks of Father, Son, and Spirit – there is Trinitarian theology right here. Look at how he speaks of the cross, not just as something that men did or something that happened, but as something that was part of God's purpose and foreknowledge, planned by God. Look at what he thinks of Jesus. He talks about this Jesus of Nazareth, but then look at the theology: "God has made him both Lord and Christ, this Jesus whom you crucified." That is theology. It is not just being a "Jesus person", it is understanding "Lord" and "Christ" and what they mean.

This preaching is *personal*, and all good preaching is. A bold preacher is prepared to use a little word of three letters, which people do not like a preacher to use, and which can cost a preacher a great deal if he uses it regularly. This is the word "you". It takes holy boldness to use that word and it is all the way through Peter's sermon. "This Jesus, whom you crucified; you, by the hands of wicked men, put him to death" *You!* Oh, that's bold preaching. Peter—is this the Peter who denied Christ just two months earlier? What has happened?

This preaching is not only personal, it is *practical*. It doesn't leave people in any doubt as to what they are to do.

In the same name of the Lord Jesus I want to leave you in no doubt as to what *you* are to do. If you haven't repented and been baptised, then that is what you are to do. That is how you save yourselves from this corrupt generation. It is corrupt and it will corrupt you. God can only save you if you are prepared to save yourself. You save yourself by repenting and being baptised. He saves you by giving you the gift of forgiveness and the same power of the Holy Spirit. He wants to give you that power because, as Peter said, Pentecost isn't just for us; it's for *you* [his congregation on that day] *and your children and to all that are afar off, as many as the Lord our God calls to him.* That includes every Christian in your church. So Pentecost is not only a historical event, it is an existential experience for all who God calls to him.

That's practical preaching, let's get down to brass tacks. If one person repents of the life they have been living, a life that is in common with this corrupt generation – if one person turns their back on that life, just changes their mind and says, "I'm finished with it; I'm going to live God's way now", do you know that all the angels in heaven will strike up the "Hallelujah Chorus"?

"Repent and be baptised" – it is that simple. You understand what it is. You are in no doubt as to what it means, then *you* do it if you haven't done it.

Finally, this preaching was *powerful*. I haven't used the word "persuasive" because that smacks of a human being trying to persuade other people. Powerful preaching isn't dependent on human strength. Paul says to the Corinthians, "I came to you in trembling and weakness, but in demonstration of the power of the Spirit." It is not necessarily the noisy preachers who are the powerful preachers. It is not those with strong, persuasive, powers. Sometimes a very insignificant little person, with little apparent intellectual equipment, can just state the facts in such a way that people know this is God – and three thousand that day received the word. It was a public holiday. There were some two and a half million people in the city milling around with little to do. No wonder they came together. When a house is on fire, the people come. When a church is on fire, it will happen the same way. I once saw a big house on fire. Stopping the car, I ran over to see what help was needed, but there was one man already there and he had phoned for the fire brigade and they came quickly. The amazing thing is that within ten minutes there must have been two hundred people there. Where there is a fire, people come.

So three thousand came this time. The people came and they listened, and they were pricked in their hearts. You see, it isn't being convinced in your mind that does the trick; it is whether you are pricked in your heart. I have sometimes watched from the pulpit. Sometimes I have watched a person sitting on a drawing pin – they really haven't been able to sit still. Literally, their heart is just being pricked. Praise God when that happens. The Holy Spirit is operating. Sometimes a person will come afterwards, saying, "Who has been telling you all about me?" The answer is, "No-one, and I don't know a thing about you probably, but God knows and he pricks the heart."

Then the right response is not, "What shall I *feel* or what shall I *think*?" But very simply, *"What shall we do?"*

Repent and be baptised!

"Oh Peter, you uneducated fisherman!" How I am looking forward to meeting one of the greatest preachers there has ever been! It all happened because the Holy Spirit was poured out on that big fisherman. He could preach because he could praise. He could speak to men because he had spoken to God. He had been released, and now that tongue which had always been so uncontrollable, that tongue which had said so many things that afterwards were regretted, that tongue that Peter could never tame – now the tongue was under perfect control and could speak another language fluently in praise, or his own language fluently in preaching – and God was glorified and people were saved. Three thousand were baptised into the water with them.

Let us get on with what God has commanded. Let us pray that people being baptised in water may be drenched in the Spirit also, their tongues set free to praise and to speak of their Lord.

13

A NEW BOLDNESS

Read Acts 3:1 – 4:31

That was some prayer meeting, wasn't it? What a prayer meeting when God joins in. The biggest change I notice in Peter between the end of the Gospel and the beginning of Acts is the change between cowardice and courage. Do you have to remain a coward? The answer is a glorious "no" if Peter is anything to go by. From Acts 3:1 – 4:31, I want to single out four ways in which Peter showed astonishing confidence. The man whom a little servant girl could frighten out of his wits is now a man who will challenge the world, a man who's afraid of no-one but God. That indeed is the cure for all fear. Once you fear the Lord, you fear nothing and no-one else. It is because we don't fear the Lord enough that we fear so many other things and people.

Now the first occasion of his boldness was with a beggar. You might feel there is no call to be bold with a beggar. What's the call for courage there? But in fact, Peter's action on this occasion showed a new Peter with tremendous confidence. I was reading a book by a tramp and he said that whenever he was tramping around England, he would come to a new town and he would look for a spire and make for it and try to find a clergyman's house somewhere near because he had developed the fine art of playing on a clergyman's guilt complex. He usually could get some money from a clergyman and so he developed this. In the countries of the Middle East, beggars make for the temples, the mosques, the places of worship, knowing that a person going in to worship God will feel jolly guilty about walking past a beggar on the steps and not giving him anything. We are in a welfare state where beggars are few and far between. But I am old enough to remember the days of Jarrow in 1920s and 1930s. I can remember a stream of unemployed men who had lost their self-respect, knocking at our door to ask for bread. It doesn't require much courage to deal with a beggar, does it? It just requires a minute of your time and a slice of bread. Ah, but not the way Peter handled this beggar.

So the man was lying there—do you realise, first, that he couldn't work for himself, therefore, he couldn't get bread for himself? Did you realise also that he couldn't worship because he was lame? The laws of God were such that the temple had to be kept pure and perfect. The very laws of that temple forbade the cripple to go beyond that porch. As long as he was in that imperfect state, he was not allowed to worship with God's people, he had to stay on the steps. Peter was going to enable him to work and to worship. But let's look at Peter....

Peter looked at the man intently. Peter had learned a lot about eyes from the Lord Jesus. After all, when the Lord looked at Peter, it broke his heart. Peter looked at this man. I am speculating, but I believe he was looking inside the man's soul, through his eyes, to see whether he was a man who could have faith, to see whether he was a man who really wanted to be sick or wanted to be well, to see what state the man's soul was in. What he saw encouraged him to say to the man, "Look at us." Then he said this amazing thing, "Silver and gold have I none, but what I have I give you." It takes boldness to say a thing like that. It takes a little courage to admit you are not very well off. Peter hadn't been working for three years; he had no money. It was the honest truth, but he had very much more and something much better for the beggar. But the real boldness of Peter came in saying in public something that would make him look an absolute fool if nothing happened to this man who had not walked in forty years (he had been born this way): "Get up and walk." This is a Peter who has got tremendous confidence and he set him on his feet.

This takes me back to the time, many years ago, when my wife was suffering from cancer. She had one operation and then needed a second one. For some reason she said that she wanted to go in to the hospital a day early. It is not everybody wants to go to hospital a day early and she went in on the Wednesday. This meant she met an Australian nurse, who had listened to a tape of Psalm 121, which was then going around the hospital ward.

The Australian nurse, who was not a Christian, took my wife's particulars down, then went off duty and happened to say to another nurse who came six months earlier from New Zealand to this country that she had received my wife and completed the papers. The New Zealand girl knew nothing about my wife but had been a Christian for two months. She had come to this country as far from God as you can get. But she was converted, baptised in water and baptised in the Spirit in the space of about two days.

The Lord just took hold of this very sensible and balanced girl, but swept her off her feet I think. When she heard about my wife, she became very agitated and burdened. She said, "I must go and see her." This was now the Thursday and the operation was to be Friday morning. This second nurse was due to go away on holiday starting on the Friday morning. So she said, "I must go and see her tonight." She came into the ward and was so agitated that she blurted out, "I've come to minister to you." My wife had to minister to her first to get her calm enough to talk it over! The nurse, a two-month old spiritual baby said, "I feel such a burden, I feel the Lord wants me to minister to you." So my wife said, "Well, we can go into the hospital chapel. We can be quiet there." My wife also said, and this is not because I've drilled her, but because it's her conviction, "I want elders present and I want men present so that it's a balanced situation."

But how do you get hold of elders and men last thing on Thursday night? At that point, the wife of the chaplain to the hospital came into the ward. The chaplain was the son of a Spirit-filled Christian, so she phoned him and he came. Next into the ward came the chief dental surgeon of the hospital, who is also a Christian, full of the Spirit. They finished up in the hospital chapel with a time of prayer and praise for an hour, but for the first half-hour, the young nurse from New Zealand was still agitated. So my wife said, "Look, you must tell us. You must share with us. You must really get it off your chest. What is it?" She replied, "Well I feel the power of evil so much. I feel Satan is trying to destroy you with cancer." Having got it out, she became more peaceful. So they then ministered to my wife. The Lord ministered in prophecy, to most beautiful effect.

The girl had written down a word of prophecy for my wife in case she hadn't been able to see her. It was only three sentences, and the middle sentence was: "Psalm 121 is my word for you." I knew nothing of that when I preached on Psalm 121 on the Sunday morning. The Lord had given that psalm to my wife privately on the previous Tuesday as well, and I knew nothing about that either. I arrived with an audiotape of Psalm 121! They ministered, and great joy and peace came. My wife went into the operating theatre that Friday morning, as if she was going on holiday. On the Saturday she was up for two hours. On the Sunday she was up and dressed. Then she was just fine and was sent home a week early.

I thank God that a nurse who had been a Christian for only two months was used by God in that way. We had known that the Lord was going to minister, but we didn't know who, how, where or when.... But he had it all planned. That nurse was able to say, "What I have, I give you. What I have, I give you"—a holy boldness to go to a complete stranger and just minister. Peter had that boldness when he said, "What I have, I give you."

Something challenging to ask yourself, in your own heart, is this: "Could I have withheld from someone else what God wanted them to have because I wouldn't give it, because I was frightened, because I was timid, because I was afraid things would go wrong, because I was afraid of what people might think, because I was afraid of *something*?"

Peter had a holy boldness now, "Such as I have, I give you. In the name of Jesus Christ of Nazareth." One can hear his voice ringing out, and one can see members of the public crowding the temple at that time (it was the time of prayer), turning around.... "Jesus of Nazareth? Why, he was the one they killed just a few weeks back." Then they really got a sight for sore eyes! The man leapt and jumped. There is nothing wrong with jumping in worship, by the way. It is scriptural. It says so: He walked and jumped and he praised God and he jumped around the temple.

Do you realise that it was the first time he had been able to go in? No wonder he jumped! Having jumped his way around the temple and gathered quite a following in doing so, he came back and clung to Peter and John. The crowd gathered and looked at this amazing pair. Then Peter showed his boldness again. He dealt with that crowd very courageously. first in making it quite clear that what had happened was none of his doing. How important this is.

I am afraid the subtle temptation always is to take even a little of the glory for yourself – give God most of it maybe and take a little for yourself. The world is being filled with healers who get a name for being healers. Therefore, their names are on people's tongues. Peter made quite sure that nobody was going to say, "Have you seen Peter, the healer? Have you been to one of Peter's healing missions?" So he said that there is one name in which this has happened – and it was not the name of Peter.

How important it is that we use only one name when we invite people. Don't you ever invite someone and say, "Come and hear Mr. So and so." Say to them, "Come and meet Jesus." Then things are likely to happen. If you say, "Come and hear Mr. So and so," you're likely to be very disappointed. All the way home, you will have to be explaining, "Well, I've heard him better than that. It was probably one of his off days. After all, you know...." That's what happens when you use any other name.

Peter boldly told the crowd that it was not his own power or piety. It was Jesus who had done this. Then his courage gave him this incredible power to use the word "you" again and point to the people who had gathered around and say: "You killed him, God raised him, He's doing this. You murdered him; you preferred a murderer to him—that's where you stand." What boldness! How did Peter dare – he who ran away from the cross – to accuse the murderers of Jesus of such a terrible thing? So the second way in which he showed boldness was dealing with the crowd and accusing them of murdering Jesus whose name had done this healing.

The third way in which Peter showed boldness on this occasion was in court the next day. The sad fact is that the world does not welcome men who perform miracles. The world does not show gladness when men do good, not if their own vested interests are hurt. Sadly, men are glad to hear about miracles unless that miracle is going to alter their position in some way, whether their possessions, power or position. If something is going to be altered, men run away from the name of Jesus and from those who minister in his name.

So they arrested Peter and John – as even now men and women are being arrested for preaching Jesus. In many countries in the world it is a crime against the state to preach the name of Jesus publicly. In some cases, it is a crime against the state to preach the name of Jesus to your own children. There are families in the world where children have been taken away from their own mothers because their mothers preached the name of Jesus. We need to recognise that this world is in Satan's hands. He is the god of this world, the prince of this world, the ruler of this world. Therefore, this world does not like it when Jesus does things. The sufferings of Christ continue in the sufferings of his body on earth.

It is interesting to see why they arrested Peter and John. They arrested them because they were disturbing the peace and Christians are always doing that. But more than that, they were arrested because they were preaching something that was contrary to the official government view. The government was in the hands of Sadducees and they didn't believe in the resurrection from the dead – and here, within a few hundred yards of the tomb of Jesus, the resurrection was being proclaimed – that's what's stuck in their throats.

The world doesn't mind Christians doing good, provided they don't put in the "religious" bit. The world doesn't mind money being sent for refugees, provided there isn't a tract in with the sandwich. The world doesn't mind us helping our fellow men, provided we don't say, "Jesus is alive and we wouldn't be doing it if it wasn't for him." That's the bit that sticks.

So they were arrested and taken to court. Now Jesus had

promised that the Holy Spirit would tell them what to say. I find it amazing to see how Peter was able to defend himself.

Here now is another example of his boldness. Here he is, an uneducated, simple fisherman, who has only worked with his hands, standing in a dock before the most intellectual, powerful people in his nation. Peter runs rings around them! He defends himself because they give him no counsel for the defence. This is the Sanhedrin, the very courtroom in which Jesus was condemned to die. Peter is in the same dock, where just two or three months previously his master stood.

Peter now accuses his judges of the crime. He starts in a remarkable way, saying, "Since when has it been a crime to help the helpless?" That's not a bad beginning in your own defence, is it? Then he moves on, "If you count it a crime to help a cripple to walk, and to work for his own living, then you have arrested the wrong man because I didn't do it, Jesus did it. So you had better go and arrest him." Now can you see their faces when he said that? "I didn't do it," he said, "Got the wrong prisoner." To cap it all, then he said, "I accuse all you lot of murder." He looked straight around at Annas and Caiaphas and the priestly families and said, "You're the murderers and I put all of you in the dock before God." I'm paraphrasing, but what a defence.

Is this same Simon Peter, who wouldn't even acknowledge to a servant girl that he had anything to do with Jesus? Yes, it is – the same man, full of the Holy Spirit and therefore, full of holy boldness. No wonder they suggested an adjournment and put Peter and John out of the room. Then they chatted together, "What are we going to say about this man?"

Do you know there were three bits of evidence? They wouldn't face one of them; they had to face the other two, but all three put them on the spot. The first evidence was the empty tomb. Do you realise it was nearby? If they could have produced the body, that would have finished the case, but they never did. They never even considered it. Why? Because they knew that tomb was empty. But the two other pieces of evidence were the evidence of changed lives. Peter, standing there – they had to take note of this uneducated fisherman who could be so bold and speak so eloquently. The other evidence was standing there: the lame man was standing upright. He had walked on his own two feet into the courtroom. They simply wouldn't consider the evidence.

They are perfect examples of those, who because they have a vested interest in their own position, will not face the evidence. They knew it would mean a total change in their outlook so they refused the evidence. This was supposed to be the highest court of justice and law in that land. So they decided to pass a law forbidding them to preach in the name of Jesus. Now believe me, this is what totalitarian regimes do. If they can't pin a crime on someone, then they produce a new law which will turn them into criminals.

Believe me, there are vested interests, even religious vested interests, that are being profoundly disturbed because people are being set free. The days may not be too far ahead, when we shall be suffering legal limitations. How do you face that one?

Listen to the new Peter, not the reed now, Simon, but the rock, Peter. Listen to what he says: "You must judge for yourselves whether it is right to obey God or man. We have made up our minds. What we know to be true, what we've seen and heard, we're going to talk about." Isn't that boldness? He's saying it in love; he's saying it wisely. He's leaving them to judge. He's saying: "What ought we to do in your view? If God tells us one thing and man tells us another, what choice is the right choice?" But then he says, "We have no choice because we've seen and heard." In other words, he's standing by God and by the truth. There's nobody so bold as someone who is sure that God is with them and that the truth is on their side. A holy boldness comes with both.

Someone once said to me, "Do you think you have the truth then?" My answer is, "No, but the truth has me." If God be for us, who can be against us? If it should come that we should find ourselves on the wrong side of the English law because we do what Jesus told us to do, then may we have the same boldness Peter had, and the same Holy Spirit, the same wisdom, to stand up for the Lord Jesus.

The final act of courage Peter showed in this account is the secret of the other three: how bold he was before a beggar, how bold he was before a crowd whom he accused, and he had no bodyguard when he did; he was accused of murder, how bold he was when standing in that court, to accuse his judges of a crime, to twist them so badly in their thinking, that they had to push him out of the room to talk about what to do with him. But now here is the secret of the boldness: it was boldness with God.

The first thing they did when they got back was report the threats, report the new law that they weren't to preach any more in Jesus' name. They came back to the people and the people had a prayer meeting. What did they pray? Was it, "Lord, forgive us because we can't mention your name any more. Lord, keep us safe from these threats. Lord, keep us comfortable. Lord, keep us happy. Lord, protect us"? No, they didn't pray like that. They said, "Lord, you made heaven and earth, and, Lord, you've said in your Word that the nations may rage, but you just laugh at them." You see, they were lining up with God in their prayer. What a holy boldness in their prayer. They were putting themselves on God's side. They were seeing things from heaven's point of view, so they were going to laugh at these threats.

They are really pathetic, the nations of the world. It is happening in many countries. Christian schools are closed, religious lessons in schools have been stopped.

It is tightening in country after country – and God sits in heaven and laughs. He says, "You think that you can stop my kingdom. You think that you can have the last word? I'll laugh at you." So this is how they pray with holy boldness. Lord, we're going to laugh with you. We'll get on your side."

Then they prayed for just two things. They said, "Lord, will you help us to go on using the name of Jesus and will you go on doing miracles?" In other words, "Will you just go on doing the very thing that got us into trouble and will you give us the boldness to go on doing it?" What a bold prayer. But, you see, if you are going to be bold with beggars and bold with crowds and bold with enemies, you need first to be bold with God.

What a bold prayer. Not, "Lord, get us out of this trouble." Not, "Lord, keep us safe," but, "Lord, just help us to go on into trouble. Lord, just help us to go on using the name of Jesus." They recognize that it was the name of Jesus that had the power in it. Just ask yourself: "How often does the name of Jesus pass your lips in public?" Sometimes we tend to use other synonyms to talk about the Master or something else, but, you know, the power lies in the name of Jesus.

Someone recently told me he went into the works lavatory. There was a group of men and one of them was just saying the name "Jesus", but in a totally wrong way, using the name as a swear word. So my friend just said, "Would you mind not using that name like that. That's the name of my best friend, Jesus." That lavatory became a holy place because of the power of the name of Jesus.

That's the name that has the power in it. That's the name that has the power to conquer evil. That's the name that can deal with sickness. That's the name that nurse used over my wife. That's the name that has all the power and authority of heaven and earth vested in it. You can't use the name of a person after they are dead because people will just say,

"Oh, yes, they're dead—poor souls." The name ceases to have any power in it when the person has died, but as long as a person is alive, and in a position of authority and they say, "Use my name," then that name has power in it and you can go and you can use it and say, "So and so sent me." The door opens. If that can apply in human society, how much more now that Jesus is risen from the dead?

Where did Peter get this holy boldness? How did he change the cowardice for courage? How did he change from a man who would run away and hide in a hole and sob his heart out, because he was such a coward? What changed him into this man who would challenge the world? The name of Jesus and the Spirit of Jesus did it. Those who are filled with the Spirit of Christ will use the name of Jesus more often – will use it for themselves, calling on the name of Jesus.

When you are in need, this week when you're in a real crisis, may I commend to you the practice of just saying aloud the name of Jesus? Call on him, "Jesus, Jesus," until he comes. If you are meeting a need in someone else, without being tactless or aggressive, I want you to ask whether you should use the name "Jesus" in conversation to them, whether you should just say, "I think Jesus could help you, if you asked him. Would you like me to ask him for you?"

When you pray for someone in need, use that name. Use it frequently in your prayer – "Jesus". Get a holy boldness in the name of "Jesus." You can command circumstances to sort themselves out, you can command problems to go, you can command temptation to go, you can command Satan to depart, provided you use the name of Jesus. If you're filled with the Spirit, then that courage to use the name will come.

I was at a meeting in Doncaster one Friday night, in a very large Church of England building – built on the principle of pulling down barns and building greater. It had two naves and a towering roof. It had old-fashioned high wooden pews. At the end there were hinged flaps on the pews. You could lift them and prop them up with something underneath. They had never seen that church full for a hundred years, but that night it was packed. They had these flaps up for the first time in living memory. There were people of all ages there; about a quarter were immigrants from elsewhere.

The Spirit of God moved in that meeting. I emphasised the name of Jesus and then said, "I want you to ask him, right now, ask him, in his name, to deal with a particular problem in your life, a particular need. I want you to tell me, as you go out, as you shake my hand, what Jesus has done in your life." I never made a greater mistake in my life; my hand was just worn out. It took about an hour to clear that church because I suppose two-thirds of the congregation had to tell me of something.

One man said, "I know he's delivered me from smoking — just like that." A housewife said, "He's delivered me from this fear." Another one said, "He's given me love for my husband." It went on; they were such practical things, such down to earth things. The name of Jesus had proved powerful right through the congregation, right through that meeting. It was so exciting. The power of the Spirit had been moving.

You have got needs. They may be physical needs, mental needs, spiritual needs, need of forgiveness, need of reconciliation with someone, need to be delivered from a fear of something or someone. I don't know what your need is; I don't want to know because God knows. Have a moment of prayer and I want you to bring that need to him and use the name of Jesus. Don't just say "God", say "Jesus". I want you to ask Jesus to do something quite definite for you.

To those who are timid by nature – shy, retiring, you don't like to open your mouth, and because of this you don't see much of God's power working because you don't say much about Jesus either – I want to give a special word of encouragement. Timothy was like that. Paul never was, but Timothy was very shy, but the Holy Spirit kindled in him a boldness. In the name of Jesus seek holy boldness – that the Holy Spirit can give you – so that you will find yourself ministering to someone else soon, find yourself talking to a stranger, find yourself just bursting to say, "I was a shy, retiring person. Here I am, talking to you." What a lovely thing that would be.

14

PETER THE PASTOR

Read Acts 4:32 – 5:42

I wonder how you would like to have Simon Peter as your pastor if we could get hold of him and just ask the Lord to send him down from heaven to take over the pastorate of your church! Would you welcome that – the big fisherman, this man whom the Lord had moulded and changed from a reed (the meaning of the name Simon) into the rock, which is the meaning of the name Peter? There are many features of the church of which he was pastor that one would love to share. It was an exciting church to be in. Things were happening; you never quite knew what would happen next. It was a growing church, and it was constantly expanding by the hundred; but it was more than that. It was a caring and a sharing church in which nobody had any need. Wouldn't you love to be part of that church with such a pastor?

Well, let me remind you that the cost of having that kind of a church is that you have all of it. It was not only an exciting, growing, loving church in which to be, it was also a church in which sin was exposed. It was also a church in which there was great fear. It was a church in which people died on the spot when faced with the truth about their own hearts. It was a church where you never knew when you would be dragged off to jail. It was a church in which your leaders would be flogged by the public authorities. Well would you like to be in this church? It is the kind of thing that would happen when Simon Peter is your pastor, and frankly I believe that this church of which we read in Acts is not an unattainable ideal, something that happened two thousand years ago that couldn't happen today. I believe that in Acts we have a mirror to the church saying, "Look into this mirror. This is what you ought to be."

There are some events, all related to Simon Peter, of which we need to be reminded. Then we shall find ten profound lessons which the early church had to learn and which we may learn, by God's mercy, from their experience without having to go through the hard school in which they learned them.

We look first at this remarkable event in which a man and his wife who were members of that church died on the spot in a church meeting and were carried out by the other church members and, as has to take place in the Middle East, were buried within a few hours. It happened because the church gave, and because people cared so much that they shared. There are many attitudes to possessions in the world. Here are four different ones. Ask yourself which of them is yours. Attitude number one: "What's mine is my own." Attitude number two: "What's yours is mine." Attitude number three: "What's mine is yours." Attitude number four: "What's mine is his, and therefore ours."

I have heard some people say that communism was first practised by the early Christian church. Nothing of the kind! The sharing they had here could hardly be further from the communism we know today. For one thing, the sharing here grew out of a united faith in God. Since when did communism grow out of that? It also grew out of a deep love for one another. Since when did communism grow out of that? For another thing, the sharing was spontaneous and voluntary. No one was forced to share; people could keep private property if they wished. Since when did communism allow voluntary sharing? There are many other differences, which we could go into. There was a man called Barnabas who had a field and he sold it because there were other Christians in need. He brought the money and he said to the apostles, "I've sold the field, here's all the money, share it among those in need." Barnabas was a good man. The tragedy is that whenever someone does something beautiful, Satan sees to it that the whole atmosphere gets spoiled by something ugly. As soon as Barnabas did something beautiful, two other members of the church, seeing what happened, did something terribly ugly. We need to realise that God is not interested in how much we give, but why we give and how we give. The way that Barnabas gave was a beautiful act; the way that Ananias and Sapphira gave was ugly.

This is what happened, very simply. They also had a property, they also sold it. They then split the money into two parts – they put half in their own pocket, which they were perfectly entitled to do, there was nothing wrong with that, but then came the ugly thing. They brought it to Peter and they said, "Peter, we also have done what Barnabas has done. We have sold a property and here's the whole proceeds." What fools they were. If you ever do that kind of thing, you have forgotten one very important fact: that God is listening. You may get away with it with people; you may keep up a deception indefinitely with them, but you can never get away with it with God. Therefore, in a sense, if we behave in the church as if God is not listening, then we really are in a serious state of unbelief. They were trying to deceive the church, but God knew all about it and Peter was given what the Bible calls a word of knowledge. It is a gift of the Spirit and God gave Peter immediately the knowledge that the money they were putting at the feet of the apostles was not the whole proceeds. They were guilty of what many of us have been guilty of, alas, and that is wanting more credit than we deserve; wanting the glory without the cost.

A man said to me once, "I really think an ex-missionary would be a marvellous thing to be. You know – to go around talking about it all, but not having had to go through it all so that you could just be on permanent deputation." Mind you, a real missionary doesn't see permanent deputation as anything approaching heaven! To be an ex-missionary... that was a very human and honest remark – to want the glory without the cross; to want the crown without the death; the credit without the costliness and the price to be paid. That was what they were wanting. In trying to deceive the church, they had lied to the Holy Spirit. They had tried to tempt the Lord their God. They had pushed him too far and they were filled with Satan. It is amazing that just a year or two before, maybe less, Jesus had said to Peter, "Get behind me, Satan." Now it is Peter's turn to say to two members of the church, "Satan has filled your heart," and he recognised this for what it was. Peter realised how serious this was and that this kind of deception and hypocrisy would wreck the church. It would be a cancer in the body of Christ, so he dealt with it. With that word of knowledge he spoke to Ananias: "How could you agree to do such a thing? You have been lying to God."

Now here is a profound principle. **If the church really is the people of God, then to lie to the people is to lie to God.** This is a principle that runs right through the scripture. "Inasmuch as you do it to the brethren, you do it to me," said Jesus. "Saul, Saul, why persecute me?" Saul could have said, "I'm not after you. I'm after these Christians," but he didn't, he realised that whatever you do to Christians you are doing to Christ. Whatever you do to the body, you are doing to the head. Whatever you do to the people of God, you are doing to God. Lie to the people of God, you are lying to God.

Laugh at the people of God and you are laughing at God. This is really teaching us to take the church very seriously; to realise that however poor the church may be, however mixed a bag it may be, it is God's people. He has given his name to them and he is in their midst. What happens among them he knows about, and he wants reality and truth; he wants honesty. All right, if you have kept half the proceeds then make it quite clear that is what you have done. You are perfectly entitled to do so. Don't profess to be more than you are. I find that a very profound and challenging principle.

So Peter dealt with it, and then the wife came in a short time later and Peter gave her a glorious chance to confess it. He said, "Sapphira, was this the price you and your husband got for this land?" She could have saved her life, saved everything, by one simple word. "I'm sorry, it wasn't." But she kept up the deception and she was carried out and buried.

Now this is an amazing Peter. This is the Peter who had his own weaknesses in years gone by. This was the Peter who had himself been filled with Satan when Jesus spoke to him. This is the Peter who had denied Christ. But here is a Peter now so filled with holy boldness that he will deal with that in the church which is going to destroy the church. It is a very bold Peter. He knew that opposition from outside the church is not nearly as dangerous as corruption within it. So he had to deal with it.

The next little event is out among the public, where not just words but wonders were seen from the apostles. They met regularly in the temple, and such was the impression they made that two things happened. First, unbelievers didn't dare to come near them; second, believers joined them in ever increasing numbers, and those two facts are related to each other. I think it is precisely because people are not afraid to approach the church today that not so many join. It may sound crazy but, if you think it through, when the church is that which makes people respect and even fear the church, more will be converted and come to the Lord. Where people can dismiss the church and despise it as an ineffective, weak body, they don't join it. Is this not true? "Of the rest, dared no man join them, but believers were the more added to the Lord, both men and women." In other words, God can do more with a small, powerful church which makes people scared than with a large church that people can look down on and despise.

One thing is said about Peter in this little picture of their public ministry, and that is by this time even Peter's shadow was serving the Lord. Jesus had said, "Greater things shall you do than I've done," and I think this is one of them. There is no recorded case of Jesus' shadow doing any good but Peter is now so full of the power of the Holy Spirit that even his shadow is doing good. They would bring sick people into the streets and lay them on the pavement so that when Peter walked by, if his shadow crossed them, they believed they would be healed.

Now you may dismiss that as sheer superstition, but I put it in the same bracket as a woman who came and reached through and touched the hem of Jesus' garment. Yes, it is a naïve way in which to exercise faith, but it is a real way. It is a simple way and it is a misunderstood way; I know that the person who comes this way needs education, but nevertheless, when the woman touched the hem of Jesus' garment there was no power in the hem. It was her expression of faith in Jesus, and in the God who was in Jesus. We should not despise an approach of faith, however strange it may seem. I believe that the people who wanted just Peter's shadow to fall across them were exercising true faith in Peter's God. It was the only way they could think of getting through to that God and having some contact, some channel of power, and so Peter walked by, and as he walked by, here's this big fisherman – so weak and helpless in the early days – striding along and his shadow is healing the sick. It is marvellous, isn't it?

Alas, whenever anybody ministers like Jesus, people get upset, and it is often the religious authorities who do. I am afraid the great enemy of Christianity is religion. It is so often the religious authorities who are troubled and begin to put blockages in the way of the free movement of the power of Jesus Christ through his followers. Sure enough, when a fisherman walks through Jerusalem and his shadow changes lives and he is not even an ordained man, not recognised by the religious leaders, then the religious authorities get jealous. That was what happened here, so they flung Peter into jail. This comes to the third thing – the jailbreak. It seems gloriously funny. They put them in jail, then the angel comes, unlocks the door, lets them out and says, "Go right back to what you were doing" – then, being a very polite angel, locks the door behind them. Did you notice that? He turns around, shuts the door. No burglar was ever so careful. The angel brings them out and just puts them right back in the temple the next morning, preaching, teaching, going on doing the same thing. Man may have put them in jail, but the Word of God cannot be bound, and if God wanted them out of that jail, he would get them out.

Someone in my church told me they went home late at night and, when they got home after church, found that they had pulled the front door to with a Yale lock. It was tight shut and locked and the key was left on the inside. They couldn't get help. Despite trying the door and pushing it, nothing would happen. Then they said, "Lord, I need your help," and put their hand on that door and it just opened. God can deal with locks!

The angel just unlocked the prison, let them out, and sent them back to where they were. Now come on to the trial; a real Gilbert and Sullivan atmosphere if ever there was one. It is marvellous to see how these prisoners are delivered from concern about themselves, and there's nobody quite so free as those who are not concerned about themselves.

These men have been delivered from fear even of death, so when they were put on trial there was no abject concern, trying to get out of it, trying to explain it away. There is just a holy boldness. This is the same court and the same judges who condemned Jesus to death, and they start by saying, "What on earth are you doing? We forbade you to speak in this name. You are trying to pin the death of this Jesus on us." Peter, again with holy boldness, the man who once ran away to save his skin, stands there and says, "You are trying to make us disobey the God whom you represent." It was a religious court, not a civil one. It was the Sanhedrin. These were the representatives of God, and Peter says, "Are you going to insist that we disobey your God?"

Now could anything be more devastating? He goes on to say, "You are in the wrong. You are on the wrong side. You are against God. He sent Jesus, you killed him. God raised him up and God exalted him and we are witnesses of it. We are the witnesses, we're not the defendant, you are the defendants." Peter stood there in that dock, and in four sentences he gave them a magnificent theological sermon. He had the Trinity in it. He mentioned God, Jesus Christ, and the Holy Spirit. He mentioned the death of Christ, the resurrection of Christ and the ascension of Christ. He mentioned the history of the Jews and of Israel in four sentences. He mentioned the offer of forgiveness, conditional on repentance. He talked about the Holy Spirit being given to all those who obey him, and the Holy Spirit witnessing to the truth of what they had seen by wonders. All in four sentences! In four sentences he got all that packed in, put them in the dock said, "We are the witnesses and the case is proven against you. You are trying to make us disobey God, but before this court I tell you we must obey God rather than men." Oh, what a change in this man Simon Peter!

Then comes what some people think is a happy sequel, but I think it is a sad one. A man called Gamaliel gets up and with apparent human wisdom he says, "Put the men out. I'd like to say something." Then he says something like this. He said, "You know, we've had this kind of problem before. We've had rebels before. We've had men who've followed them before. There's Theudas, then the Galilean, Judas was his name, and it came and it went. Just give it time; wait and see. It's all right; the leader's dead and look what happened when Theudas was killed and when Judas was killed. It was only a matter of time until the followers dispersed. These things don't last once the leader's dead."

It all sounds so clever, so wise, but it was very silly and I will tell you why he said it: Peter had got him worried. The others, Peter just made them angry – so angry, so furious in the blindness of their jealousy, they couldn't listen to reason and they wanted to kill these men, but Gamaliel had been hurt. Gamaliel thought, "My, just suppose I was fighting against God." You see, he was a professor of theology and he taught about God. He couldn't afford to be wrong, and so he played for safety. He said, "Let's wait and see. It might just be that it's of God, and if it is, well we wouldn't want to be on the wrong side, would we?" That's how he talked.

Some people have held up Gamaliel as a marvellous example of wisdom. I hold him up as an example of folly. Why? Because this man is never heard of again – the man who will not make up his mind; the man who will not come down one side or the other; the man who wants to hold off and become neutral in the situation; the man who wants to get out of the situation, is the man who will never get related to God. At one youth club I went to there were thirty young people, and when I came home my wife asked, "How did you get on?" I replied, "Well, there's hope for two of them." She said, "Why?" I answered, "They were so angry with what I said there were tears in their eyes; the rest were indifferent." Within six months both those two were baptised. They are both serving the Lord now. They weren't Gamaliels! Gamaliel sits on the fence. That is the position he likes to be in. He feels safe there because he can jump either way, seeing which way things go. He doesn't want to be caught on the wrong side, so he goes on no side. Gamaliel disappears from the Word of God. I don't expect to see him in heaven, wise though he seems to have been in worldly eyes.

"Wait and see. Let's see if it's of man or of God." They didn't need to wait and see when a man's shadow is healing the sick. When Peter, the big fisherman, is transformed, they didn't need to wait and see. When a beggar of forty years, a cripple, is leaping around the temple, they didn't need to wait and see. He had got all the evidence in front of him, but he wanted to play for safety and he said, "Some time, some other time. Let's wait and see."

But in his theological seminary there was a young, fanatical student called Saul, from a place called Tarsus, and I praise God that the young Saul did not take his teacher's advice. He did not wait and see. He said: I'm going to get rid of this Christianity; I'm going to fight it. I'm against it. He came down firmly on the wrong side. Because of that, we got the apostle Paul. Thank God when people don't sit on the fence. You can't sit there. It's not really a very comfortable place to be. When you are faced with men of God, you have got to be "for" or "against". "He that is not for me," said Jesus, "is against me."

So Gamaliel disappears, but they accepted his advice. They flogged the apostles, and I don't know if you know what that means. It means flogged with thirty-nine strokes, which were enough to drive a man insane and certainly to tear his back to bloody ribbons. Peter came out with a bleeding, burst back. He said, "What an honour." What did they do then? Make for a convalescent home somewhere in Greece where they could recover? No, they went right back into the temple again. There with bleeding backs, they never ceased, it says, to preach and to teach that Jesus is the Christ. You know you can do nothing about a church like this, can you? You just can't win; you just can't get rid of them. The more disgrace you give, the more honour they feel. The more you hurt them, the more they go on preaching.

Here are ten lessons, and I want you to ask the Holy Spirit now to take one of these ten lessons and give it to you, individually.

Lesson number one: **If you fear God, you don't need to fear anyone else.** Do you notice all the mention of fear in this chapter? Do you notice that in the beginning it's great fear inside the church? Fear of whom? *Fear of God* – and where there is great fear of God there is no fear of man. We are only afraid of men because we are not sufficiently afraid of God, but when you are afraid of God and have a healthy reverence for him, it delivers you from fear of anyone else. Peter was bold before men because he feared letting God down.

Lesson number two: **Purity inside will mean power outside.** It was because wrong things inside the church were dealt with that, when the church went outside, such lovely things happened.

Lesson number three: **Christians are called to death for themselves and life for others.** How that comes through in this chapter. It begins with two Christians dying, but it goes on to people receiving health, and the apostles being told by the angel, "Go and preach in the temple this word of life." This should be the attitude of Christians; death to self, life for others. That was the concern of the early church – not life for themselves, but they were willing to face death for themselves, that they might give life to the world around them.

Fourth lesson: **The clearer we draw the line between church and world, the more people will be converted.** That is a profound lesson which this country desperately needs to learn, for the fact is that many British people are baptised as babies and many are buried with a Christian burial, but few of them are real Christians and the result is that in this country we don't know where the line is drawn. One of my deep convictions is that when the whole church of Christ in this land returns to believer's baptism, the line will be more clearly drawn. I think we will know then who is in and who is not; where the believers are and where the rest are, who dare not join. I believe that the clearer we draw the line between church and world, the more believers will be added to the church, but we have so blurred the line that nobody knows who is a Christian and who is not.

The fifth lesson I have already mentioned: **Religion is the enemy of Christianity.** A candidate for baptism I was interviewing said to me quite simply that they had finished with religion – and my heart bounded with that! Hallelujah! It is great to be finished with religion; it is religion that gets all upset when Christ gets busy. The religion in this country is church-ianity. There are other religions, and it is a sad thing to see that the confusion is entering in so many ways. It was the Sadducees and the Pharisees who opposed what Peter did. I believe we have to learn that the more religious we are, the more difficult it is to be Christian. The more committed we are to an institution, the more difficult it is to let Christ form his body in us.

The sixth lesson is this: **The angel's message to Peter when he let him out of prison was, "Go out and tell."** God sets us free to go and tell. Why did he set me free from me? Why did he set me free? To go and tell — that's why you are brought out of prison.

Seventh lesson: **It is an honour to suffer dishonour for the Lord Jesus.** If people embarrass you, if you are subject to any kind of social isolation because you are a Christian, count it an honour. There are many people in our world who are suffering very deeply for the faith. They are honoured; it is an honour to suffer disgrace.

Eighth lesson: **Obedience is the condition of victory.** Peter, to the trial court, says this, "The Holy Spirit is given to those who obey him."

Ninth lesson: **The closer we follow Christ, the more we will be treated as he was.** The more you walk in his ways, the more you will find the world's attitude to you will be the attitude it had to him. It is important to realise that in being baptised we are being identified with Christ. We are saying, "Christ, we want to be closer to you than we have been before. We want to be buried as you were buried, raised as you were raised." So Christ says to us, "Then will you suffer as I suffered?"

The tenth lesson: **The real change in Peter was that Peter had become a man of God.** I mean that he looked at every situation from God's point of view. Do you notice how that came out in incident after incident? Faced with Ananias and Sapphira, he did not say, "Well now, you've let the side down. You've let your fellow members down." He said, "You've lied to God, not men." He is now looking at the whole scene as God would look at it, and he could say: "I can see now what you've done. It's not what you've done to the church. It's not that you've tried to deceive us. It's God you've been dealing with."

When he stands in a courtroom, he says to the judge, "We must obey God, rather than men." Do you notice this constant refrain: God; man? The Gamaliels of this world sit on the fence and say, "If it's of God; if it's of man," but the Peters of this world say: "We must obey God, not man." "You've lied to God, not man." He has come down firmly on one side of the fence. From now on everything is from God's point of view, and that is the strength of this man.

God himself is waiting for men and women who will not just sit on the fence and say, "Let's wait and see. Let's give it time. I want to make up my mind thoroughly. I'm going to wait and see if it is of God or if it is of man." God is waiting for men and women who will say, "It is of God, and I want to be on God's side and I want to have his compassion, I want to have his love, I desire his holiness, I want to be a man of God, a woman of God, I want to be right that side of the fence." That was what made Peter the rock.

15

GOD USES NOBODIES

Read Acts 8:1b – 25, 9:31–43

God loves to take "nobodies" and use them to confound all the "somebodies" in this world. Peter was a very ordinary fisherman. His hands, big and tough, had worked on nets, but now those hands were being used to release the power of the Holy Spirit in other people, to heal the sick and to raise the dead. Just a fisherman!

So there is hope for every one of us that we can be used by God – for if God limited his work to those who were naturally gifted, or those who were above average, or those who were already somebody before he got hold of them, then there would be no hope for most of us. But if ever you feel you are a nobody, and inferior, and that God couldn't do things with you, read 1 Corinthians 1. By the end of that chapter you will have lost your inferiority complex and believe that God can do extraordinary things through very ordinary people.

We have been studying the life of Peter and learning a lot from it. We now look at Peter's ministry in just three places and try and learn something from the events in all three – Samaria, Lydda, and Joppa.

I do not know if you get the flavour of the word "Samaritan". It probably just reminds you of the parable of the Good Samaritan, but to a Jew it was a horrible word. If you have ever been out to the Middle East you may well have been to visit the few remaining Samaritans. They were nearly dying out, but they have turned the corner and there has been a little bit of a population increase. They are the remnant from over two and a half thousand years ago when the Jews were taken out of their land to Babylon. Some of them managed to stay behind, some probably hid from the invading forces or were way out in distant parts of the country. They were so short of people to marry that they married outside the people of God and became a kind of half-caste group. When Jews who had suffered much in exile came back, they would have nothing to do with this mixed group. Jews so hated the Samaritans that they would go an extra seventy miles from Judea to Galilee, right around the other side of the Jordan, to avoid having to walk through Samaria. A Samaritan would do likewise. That is the situation behind the account of the Good Samaritan. The fact that it was a Samaritan who did that for a Jew – that's the rub in the story, not that somebody was kind to somebody else, but that somebody was kind to a person who would hate his guts for doing it. The Jews and the Samaritans wouldn't even eat or drink in the same restaurant.

When Jesus asked a Samaritan woman to give him a drink, she was astonished because, as it says in the scripture, "Jews will not use the same drinking vessels as Samaritans." It was he, who on that occasion said, "I must needs go through Samaria." Later, the Samaritans' reception of Jesus was so bad that, at one stage, John – the beloved disciple – said to Jesus, "Are we going to let them insult you like this? Why don't we call down fire from heaven and burn them up...?" The amazing thing is that when Peter finally got to Samaria, the man who went with him to bless them was John. It is when you read between the lines of scripture that you get the miracles of grace that happen and you see the change that can occur in human nature. God can do extraordinary things with ordinary people, provided those ordinary people are willing to be changed and made extraordinary.

Peter and John came down to Samaria. Why? Because a revival had broken out. When Jesus left his disciples and went back to heaven, he left them with marching orders – a clear, overall project to work at while he was absent. He said, "You're to begin preaching in Jerusalem and you're to be my witnesses there. Then you're to move on to Judea, then you're to move on to Samaria, and from there you can go anywhere in the earth, to the uttermost parts...." The fact is that until Acts 8 no-one had gone to Samaria.

Do you know how God got them there? By persecuting them in Jerusalem. I believe they would not have fulfilled the Lord's programme unless he forced them to go. Because God raised up a man called Saul who began to put the Christians in prison in Jerusalem and the members of the church in Jerusalem just had to get up and go and get out of this situation. They fled anywhere they could, and some of them fled to Samaria and that was how the gospel came to Samaria. Almost, it seems, by accident.

The apostles didn't go, but the ordinary members went, and this is the exciting thing. In the old Anglo-Saxon New Testament, 8:4 says, "And they went everywhere, gossiping ye word." Oh, when the members of the church gossip the word, you are really going places. There will be revival when that happens.

It was a Spirit-filled deacon, Philip, who had been set aside to look after the finance, who led the revival. If you choose your deacons because they are full of the Spirit, you can expect revival. If you choose them just for the job, then you can't, but if you choose deacons for a practical job who are full of the Spirit, wait and see what happens! Philip went to Samaria and started preaching, healing, casting out demons. Philip, I thought you were called to serve tables! It is exciting, isn't it? There is great joy in the city. All kinds of things were happening. He baptised them, but – this is the "but" – the Holy Spirit was not poured out on them.

Many people today, if they had been sent to Samaria to look at what Philip was doing, would come back and say, "They've no need of anything more. It's tremendous, there are crowds coming to the Lord, people are getting healed, people are getting baptised, the whole place is so happy you can sense the joy as soon as you get into the city." But the Word of God says – and the "but" is one of the most important buts there can ever be – *they had not received Holy Spirit.*

From this scripture alone, even if there were no others at all, we would know that *believing* and *receiving* are two distinct operations of the human heart, but we have confused the two. So confused have we got that preachers and evangelists talk about "receiving Christ". The apostles were wiser, and the New Testament preachers didn't make this mistake. There are only two places where the verb "receive" is ever applied to Jesus. One is when he came in the flesh to his own people, the Jews. "And he came unto his own people, and his own people received him not. But to as many as received him, to them he gave power to become sons of God." But that was in the days of his flesh, it was before the Spirit came, so the word "receive" was applied to Jesus in the flesh because it literally was a case of receiving him in the flesh into your home, into your town.

The only other case is in Colossians 2, which is addressed to Christians, where Paul says, "As you received Christ, so walk in him." (The Greek word for "receive" here is different, literally translated "beside receive" and can mean: "to be taught about".) But on no occasion after Pentecost does any preacher exhort people to "receive Jesus". Their preaching was clear and simple, and if we had not got it confused I think we would understand the situation better today. Their preaching was: "Believe in the Lord Jesus Christ and receive Holy Spirit." Those two are so distinct that Paul can say to one group of disciples, "Did you receive when you believed?" which is a very important question to ask.

The fact is that in Samaria hundreds had believed on the Lord Jesus, had been healed and delivered, had been baptised, but the Holy Spirit had not "fallen on" them – and that's a very strong description. It was not describing some unconscious or automatic spiritual event, but something which is discernible, something which is known, something of which people are conscious.

The fact that there was a "but" in Acts 8 proves this – and I hope you can follow me in my argument. It means that up till that point there had never been such a "but", and that up to that moment it had been normal for Christians who believed and were baptised to receive and have the Holy Spirit fall on them. Until that moment it was normal to have both, and here was the first exception, which meant that there was an urgent need to remedy the situation, which required help from elsewhere and a more varied ministry then they had had thus far. They needed someone more than Philip to come.

Why had Philip not been able to help them in this matter? He had done so much for them. He was a man full of the Holy Spirit. There are many reasons, and they are all speculative since the scripture doesn't say. Some have felt that Philip was inexperienced in these matters. Was it that they had only been baptised in the name of Jesus, and the Holy Spirit had not been included in the formula? I don't think that is so. I think it is reading far too much into that verse, because I notice that, in Acts 10, Peter baptised in the name of Jesus. In Acts 19, Paul baptised in the name of Jesus, so I don't think there is any clue there. It was normal practice for them to do that.

Is there, then, something in the scholars who say that God withheld the Holy Spirit until Peter and James came down from Jerusalem, so that the Jewish and the Samaritan church might be one, not split into two denominations from the beginning; so that they were mutually dependent for spiritual gifts? I think there may well be a truth in that, but then Philip had come from Jerusalem, so he was a representative of that church also. Was it that the Samaritans might thus, from the beginning, be led to recognise the apostolic authority in their teaching? Maybe, but I find myself more and more thinking that it was God's way of ensuring that the church in Samaria did not look to one man alone, but realise that God blessing a group of people is a shared ministry, and that God wants to use more than one channel so that one person should never get the limelight and be too prominent.

So Philip was able to help thus far, then John and Peter came down to the Samaritans, to the very place where they had wanted to call fire down from heaven. Now they did precisely that, but it was a different sort of fire. We want fire on everybody's head. We do want to see coals of fire on people's heads, not in malice but because we want to see the Holy Spirit of God burning on others.

I believe that God in his mercy was saying, "Philip, that's what I'm going to allow you to do. Peter and John, that's what I'm going to allow you to do." So Peter came down, and when he laid his hands on them he was taking part in a very strong form of prayer. I think the strongest form of prayer you can pray is to lay hands on someone else. I do not believe that here we have a confirmation rite, though this is the very scripture from which the Church of England and other churches have taken their practice of confirmation by bishops.

Laying on of hands is a most potent form of prayer, for

it adds to the verbal prayer a number of other aids. First, it directs the prayer very definitely to one person, and that as it were, concentrates the prayer. It is so much stronger than a prayer that says, "Lord, fill everybody who needs your Spirit." Secondly, it is adding a physical aspect to a mental or spiritual act of prayer. It is engaging the whole of a person in prayer. One of the constant dangers is to separate physical and spiritual and keep them too far apart, without realising that we are to give our bodies as an act of spiritual worship. Laying on of hands I believe is a sacramental act in the sense that God can use a physical agency for spiritual power. Otherwise, why did Jesus spit on the ground and make clay with the dust, and smear a blind man's eyes? He was using clay as a sacrament. Peter was using his whole body, as well as his heart and spirit and mind, to pray for those people, and, as he did, the Holy Spirit came down upon them.

This was not invariably the pattern. There are cases where the Holy Spirit came down on someone without any hands being laid on them at all—Cornelius, and indeed all his household. There is a divine and beautiful freedom in this. I am scared stiff of getting into a confirmation ceremony that becomes an empty rite. That is what it has become for thousands. It is said when it is done that the Holy Spirit may be poured out upon that person, but I have only heard of one case where a bishop did that and it happened. He nearly shot out of his mitre – never had such a thing happened before.

I am always thrilled when somebody says, "I've been filled with the Spirit – I was all by myself and I was asking the Lord to fill me." I remember one dear girl, who later went to Bangladesh, who simply said to me, "You know, I was in my room, praying all by myself, and just asking the Lord to fill me, and suddenly he did and I didn't quite know what was happening, but it was so beautiful and I just love the Lord so much." The Spirit came down on her. The important thing is not whether hands were laid on you or not. The important thing is: did the Spirit fall? One cares not how he came, as long as there is no "but" in my life. "Lord, I have much joy. Lord, I've been delivered. Lord, I'm baptised. Lord, I believe, but...." Peter wanted to sort out that "but" quickly.

At this stage, Peter found someone else bearing his own name, Simon, and that must have been a bit difficult for him. It would remind him of his past. The name of this other Simon (in the form "Simony") has been given to those who try to buy God's gifts with money and trade in God's blessings.

The other Simon loved the power and prestige of magic, and he was dabbling in the occult. He got powers and he could do things, but he had never before seen anything like Peter ministering and others being filled with the Spirit. Offering money, Simon the magician revealed how he usually got his tricks. He had believed and he had been baptised, but there were two "buts" in Simon's life. First, he hadn't been filled with the Spirit himself, but the second "but" was more serious in his case and it was this: he had believed, he had been baptised, but *he had never repented*, which meant that the same desires were still there. He had not said good-bye to his old inner attitudes. This inner attitude loved power and prestige and he saw that gifts of the Spirit would give him a power and a prestige.

When the Holy Spirit is moving, we have to be very careful to examine our motives. If we desire a gift, we have to be absolutely sure we want it to edify the body and glorify the Lord, and not to gain any power or prestige for ourselves. Peter, with that rare gift of discernment and the word of knowledge which he had shown with Ananias and Sapphira, said: "To hell with you and your money. I can see that you've never truly repented."

Now Simon reacted rather differently from Ananias and

Sapphira. They both tried to brazen it out and so they died. Simon immediately said, "Pray for me." I can't judge from his words whether he was more worried about his skin or his sin, but nevertheless he prayed. He said, "Will you pray for me that this will not happen to me?" Once again, Peter with discernment sees that when the power of Almighty God is let loose that power can corrupt, and it is important to deal with that corruption straight away. This uneducated fisherman has total command of the situation.

Now we move on to Lydda. You can see it just on the edge of Lod Airport today, visible at take off. One of my most precious memories is of a house meeting in Lydda, in the very place – a gathering of the saints in a little Arab bungalow with the main living room then, off it, the bedrooms and kitchen. That main living room was packed to the ceiling! New things were happening that night. It was the first time there that Jews had come to an Arab home for fellowship, and people could hardly believe it. They were praising the Lord to see Arabs and Jews together in an Arab township in an Arab bungalow praising the Lord Jesus Christ. The man whose bungalow it was, a dear saint of God, was an Arab man who had been in prison more than once for various reasons – never for crime, always because of his principles, but there was no bitterness. There he was, he had four fine grown-up sons, all Christians and all praising the Lord with this father. What a joy to see the whole family! As I spoke to them, crowded into that little room that night, through an interpreter, one could feel that the Holy Spirit was blowing a breath of fresh air through the company, and I thought of this occasion when Peter was in such a meeting.

It has been a place of many battles. It was here that George fought the dragon. Did you know that Saint George came from Lydda? Did you know that the dragon was actually Dagon, the Philistine god? The patron saint of England fought the god of the Philistines. It is all very much involved with Lydda. Just on the outskirts of Lydda, David slew Goliath. They will show you the Samson garage and the Samson coffee bar next door where they said Samson used to meet Delilah regularly at the disco, and this has been a battlefield. If you come outside the bungalow and look up to the hills, you see the Valley of Ajalon where the sun stood still for Joshua. Many battles have been fought there, and here was Peter fighting the battles of the Lord. In that house was Aeneas, a saint who had been a cripple for eight years. Peter, who came to fight the works of Satan, simply said with such boldness, "Aeneas, Jesus Christ heals you." Oh, how humble the man is. Not: "I'm going to heal you; I've been given the gift of healing; I've experienced such things that I can bless you." No, "Aeneas, Jesus Christ heals you." Peter had almost forgotten that he was the channel; that he was the postman of God's grace. Indeed, this is the mark of a true healer in the name of Jesus, who says, "Jesus heals you." That's why Peter didn't become the centre of a cult or a fan club. It says the people of Lydda turned to the Lord, they believed in the Lord. God is waiting for people who will say, "Jesus Christ does this," who are conscious not of the channel, but of him.

It is interesting that Peter had learned a great deal from being with Jesus. He knew that when a man is healed, the best thing you can do is to tell him to do something for himself and to use the health God has given him to work. "Rise, make your bed. Arrange your things. Tidy the place up." How wonderful that the man who had not been able to do a thing for himself in eight years was now ordered by Peter to take his part in the service of the home – to make his bed, which had always been made for him. It is a lovely little touch. When the Lord delivers us he tells us to find a job and get busy.

In Joppa, six and a half miles away, at this very time a woman died. Her name was Gazelle. If ever you have seen a gazelle, you know that's a beautiful little animal, with very thin but athletic legs. Maybe it says something just about this lady—Dorcas was her Aramaic name, or Tabitha the Hebrew name, but it means the same thing: little beauty, gazelle, but she was a little beauty in more ways than one. In the Middle East in those days, a widow had nobody to look after her – there was no state scheme or pension. A widow was worse off than anybody, except perhaps an orphan.

This dear lady had gathered the widows together and had put new morale into them. She had said, "We are not finished, we are not on the scrap heap. We can now give ourselves to other people." She gathered the widows around. She said, "Get your needles and thread out. We are going to be useful. We are not going to be despised as being on the scrap heap. We are going to get together and we are going to serve." So the widows got together with Tabitha and there she was in the centre of a working party. It's part of the Lord's work. It was a very beautiful thing and this lady was essential to that group. They no longer felt unwanted, useless. It is a beautiful little picture. And then she died.

Now there are many questions in the next bit of the story. Unbelievers want to ask, "Was she really dead?" or "How was it done?" I accept the straight statement of the Word of God that she was dead and that she was brought back to life, but there were still many questions in my mind which a believer may ask. First question: why did they send for Peter? To give her a good funeral? To come and comfort those who felt the loss? To come and try and explain why such a servant of God should be taken, presumably before her time? Or did they already believe that, since Jesus rose from the dead, even death need not have the last word? If that is so, what faith!

Peter came the six and a half miles quickly. My second question then: why did he turn them all out of the bedroom before he did what he did? Why did he want to be alone? Peter could have made quite a show of this. He could have enjoyed an audience. I think it is a mark of the Spirit's dealings with him that he wasn't going to make this into a show. He knew the danger of the sensational in Christian service. He shut them out. Was it because he wasn't sure what he was going to do? Was it because this was the first time he had tackled a resurrection and he wanted to try it out in private? I just don't know. When I get to heaven, I'll say, "Peter, why did you turn them out?" Maybe Dorcas will tell me, but he turned them out and he was alone, and then it says, "He prayed."

What did he pray about? I have the feeling that he had just one thing that he wanted to ask the Lord. "Lord, do you want Dorcas in heaven, or may we have her back here?" You see, the plain fact is that Peter didn't then start a ministry to undertakers' parlours. The fact is that he did not then go on to the next corpse he could find and raise that. In fact, as far as we know, this is the only one he ever raised. It is a shallow and superficial understanding of the scripture to think that because one has been healed, therefore you should make for the nearest hospital and empty it; that because a thing happened once that it should happen all the time and everywhere—that is a very big mistake. It is vital in any one situation to find out whether the Lord wants someone in glory or back on earth – to know the will of God and to know what he wants to do in the situation. That is not the kind of resigned prayer, "Well, whatever the Lord wills shall be done." It is a positive attempt to find out the Lord's will before acting.

On two occasions in my own life this happened. First, where I went to lay hands on one person who was gloriously and permanently healed of the affliction that had been with him for many years. Within a week or two, a dear lady who was very seriously ill with cancer in the bones, having heard of the first case said, "Will you come? Will you lay hands on me, that I may be healed?" I went, and I said, "We're going to seek the will of the Lord. Let's pray about it and then we'll come together." As I prayed, the Lord told me clearly he wanted her in glory. When I went to see her, I didn't know how to tell her, but when I went into the bedroom, she told me. She said, "It's all right. I know." She went to the Lord a few days later.

How important it is to have that time alone with the Lord before attempting anything, and to get in line with what he is doing and planning. I am quite sure that Peter, alone in that bedroom with a corpse, was saying, "Lord, she's vital to the work here. Look what she's doing. We can't see these widows carrying on without her. She has been the one that has led them, but Lord do you want her in heaven or on earth?"

The Lord said to Peter, I believe, in that prayer, "I want her on earth, Peter. Satan has done this; now let's conquer him together," and he did. Of course, again, he had learned from Jesus in the case of Jairus's daughter to put out the crowds who would simply observe with curiosity and morbid delight. He wanted it private, but then of course it had to come out, and he presented her alive.

Notice, that in the case of the healing of Aeneas it says, "All believed...." In the case of Dorcas it says, "Many believed...." I can understand the reduction in numbers believing. The more extraordinary a way in which God works, the more people refuse to believe, and that doesn't matter. God had moved, and a big fisherman had brought a woman back to life. As far as I know, he never did it again, nor does it read in the next sentence, as you might expect:

And throughout that whole region they brought corpses to Peter and he raised them, every one. It doesn't say that, but Peter had now been used of God to do, I believe, the ultimate miracle – life from the dead, which is surely the ultimate, for death is the ultimate enemy.

As I read through these three stories – Samaria, Lydda, Joppa – I had been blinded. I had been dazzled, as I am afraid we so easily are, by the mighty works of God, and I had missed what God had really been doing with Peter through the three events. What do you think he was doing with Peter? Do you see yet? To understand, you need to get out a map, and you've got to put Samaria, Lydda and Joppa on it. When you put those three points on a map, and when you also put a point for Peter's home on the shores of Galilee at Capernaum, you will find there is a line: everything Peter did took him further away from home. What God was doing with Peter was thrusting him out into a world and pulling up his roots from his background and culture. As he had been brought up, he would not have gone to anyone but Jews. He had now had to go to Samaritans, and he finishes up at the end of Acts 9 in the home of a tanner. Do you realise what that meant to a Jew? If I said that he stayed in the home of a pimp or a pornographer, you would begin to get the feel of what it was to a Jew to stay in the home of a tanner.

Peter's cultural background is being uprooted. He is having to get over prejudice after prejudice. He is having to be set free from his past; free from his religious upbringing; free from his tradition. Now he is on the shores of the Mediterranean itself, which was called in those days by the Jews, "the sea of the Gentiles". From his bedroom window he looks out over the sea that is so much bigger than his little Sea of Galilee where he once fished, and facing the question, "How much further? Where is the gospel to go?" He has come right away from his home and he has come as far as he can – to the seashore. Where does it go next? He is poised for a great leap forward that will take him into a Roman house – the first step in a journey that will lead Peter to the city of Rome itself and to death for the Lord Jesus.

So the deeper, underlying message here is not just that the Lord can do extraordinary things through ordinary people, and greater and greater things through them if they let him. The message is also that he must uproot from the past; that we must be free to go where he wants us to go, and he may take us far from our culture, far from our background. Here am I, a Geordie in the south of England. That was quite a jump for me. One would much prefer to stay back home where you feel secure, but God says, "I can do more if you're willing to go."

Are you willing to go? Jesus said, "Go into all the world." He said nothing about coming back. Are you where you ought to be? Are you where God can use you most? You may have to get up and leave, to go somewhere else to be used by him. Peter was willing to go. The very next thing would be a dream, and a call to come and preach, from a Roman regimental sergeant major up in Caesarea. Peter was going to have a real battle about that, but the Lord would win and Peter would go.

Peter finished up far from the little village where he had been brought up to be a fisherman, and that is sometimes the cost of doing wonderful things for the Lord – to be willing to be where he calls you to be; to leave behind the inhibitions that you were brought up to have; to leave behind even religious traditions that hinder the Spirit's leading, that God may work mightily through us.

16

GOD HAS NO FAVOURITES

A little bit in the middle of Psalm 32 reminds me of something I heard about John Wesley. His mother, Susannah, was a very remarkable woman. She had nineteen children of whom twelve survived. That was about the toll in those days. But of the twelve who survived she would spend one hour each week with every child to help that child to grow and mature, face life. But one of the things she said to all of those children was this: "If you have done wrong and you come to me and say sorry before I find out, I will forgive; and if you don't and I find out, I will punish you." She kept her word and she taught them that there is forgiveness for those who confess straight away.

Read Acts 10:1 – 11:18

One of the hard facts of life is that it is always easier to learn something than to unlearn it. I used to meet a group of ministers every Monday morning for a game of golf. (Mark Twain used to define golf as a good walk spoiled!) We had good fellowship, we used to work off a lot of our inhibitions just smacking that ball hard, but I could never get into two figures. The fellowship was good but I was deeply put off when a robin redbreast followed me around one day. As you know, they always go where someone is digging!

One day I decided I would try to be a better golfer, so I had one session with a pro, but he told me he wished he had had me at the beginning. I had learned too many bad habits; I had a bad swing and I had done it too long, and my problem was not to learn how to swing a club but how to unlearn, and it was just too hard. I am still in three figures for my annual game. Whether you play the piano or do anything else, if you learn the wrong way, how hard it is to unlearn that!

One of the lessons Christians have to unlearn concerns scruples. You are likely to have more scruples if you had a strong religious upbringing than if you had not. Simon Peter, if I may dare to say it, suffered from a strong religious upbringing. He was a Jew and his parents seemed to have been devout, and while there is much to praise God for in that situation, there are also handicaps.

It makes an interesting debate as to whether it is an advantage to be brought up in a Christian home or not. On the one hand it can be a handicap to coming to a first deep love of the Lord through sins forgiven, because you have in a sense always been familiar with these things. On the other hand, once you have become a Christian how grateful you are for the many things you have learned almost subconsciously and just accepted as normal: that people are to love each other; that people are made for God – and all this becomes fruitful after you have come to the Lord. So there are advantages and disadvantages. But one of the disadvantages is undoubtedly that you inherit certain religious scruples, and sometimes the people with greatest problems in a church where the Spirit is bringing liberty are those who have been brought up all their lives in church circles and don't come fresh to the Lord. Some of the scruples that we have inherited may have been good in their day and place, but God may want us to move on from those things. The important thing is that when the Lord wants to set us free from a scruple we must respond to that freedom – when *he* wants to set us free, not other people.

Peter had been brought up with two scruples which thus far he had observed all of his life faithfully. One was that he was very careful about the food he ate. To every good Jew there were certain foods you could eat and certain foods you could not eat and the line was rigidly drawn. It came from their own law, in the book of Leviticus. Whereas you and I have no qualms whatsoever about eating a good ham sandwich, if I had been brought up a Jew I would choke over it.

Secondly, Peter had a scruple about the homes he went into. There were certain homes in Capernaum he would visit, and there were other homes where he would not darken the door. The homes that he would go into were the homes where the men were circumcised and the homes he wouldn't go into were where the men were not circumcised. He had been brought up on these scruples, and they were good in their time and in their place. God had commanded this line to be drawn because it taught the children of Israel a profound truth, that some distinction must be made in life between clean and unclean.

Now God was going to bring Simon Peter to the point where he was going to redraw these lines. To redraw the lines that we have been brought up to observe is a very difficult thing to do. We must be very tender towards one another and sensitive. We must bear in mind that it is the brother with the weaker conscience who has most scruples and we must love that brother and observe his scruples. On the other hand the Lord wants us to enjoy freedom in the Spirit and has given us all things freely to enjoy and he wants us to be free.

In Acts 10 – 11 here were two men who normally would

never had been in each other's homes. One of the glorious things that Jesus does is to put you in homes you would never otherwise visit.

In Brazil, within twenty-four hours I had two contrasting experiences. One day I was in one of the wealthiest homes there, the home of an ambassador. The wife had come to the Lord, the husband was interested. Their home had a sitting room with a sunken lounge in a great hollow at one end, grand pianos littering the place, bedrooms stretched down the massive garden. Each bedroom had its own sitting room, marble bathroom and shower, and was a separate unit linked with beautiful walkways through the garden. It was the most luxurious home I had ever been in.

Within twenty-four hours I was in the Amazonian jungle, sitting in one big mud hut with a thatched roof with about twenty people (mostly wearing string) with dogs, a fire in the middle filling the place with smoke. I was sitting on a lump of wood and they were offering me a glass of tea which had been boiled in a pan with sugar cane, and the glass was so encrusted with dirt I couldn't see through it. It was rough to my lips and I had to just turn off mentally and swallow it. The Lord enabled me to forget what I was drinking from, and it was beautiful and refreshing. I was in that home talking to these men. Here was a man sitting, squatting down at my feet – a naked man in the middle of the jungle and he was talking of Jesus. I would have never got into those homes if I didn't know Jesus Christ. It is the people who don't know Jesus who live a narrow life. They are locked up in their own social set and they can't get out of it, up or down – what a miserable life that is. Peter was going to learn this at a much deeper level than I learned it. The only scruples I had in that case were hygienic scruples on the one hand and financial scruples on the other. Peter was going to have to unlearn religious scruples and that is very hard. Cornelius and Peter were in homes about thirty to forty miles apart on the same coastline. Peter had already gone as far as he thought he ought to go. He was as far from his birthplace as he had ever been. If you trace it on a map you will see it – Capernaum. He had been moving steadily southwest, and he had now reached Joppa on the very coast of the Mediterranean.

Peter was also on the very edge of his scruples because he was in a home that he had severe doubts about. It was a Jewish home, but not an Orthodox Jewish home, because the Jew was engaged in an unorthodox occupation. He was a tanner, which meant the house stank, and there was blood and skins. So Peter was already feeling a little doubtful about his lodgings.

So he went up to the flat roof at lunchtime to snooze. Have you ever noticed how dreams usually link up with things that have happened during the day? All kinds of features keep coming back in. Well at least three features from his day came in. First, he was hungry so he dreamt about food. You can understand that, a natural thing. Secondly, he was in the house of a tanner and as he went to sleep he could smell the tanner's occupation, so you can understand him dreaming about unclean animals. Then on a flat roof they would have a sail or a large cloth on poles to keep the sun off those who were resting. He dreamt about a large cloth suspended at the corners being let down. You can see how he just fell into a trance.

How do you know when God speaks through dreams? One of the glorious things is that God can speak to you while you are asleep as well as while you are awake. Sometimes this is even better while you are asleep because when you are dreaming you will accept things that in the daylight you would question. So how do you know a dream is from God? First, I think you will always remember the dream vividly after you have woken up, and you will recall every detail. There is no use God speaking to you if you don't remember it. Second, he will also speak after you have woken up – to apply the dream. Third, you will find that circumstances beyond your control fit the dream.

Those are three confirmations that a dream has been from God, and all three occur here. When Peter woke up, he remembered it; after he had woken up, the Spirit said, "Now this is how you are going to work it out. Three men are at the door – go with them." Also, circumstances fit, because those three men were at the door without Peter trying to engineer circumstances. When God spoke in a dream, and Peter saw clean and unclean – the old Peter, the reed, the Peter who when Jesus came with a towel and a bowl of water said, "Never, never, he'll never wash my feet" – the same old Peter comes back. Don't you find this comforting and encouraging, that Peter still had to live with "old Peter"? The old man was still around, the flesh was still there.

Peter's reaction when God showed him all these snakes and horrible animals! Is there something of which you would say, "I would never eat that"? Tripe is one of mine! Somebody took me into a restaurant in Chinatown in Vancouver and said, "Which will you have, shark's fin or bird's nest?" I just stopped mentally at that. We finally settled on squid, which is horrible, like synthetic rubber.

"Never, Lord, I've never touched food like that. I just couldn't eat that." If you have been on the mission field you may have had those moments when you have had to swallow hard and eat what was placed before you – no questions. If you are among the Bedouins, you may have a feast laid out for you, and as a special guest be given the sheep's eye; that is your delicacy. If you don't accept it thankfully you are in trouble! Now your reactions at such a moment, how you would feel inside – multiply that by about ten and you have got about how Peter felt in the dream. "Never, Lord, I've never done that. It's against our laws." I'm glad he didn't say "It's against your laws." He said, "It's against our laws. I couldn't do it, I'm sorry Lord, I couldn't do it." God is teaching him: Don't contradict me Peter. I say something's clean, you mustn't say it's unclean, I'm trying to teach you something, trying to broaden your outlook in the real sense, in the deepest sense.

Three times he spoke, and Peter usually had to have things said three times. He had denied the Lord three times. Three times the Lord said, "Do you love me?" Three times God was saying: "Don't contradict me, Peter; don't say 'never'." So Peter woke up and shook himself. At first he must have thought, "Well, perhaps the Lord is preparing me for lunch; maybe there's something on the table downstairs that I wouldn't like to eat and I've got to face it," but it was something much deeper than that: three men at the door.

All of this had started at three o'clock the previous day back in the house of Cornelius. Cornelius was a man who answers a question. You can be too exclusive in Christianity, or you can be too inclusive, and Peter had said (you can look it up in Acts 4) that in no other name is there salvation except in the name of Jesus, which had narrowed his outlook very considerably. You see, before that he believed that the Jews at least were going to heaven, whether anybody else did or not; probably not, but at least the Jews are going to heaven. Now he had narrowed that view down considerably and he had said to the leaders of the Jews, "The only way you'll get saved is through Jesus, there's no other name."

So he had become even more exclusive than he was as a young man – from thinking all Jews would go to heaven, he now thought that only Jews who believed in Jesus would go to heaven. But now he was going to have his outlook so broadened that he could believe that a man who had never heard of Jesus was acceptable to God. Now this is the contradiction, in a sense, the apparent contradiction that all of us have to come to. We have to come to the exclusive view that in no other name is there salvation, no other name given among men by which we must be saved. We must also have the widest possible view as to who might be seeking after Jesus even without knowing about him fully.

So that's the kind of struggle that was going to happen and it is a struggle every Christian has to go through. You must become exclusive and inclusive. You must be narrow and broad. Where you started was probably the wrong position, starting with all the Jews going to heaven. You have got to get narrower than that and then get broader than that. If you were brought up in church you probably thought that everybody in church was going to heaven.

I say you have got to get narrower than that and realise that every churchgoer who believes in Jesus will go to heaven, and then you have to get broader than that and believe that God may have much people in the city who are outside of church, and who deep down are looking for him and seeking him. We have got to start looking for those people. So it is the narrow and the broad, the exclusive and the inclusive. How difficult it is to get the balance right.

Cornelius was a man who genuinely wanted God. Now he wasn't just a man who believed God. I don't believe that a person who believes in God is acceptable to God because the devil himself believes in God and he trembles but he's not acceptable to God. Cornelius feared God, and there is the key, that's the beginning. He knew there must be a God and he knew that this God must have a life that was lived right. He knew the two basics. It was a religion that didn't bring him peace or power, but it was a religion of utter sincerity based on fear of God. Peter had to learn that God is prepared to begin with a man there. He will get peace when he finds

Jesus, he will get power when the Spirit comes upon him, but at least he fears God and that's the basic minimum. I believe there will be people who will be in heaven because they have feared God even if they have not had the opportunity of hearing about Jesus. The proof that they are acceptable to God is very simple. The proof is that as soon as they hear about Jesus they respond totally.

Stanley Jones tells how in India he preached Jesus to an Indian who said, "I've worshipped him all my life but I never knew his name – now you've told me," and immediately accepted Christ. There are those in our cities – we may not be aware of them but we need to be listening for them, watching for them – who do, in their heart, fear God.

Peter had to learn that although in no other name is there salvation, yet God is prepared to start with fear of himself and the desire to live right. That's how Martin Luther began, that's how John Wesley began; you'll find that many great men feared God and tried to live right They tried to save themselves. They didn't manage it, but God met them because they meant business with God. They didn't just *believe* in God, they *feared* God.

So Peter and Cornelius met up, and there was Cornelius with a household, people who were praying, but until the angel answered they had not had an answer. It was a one-way traffic but they prayed, they called on God. Mind you, when he feared God, as he prayed, when he got the answer it says he was terrified. It is interesting that you fear God and when you get the answer you are terrified.

So Peter went into that home, and when they looked at those faces he realised that his attitudes had been wrong. He also realised that Cornelius's attitude was wrong. There was a lot of correction of attitudes going on here. You know, the Lord can really do mighty things, he can pour out his Spirit when correction of attitudes is going on.

Cornelius's attitude was: "Peter, I worship you, you're a man whose name and address is known to God, you're a man who angels talk about, you must be great," and he fell down. Many enquirers and many new Christians make the same mistake, thinking that the man who speaks to them from God, who brings the word of God to them, must be some great man. That attitude has to be corrected. That man is just a man, he's not a god. "Cornelius, I'm not God." It is very important that we should never give to each other the glory that belongs to the God who alone knows our name and address. We are all ordinary people – so Cornelius, get your attitude right.

But Peter's attitude had also been wrong and he confessed it publicly. He wouldn't have come into that house two days earlier, regarding others as untouchable, outcast. God had to put him right. Who do you mix with after a service? Just those of your own type? Just those you would like to know? Who do you invite to your homes? Just those who have a comfortable lifestyle? Let's confess, our attitude is often very human and God has to correct it and put us in homes that we would never be in otherwise, and bring people into our homes whom we might never have invited.

In such a situation, where you have got sincere people who fear God, who know that he wants them to live right, who pray and who correct their attitudes to one another by the guidance of God's Spirit, something's going to blow. So Peter began to preach. He said, "Now I can tell you the rest of the story." First of all he said, "I'm amazed; I realize now God has no favourites."

If we have scruples about this, let us get rid of them straightaway. Whoever in any nation fears him is acceptable to him. That word "acceptable" doesn't mean saved, so don't read too much into it; it means we'll get a favourable hearing and we'll get a response from God, and the response will be to give them the truth they seek.

So Peter began to preach and he talked about his beloved Jesus and about God. He talked about the Holy Spirit – sound Trinitarian preaching. He talked about Jesus' birth, his baptism, his ministry of healing and deliverance, his death and his resurrection, his coming again to judge. It is all there in a short sermon. This may be a summary of it, but almost the whole of the Apostles' Creed is there.

Look at the growing understanding of Jesus of Nazareth. If that is as far as you've got, it isn't far enough. Jesus of Nazareth became the Christ of Israel – Saviour. Do you believe that? That is better still but still not high enough. What is the third aspect that Peter mentions? Jesus of Nazareth, Christ of Israel, Lord over all creation. Here is a view of Jesus that is big enough.

Now comes the great deathblow to any remaining hesitations or scruples Peter might have had. As he looked at his congregation he saw Gentiles whom he thought were not interested in God, eager for the truth. Sometimes someone outside the church is more interested in the things of the Lord than someone inside. You can get the biggest surprises provided you are willing and ready to talk, and to go into unlikely situations.

I have mentioned an occasion when a prominent Methodist preacher and a friend of his responded to a challenge from a Sunday newspaper to go to the worst nightclub in London at midnight on a Saturday night and preach the gospel to people there and see what happened. The newspaper swore them to secrecy then arranged for them to be taken to the back alleys, down some steps to a door with a little peephole that pushed aside. A big bruiser looked through and let them in.

In their clerical collars, they went down into a cellar, under an archway decorated with women's underwear which said, "Abandon hope all ye who enter here." Down and down, through the smoke, in the darkness, they saw couples and the manager said, "Right, you're on at midnight," and there was no warning to the customers. At midnight they stopped the band and the manager of the club announced that someone was going to speak.

One minister said to his friend, "Well now, you open up and I'll follow you up afterwards." He said "But no, I think you're better at starting off, you're good at stories and so on." Finally, he found himself standing on the platform in that situation. He just sent up a quick prayer to the Lord "Tell me what to say." Then he began speaking: "My wife doesn't know where I am at this moment. She's wondering where I am." He continued, "Are any of your wives wondering where you are?" There was a dead hush and then he started preaching Jesus.

What happened? They preached till dawn by the request of the patrons! The band went home, the dancing stopped permanently and they preached, and those people said, "Tell us more!" There was no looking at watches "My, look at the service – so long tonight; we'll never get home, he's going on...." They didn't get away till dawn. They found the hunger for reality in those hearts – so unexpected. They had to overcome scruples. The Spirit had led them to a different situation but they found people hungry for the gospel. I think sometimes we underestimate the hunger that there could be out there, the interest.

So Peter saw a crowd of hungry people and things happened almost too quickly for him. Normally they would have asked him, if the Holy Spirit convicted them, "What should we do?" He would have then gone through the routine: repent and be baptised, and you shall receive forgiveness. He didn't get any of that out! The Holy Spirit came on those people before he finished his sermon, the whole thing was taken out of his hands and God gave these sincere seekers his power. What a moment! There are people today would then have said, "Speaking in tongues—hmm," and they've got scruples about that. It was a situation in which Peter had to bow down before the Lord and see that God was ahead of him. He said they would have to be baptised in water – and that was because the outside and the inside belong together. Some may think that the spiritual and physical are poles apart, and as long as you have got the spiritual it doesn't matter about the physical. Don't you believe it – God wants all of you. It is as important to be baptised in water as to be baptised in Spirit. God wants everything for you.

So Peter's message meant: we have to complete this, God has confirmed them so let's baptise them. It is an exception for it to be that way around, but I have known it today, and it is God who does confirmations, not man. Peter said, "Can we forbid it?" I noticed this: Peter was not amazed that this had happened. The Jewish believers he had brought with him were amazed, but not Peter. So they had a glorious baptismal service and Peter's scruples vanished as the morning mist.

What a big lesson he learned that day. He learned that the most unlikely people – people he had written off, people he really thought would never make Christians, never come into God's people – would come. He realised that God has no favourites. Oh, what a lovely lesson that is! He doesn't like any of you better than anyone else. Does that help you? He has no types that he prefers.

I find it sad when people come to a church service (I know it may be different from another church) when people say, "Oh well, it's just those with a certain kind of temperament who are attracted by that kind of service."

Let me underline this: God has no favourites among temperaments. There are no "religious types". Peter's scruples vanished and he came into the freedom of recognising wherever God was working.

Here is how I lost a scruple. It happened at a conference in Nottingham. I had said to the organizers, "You know, the one thing you don't seem to have at your conference is to me one of the most important – you should have solid Bible exposition as a foundation because heat without light can go astray, and emotions without understanding can let you down."

So the organizers said, "Right, well you can come give us some Bible studies."

What could one say? I said, "I want to come and I want to go through Galatians because I know you've got a lot of Roman Catholics coming to that conference and I believe that Galatians is the one part of the New Testament this ecumenical age won't face, because it raises some of the deepest, divisive issues of the gospel."

They replied: "Fine, do Galatians." So that removed that excuse.

When I got there they said, "Now, your chairman will be Father so and so from Dublin."

I said, "Now what are you trying to do? Is this your sense of humour? Are you trying to clip my wings and tone me down? Look, my first talk will be about Martin Luther and how as a Roman Catholic monk he discovered freedom through Paul's letter to the Galatians and his reading of Romans, and that this split the Church into Protestant and Catholic. I'm going to go right in there because that's what I believe."

They said, "That's alright."

I replied, "Well, I don't want to embarrass this man because really it could be very embarrassing for him as well as for me."

They said, "Well look, try him for one lecture and if it's no use then we'll change the chairman for the second talk."

So the first morning came, and I just sailed right in –

good Protestant stuff, really solid. I laid it down heavy and I thought, "Well, how's he going to react to that?"

This dear little Catholic priest, all in black, got up at the end to make his chairman's remarks, and he said, "I want to tell you that two years ago I was a priest trying to get to heaven by keeping the commandments. Two years ago someone took me to a sitting room in a house in Dublin for a prayer meeting. I was baptised in the Holy Spirit that night. The first thing I read after that meeting was Paul's letter to the Galatians and it is my favourite part of the Bible, and it describes the freedom which I now enjoy."

Thereafter, after every exposition I gave, try as I might, I couldn't prevent him from giving a testimony at the end to the truth of it in his own experience – until the last morning. Then he got up to speak, and he said something, and my theological ear said, "I know what's coming next. Here's the pill in the jam now. Here's the dogma coming, I can sense it."

He stopped, paused, grinned and said, "The Holy Spirit has just told me to shut up. I must have been going to say something that would grieve him," and he sat down.

I had to ask myself, "Are you sensitive to the Holy Spirit to know when to shut up, when to sit down?"

I asked him, "What are you doing now? Are you looking after a Catholic church?"

"No," he said. "I'm in Belfast, organising prayer groups down the barbed wire line. We have Protestants risking their lives to go to Catholic homes to pray and read the Bible, and Catholics risking their lives to go to Protestant homes to pray and read the Bible. At our last meeting a Catholic girl knelt at the feet of a Protestant and begged the Protestant's forgiveness for the bitterness in her heart that her brother had been killed by Protestant extremists. She was kneeling at the feet of the only girl in the group whose father had been killed by Catholic extremists." He called a prayer meeting on a hill outside Dublin to pray for that city, and thousands of people came to join him. My scruples had gone, and I'd had them at the beginning of the conference.

I found the same problem Peter found when he got back to Jerusalem. You see, the first problem with scruples is how to get rid of your own. The second problem is how to face others who still have them. When Peter got back to Jerusalem they said, "Where on earth have you been? We hear you've been among Gentiles, eating with uncircumcised people. What do you think you're doing, Peter?" People say to us, "What do you think you're doing, having dancing in your church and having actors doing drama in the middle of a sermon?"

Your biggest problem is not to get rid of scruples yourself but to face those who have still got them. There's only one way to face them in other people. Peter didn't argue, and he didn't say, "I've changed my opinion, I've now come to this conclusion, and I'll argue it out point by point." He just said "Brethren, let me tell you what happened. I can only recognise it as of God. Let me tell you, God was ahead of me. Who was I to argue with God?" To me that is the one thing that deals with scruples – when you see that the Holy Spirit is in something, using someone unexpected, a new method, a different man, someone you would not have expected to be used, someone you wouldn't have expected to be full of God, and yet they are and you just have to bow down and say, "God is ahead of me." When others question what you have done, all you can say is, "Was the Holy Spirit in this?"

It is God who removes our scruples by running ahead, releasing his power, and blessing unlikely people. We have got to run to catch up and say, "Lord, I'm sorry, I didn't expect it; I wasn't ready for it, but Lord, I'm going along with it and if people question me, I'll just say, 'Well, God was ahead of me and I had to catch up.'"

Simon Peter learned this lesson. It didn't lead him into

license, it didn't lead him into immorality, but it led him away from his religious background. It led him to that exclusiveness that says, "In no other name is there salvation." He preached that name to Cornelius, but it led him to the breadth where he could say, "I can see in every nation he that fears God, seeks to do what's right, will have a hearing from God, will get a response from God, and I can see that God has no favourites."

He is not the God of the Baptists, he's not the God of the Roman Catholics, he's not the God of this group or that group. By his determined will, he is calling out from every kindred and tribe, and every temperament, type and background. He is laying his hand on people and surprising us all.

So let us learn with Simon Peter how to bring our scruples to the Lord – the traditions we have held. Even if we have to have a trance like Peter (in a trance he lost his tradition). Let's come and say, "Lord, which scruples shall I scrap for your sake that I might have the privilege of leading more to you? But, Lord, keep your hand tightly on me lest I mistake what I think is a scruple for what is a moral principle that you want me to keep." How much we need wisdom here. Pray for that wisdom, and grow up like Peter.

One final word—it wouldn't be right to leave you with the impression that Peter learned the lesson once and for all. There was an occasion you can read about it in Galatians 2 where Peter's scruple came back, and no less a brother than Paul had to rebuke him publicly and say, "Peter, what are you doing? Why are you going back to tradition? Why are you going back to your scruples? God has set you free to eat with anyone."

Peter took that rebuke graciously and he learned from it because in his later letters he could talk about our "beloved" brother Paul. Let's walk in the Spirit, without scruples and in the fear of the Lord, and in the love and the grace of the Lord Jesus Christ.

17

LEARNING IN PRISON

Read Acts 12:1–24

Almost as far back as we can go in human history, there have been places of detention. There are two aspects to being imprisoned. One is, of course, being shut in, put in a more confined space than is normal for human activity, to be put in a small cell, to be crowded in with company you haven't chosen. But the worst aspect of imprisonment is to be shut out. The main point of sending someone to prison is that you are shutting them out – not in: out of their family, out of their community, out of their society. You are saying to a prisoner, "You are not fit to live in society."

Until recently, even in our Western world, prisons were horrible, inhuman, barbaric places. Charles Dickens did a very great deal to challenge the British conscience about, for example, debtors' prisons. Elizabeth Fry worked hard and long, in the name of the Lord Jesus, to do something about prison conditions. Even in our generation, if you have read the book *Papillon* you know something of French colonial prisons. There are prisons I have visited in the Middle East which take you right back to those barbaric days.

Christians through the centuries have had their share of being sent to prison. There are hundreds in prison now because they know, love and serve the Lord Jesus and will not deny him. We need to remember that. That is why Jesus said, "I was in prison and you forgot about me; you didn't visit me." We say, "Lord, you weren't in prison in our day or in our country." He says, "If the least of these, my brethren, was in prison, I was." He is not referring to *any* person, mankind generally; he's referring to his brethren. Any Christian, who is in prison now, if we forget them, forget to pray about them, we are forgetting the Lord Jesus. It is a serious word.

To look no further than John Bunyan, we would never have had *The Pilgrim's Progress* unless he had spent twelve years in Bedford Jail – separated from his wife and children, including a blind child. It was in that incarceration that he learned many things. He learned that the worst prison to live in is not a physical one but a spiritual one. The worst prison is not something that is outside you, it is something inside you. He incorporated that insight into *The Pilgrim's Progress*.

Now back to Simon Peter. Have you found it very moving and very profound how God took a reed and changed the reed into a rock? Peter had to get pretty used to going to prison. This is now the third recorded occasion. So he was getting quite used to that cell. He was going to learn five profound lessons about God, this time that every Christian needs to learn. We can either learn them first hand by going to jail ourselves, by going through this situation ourselves, or we can learn them secondhand by listening to this word of God and saying, "Lord, I want to learn that, whether firsthand or secondhand, so that if ever I should be in this situation I would be able to hold on to these truths."

Here is the first and it is a little surprising: **God does not guarantee safety to his followers.** Religion is no insurance policy and if we think provided we trust in God and do our bit, he will so look after us that no danger will ever befall us, no risks will ever come to us, we are safe – then, frankly, we had better think again.

We are now right up against a question I am asked frequently and for which I have no answer. Sometimes it is in this form: "Why does God heal some and not others?" That is a profound question and I do not believe it is sufficient to say, "Well, some have enough faith and some don't," because I have known those with very little or even no faith healed of God, and I have known those with great faith not healed. And why does God keep some missionaries safe and allow others to be martyred? Here is the same question in a different form: why does God allow some Christians to prosper and some to struggle?

I do not know the answer and it comes right at the beginning of this chapter, "Herod seized James and put him to death with the sword." But, later in the chapter, the same God who allowed James to die set Peter free. Why did he let James die and Peter go free? I cannot believe that that means that Peter was a better Christian than James or that Peter had more faith than James. I believe we have got to come to the point where we have to say, "God, you know best." Therefore, in some situations, God seems to prompt a group of Christians to pray for another's safety or health and God answers the prayer. In other situations, those who are sensitive to God do not find themselves praying for that.

Why did James die and Peter live? I do not know. Why does he choose some Christians to be martyrs and others live to a ripe old age? Why out of the twelve apostles did eleven die unnatural, violent deaths, but one live to a ripe, old age – John? I do not know. I just know that you've got to learn the lesson that God decides and God knows best.

Peter had to learn this lesson. He was thrown into prison by Herod. I would like to spend quite a bit of time on Herod, but I don't think it would really be good for any of us. I am surprised some of the cheaper Sunday newspapers have not serialised the life of Herod and his family! They had descended from Esau, as Jews had descended from Jacob. This Edomite king, who managed to get the throne in the Holy Land by intrigue with the Roman Caesar, was a puppet king, hated by the Jews but put in by the Romans as king, or at least his grandfather was – Herod the Great, the man who killed innocent babies in Bethlehem when Jesus was born. The grandfather of the Herod of whom we are now thinking had killed his father. Within this family there was murder, incest, adultery, intrigue, and wife swapping. You name it, it was there. They were such a perverted and degraded family, that when Jesus met up against this one's uncle, he wouldn't even speak to him – the only person recorded in the Bible for whom Jesus had no word whatever. This Herod, grandson of Herod the Great, the nephew of the Herod before whom Jesus stood on trial, the nephew of the Herod who had chopped off the head of John the Baptist because he was pleased by a dancing girl – this is the last of the line. Now he took James and killed him before anybody was aware of what was happening, presumably the same day. I don't know why he did that, maybe these Christians were getting under his skin, touching his conscience perhaps. But I do know this: he made a surprising discovery – that he suddenly began to be popular with the Jews, a thing he had been trying all his life to achieve. So straight away he said, "Fine, I've really hit the right thing at last. I now know how to establish myself. Now who else can I get? I've dared to touch one of their leaders, the apostles. Now who's the big man there? Tell me, who leads them? Who's the pastor? Who's the leader of that church?" It was Simon Peter.

So, because he saw it pleased the Jews, he seized Peter and put him in jail too, intending to execute him, and would have done so straight away, but for one thing. It was the Jewish

Passover and it was not the time for executions. During the feast days there must be no death; death was unclean. So since he was doing it to please the Jews, he had to wait. In that time, the church got to prayer. Now bear in mind that the church was faced with this same problem. James was dead; now Peter was following and it was only a matter of time until Peter too was dead.

Behind Herod, you can see Satan. Satan was threatened by this growing church now numbering many thousands, and Satan will pick off a church's leaders if he can. You can see the whole plot. In that situation the church had time to organise prayer meetings, to get down on their knees for Peter. They felt earnestly led to pray for safety in this case, and pray they did.

I believe it is instinctive to pray to God when we are in a jam. It is instinctive to ask for safety and health, but I believe when we are confronted with a crisis, we should seek to be sensitive to God and ask: God, what are you going to do for your glory in this situation? We want to be praying with you, not against you. We want to be praying; we want to be acting, but Lord, will you direct our prayer that we are not just praying as natural people in the flesh would pray for health, safety, comfort and all the rest. If this is your will in this situation, if you really reveal it, we'll get on to this with prayer and we'll really get alongside this person.

They prayed for safety and their prayer had not been answered if they had prayed that for James, but for Peter they felt they should, and they did.

That brings me to the second lesson Peter learned, or certainly the church. I guess Peter knew they were praying for him, and it is that **God does not always answer prayer immediately**. Sometimes he does; more often he keeps us waiting till the last moment. Why should God do this? Surely he loves me. Surely he knows my need before I share it with him in prayer. Why doesn't he give me an immediate answer?

For eight days, that church prayed. Can you imagine their feelings as they got nearer to the end of Passover, and knew that Peter's execution would take place at daybreak, the first morning after the Passover? Eight days, seven days, six days, five days, four days, three days, two days – still they prayed, but how do you think they felt? They went on praying, but did they go on hoping? I guess that they began to feel that it was all up.

Why should God do this? It is a profound lesson. I think he does it, first, lest we treat prayer as a slot machine – put the prayer in, put your hand out for the blessing. If that was what he did, we would treat him as a machine. But he lets us see that this need is an opportunity for us to get closer to him. He wants you close. He wants you to go on talking to him. It is an opportunity to really *trust*, because the nearer you get to the crisis; the more you have to trust.

It is one thing to pray about a thing five months ahead; it is another thing to pray for a need that is only five hours ahead. God is not teasing us, he wants to keep us close to himself and he wants us to learn to pray. He wants us to learn to have faith, right to the cliff edge, because it is not real faith if it doesn't last that far. In his mercy, he doesn't always answer immediately. He kept that church praying right till the last moment. I know that they had stopped believing in any answer to their prayer by then because of their reaction to the answer when it came, and it is a reaction that we have.

Have you ever noticed the tone of surprise in people's voice when they tell you that a prayer has been answered? Or have you noticed that tone in your own voice, "Do you know what I prayed, and what do you think happened Friday?" We give the whole show away because we talk in such tones of surprise as if it wasn't normal, as if we didn't expect it.

How often we pray and just don't really believe in our

hearts it is going to happen. The nearer we get to the crisis, the more our hope tends to decline, but God knows how to teach us and take us right to the brink before we know.

The praying church was no doubt beginning to wonder whether the prayer would be answered – but how was Peter getting on? Peter was asleep. It was the last night before his execution—the last night. That tells me a great deal about Peter. Doesn't it tell you something about him? It tells me that he wasn't praying for his safety at that point. It tells me that he went to bed that night – on the floor it would be – and he just had a good night's sleep. It tells me that he had learned some profound lessons.

Here is the Peter who once upon a time was in a boat in the middle of a storm, and who was blaming Christ for sleeping: Wake up. What do you think you're doing sleeping at a time like this? We're about to perish and you sleep. Now here is Peter asleep. I am quite sure he had learned that a Christian has nothing to lose by death. If you had woken Peter up he would have said, "You've spoiled my sleep and I was so looking forward to seeing James tomorrow morning." He could go to sleep because he had nothing to lose. He maybe knew the church was praying, but Peter was resting and trusting and sleeping. An angel really had to kick him in the ribs to get him awake. There is the second lesson: God doesn't answer prayer immediately, but without panic and without fear you can go on resting in him.

The third lesson Peter had to learn is that **God is a God of the impossible**. Not just one miracle, but a whole string of them. A miracle is something that is a natural event, for it happens in the world of nature; it is an unnatural event because it's something that happens that wouldn't normally happen. It is a supernatural event because it is caused by supernatural agency.

Supernatural things, miracles, actually happen. Think of

angels. They make wonderful cooks. I am sure you know of one occasion in the Old Testament where an angel cooked a meal for a servant of God who needed good food. They can do astonishing things. I hope you believe in angels. Do you? They surround us. Whenever we gather to worship it is with angels and archangels and all the company of heaven. Angels are real and the hosts of the Lord encamp around those that fear him. In spite of what Charles Darwin believed, man is not the highest intelligent life in the universe. There is an order of life even higher, which did not evolve from monkeys or men – angels created by God, and we ignore them at our peril.

When the first Russian astronaut came back to earth he said, "I didn't see any angels up there," but they saw him! Though we may not see them all the time, and though we may go through a lifetime without ever seeing one, you might even have had one in your home without realising it. They can appear as with the glory of heaven or they can appear as the man next door.

They had got Peter out of prison once before and they were now to do it again. But because he had already got out of prison twice, now they had put him inside the inner security block with sixteen soldiers to guard him, three locked gates, double chains chaining him to two soldiers. They really thought they had got him. But you match one angel against that kind of situation and those soldiers had had it. One angel can deal with 135,000 soldiers and did once in the siege of Jerusalem. The angels are strong, beautiful, intelligent creatures. They can act in this world even though they belong to another – and Peter was asleep and an angel came.

Look at the miracles. First, Peter would never have got out unless he'd had a light to get out. You try and find your way out of that kind of situation in pitch darkness – and it would have been. The first thing the angel did was switch the light on. The next miracle was to keep the soldiers' eyes shut with the lights on. Then the angel said, "Now shake off those chains." They fell off. Can you imagine chains falling off and sentries not waking up? There are more miracles happening here – not only the chains falling off but the sentries' ears! Clatter, clang, lights flashing, chains crashing, and the sentries go on snoring – then doors opening, the whole thing just seemed like a dream.

I am so relieved that Peter found it hard to believe. That gives me a little excuse. Peter just didn't believe what was going on. He was in a daze and he walked out after this angel. Finally, he found himself one block down from the prison in this street, in the cool night air. He shook his head and looked around. He realised it was real, he was awake; he wasn't dreaming, it had happened.

I was talking recently to a missionary, who got as far as being blindfolded and facing a firing squad, and was quietly trusting in God, and is alive today to tell the tale. It actually got as far as that, and God stepped in with his mighty power – it is exciting. Peter was learning that God is the God of the impossible, but he had difficulty believing it. I am so glad the church had difficulty believing it too. That gives me a little comfort. God understands that our minds find it difficult. "Lord, I believe, help my unbelief."

There was Peter bashing at the door and saying, "Let me in."

The maid was looking through a little peephole saying, "It's Peter. Can't be; it must be his ghost," and running and telling the others.

They are saying, "No it can't be; we're praying for Peter. He's in prison. He's going to be executed tomorrow. Maybe they brought the execution forward."

How often our prayer meetings are exactly the same. How astonished we are when God does what we ask! Why should we be surprised, with a heavenly Father, who loves us and cares for us, and wants to do for us more than we could ever ask or even imagine?

The next lesson Peter had to learn was that **God can vary his strategy**. When Christians are threatened, they are faced with a very difficult question: should they run or should they stay? Should they defy the situation at cost of their lives or should they play for safe and go? Such situations arise in modern times. One man from Canada got five hundred Christians out of Vietnam just before the communists came. Was he right to do that? Somebody who heard about that criticised the Christians for being cowards and said, "Why did they run away?" Two dear ladies, missionaries, were kidnapped in Thailand and their remains were found. They were shot in the head. Other OMF missionaries were asked, "Do you want to go home and leave?" They chose not to do so, but in some situations missionaries have chosen to do so. Are they cowards? Once again, it is fatal for Christians to be giving each other cast iron rules. God can vary his strategy. Sometimes he says to a person, "Stay, defy, die," and sometimes he says, "Leave that city, flee to another, and continue." Neither person must criticise the other. This was a problem in the communist world of the USSR. There was an underground church that believed there must be no co-operation, no compromise, and they were prepared to die, and there was the above ground church, who were seeking a more difficult course, which was to be officially registered, accept some of the limitations that that involves, but continuing to witness. The tragedy was that those two groups of Christians were being tempted to criticise each other. It is very important to be more flexible in our understanding in these situations.

When Peter was in prison the previous time, an angel got him out and said, "Go to the temple and start preaching straight away again." Peter did and was obedient and immediately found himself re-arrested. This time, God's strategy was to be very different. God had smuggled Peter out in order that he might go into hiding. I can see one of the reasons why God had this strategy this time. It was that he was no longer up against the Jewish priests, but against Herod, a man you couldn't talk or argue with. He was beyond being challenged and had lost his powers of rational thought. Annas and Caiaphas, Peter could argue with and wipe the floor with them in argument. He had never done that with Herod. Herod was too far gone—even Jesus himself wouldn't speak to this family. They were so sensual, so depraved, that they would not even be challenged by Simon Peter himself.

This time God's strategy was, "Get out, Peter, go and hide." So Peter didn't even go straight to the Christians and stay there. He went to them and said, "Tell James that I'm out, and I'll leave you so that they won't track me down to you and I won't run the risk of bringing you into difficulties. What an important principle that is – not to bring Christians in other countries into situations they have not chosen to be in. Unwise Christian interference can do this. So Peter went into hiding. He was no less a rock than when he went straight back to the temple on the previous occasion. How important it is to learn that God can vary his strategy.

We must be responsive to God and say, "God, do you want me to run or to stand? Do you want me to hide or to go into a public place? Do you want me to defy the authorities or do you want me to be discreet?" If God tells two people to do different things in the same situation, they should never criticise each other—it's a profound lesson to learn.

The next lesson Peter had to learn is this: **God expects us to do our part**. Miracles are no substitute for action. I notice that in this story God's angel did everything that was needed by way of the miraculous and not a single thing more. The angel did not put on Peter's shoes, but said, "Put your shoes on, Peter." The angel did not dress Peter but said, "Put your clothes on, Peter." The angel didn't lift him up and transport him over the top of the fort. He said, "Follow me, Peter." As soon as Peter was in a position to do everything for himself, the angel disappeared. There is a profound lesson to be learned here. We often want the Lord to substitute for our action, like the man who prayed for rain when his house was on fire!

Peter had to learn that what we can do for ourselves, God expects us to, and there is a balance. There will be moments when we need miraculous help for we cannot do a thing, but at the same time he will say, "Now do what you can." So the angel, by God's orders, left Peter as soon as he got him out of the prison. Peter was on his own, had to decide where to go and how to get there. That is an important little lesson.

The final lesson I learn from this chapter, which Peter had to learn, is this: **God ultimately dispenses justice to all evil men.** However frustrating it may be that wickedness can prevail for a time, and perverted, sensual people like Herod can get away with it and can do dreadful things, their days are numbered. God may not settle his accounts every Friday evening, but there is a day of reckoning coming for everyone. Therefore, we need not fear that a wicked man will get away with it indefinitely.

I feel sorry for the soldiers. They didn't stand a chance of keeping Peter in prison, but they paid for his loss with their lives. Herod, as soon as he knew that Peter had gone, executed every sentry, sixteen of them. Those men paid with their lives for Peter's freedom. I don't know what Peter thought about that, but I think he must have thought, "How long will God let Herod go on spilling blood? This family has spilt the blood of innocent people right down the years. How long can he go on doing it? Will I get back into Jerusalem and be able to move in public again?" Well, by Acts 15 he was back in Jerusalem – publicly.

You see, God's sets a day. He gives men a lot of rope, but ultimately they hang themselves. He gives us a great deal of freedom to hurt innocent people, but ultimately the day comes when God says, "No more, you have finally reached the point where I deal with you." Would you have it otherwise? Just think for a moment. Would you like to live in a world where God dealt with every sin, vice and crime immediately? It would include you, that's the problem. We wouldn't mind it with other people, but we claim this privilege for ourselves that God should wait before the accounts have to be paid. It is so inconsistent.

During World War 2 we said, "Why does God allow Hitler to do all these things?" The mystery is, "Why does he allow me to do all these things as well?" Oh, I may not be doing quite so much damage because I'm not in a position of such power – but, scaled down, I'm hurting people; I'm causing others to suffer. Do I honestly want a world in which God will deal with that immediately and will strike me dead as soon as I hurt one of his children? Do you want to live in a world like that? God, in his wisdom, has chosen not to act like that, but to appoint a day of reckoning, in which the accounts will be settled. Frankly, if he had not chosen that way, and had chosen to deal with every sin as soon as it was committed, not one of us would be around.

So Herod thought he was getting away with it, as many people think they are getting away with things now. We have thought we have got away with something because the heavens didn't open and the lightning didn't strike immediately. By the next week we had begun to forget it and we thought it was gone, but God remembers every single act and word and thought. There is a day of reckoning, and there was for Herod. How the church and Peter must have felt about Herod's wickedness robbing them of James, one of the inner three apostles. They must have known that this could not go on forever, that one day God would step into Herod's life. It happened in the very year when Britain was successfully invaded under Claudius. The great public pomp and circumstance of Herod's great day, here, was probably the celebration of the successful invasion of Britain by the Romans. Herod appeared in a great silver robe. He had reached the pinnacle of his ambition. His pride now was at its peak because the nations Tyre and Sidon were coming to him and begging him for trade terms, begging him to be favourable to them. He saw that his power was not just within the country of Israel but was extending to other countries. He was in a strong financial position and could hold other nations to ransom. It went to his head. In the silver robe he got up and there was a great ovation and the people said, "It's a god. It's a god." They treated him as a god. Do you know, deep down, that is the ultimate ambition of human pride? Way back in the garden, Satan said to Eve, "Wouldn't you like to be like God?" It goes to a man's head when he thinks he's God.

We have got some example in our world today of dictators. We've got some examples of pop stars. One day the Beatles said, "We are more popular than Jesus Christ." God will not share his glory with another. The ultimate point where God's patience is absolutely exhausted is when a man thinks he's God. God says, "No. There's only one God in this universe and it's not you, Herod, it's me." Herod was a man who was being worshipped by a huge crowd and there is nothing much new about that, is there? It is still happening. Herod was just catching up with the Roman Caesars, who were already calling themselves "Lord".

Herod now put himself on the same plane; "I'm God."

At that moment, he clutched his stomach, reeled and fell. It took him five days to die, according to the secular records we have – days of excruciating agony. Herod was eaten by worms before he died and God didn't even wait till after he was dead for that to happen. God said: you, a god? – you are just a man whom worms will eat up. As the song *On Ilkley Moor* has it, "Then Worms Will Come and Eat Thee Up...." Down fell Herod that day; God's day of reckoning had come. Yes, he had done a lot of evil things. He had had a lot of freedom. God had given him a lot of rope. Now he had hanged himself, and now this man Herod had been dealt with.

When Christians are under pressure, one of the lessons they can learn, and one of the things that will hold them stable, is to know that their persecutors, the dictators, the totalitarian powers, have put them in prison, but their day of reckoning with Almighty God must come. Therefore, we do not need to seek vengeance. "Vengeance belongs to me," says the Lord, "I will repay."

Now for my final word from John Bunyan's book *The Pilgrim's Progress*. Poor John Bunyan, twelve years in prison – two lots, six years first and then later. As he watched his guards he saw that they were more in prison than he was. As he watched people passing the grille, the barred window of that little cell on the bridge at Bedford (which you can still see today), he could see that he was not the one in prison; they were.

In Bunyan's book, the pilgrim, having left the cross, moves on and comes to a house where he is taught profound lessons and is shown different scenes, which bring home to him a spiritual truth. He is taken into a room and there is a man in a cage of thick iron bars in lattice style. There is no door to the cage nor even a padlock on it. There he is, miserable, sitting inside. He will never get out for there is no door. Pilgrim asks the interpreter, "Who is this? How did he get in this cage?" He is told, "This cage is the cage of his character, of his habits, and he formed this cage around himself and as he lived the bars got stronger and thicker and he can't get out now. He's in prison."

Bunyan, in prison, was writing about those who call themselves "free". He saw that they were in cages of their own character and habit, and that the iron bound them strongly.

I believe there is a profound lesson we can learn from Acts 12 – those of us who may never be imprisoned for the Lord's sake (and I'd hope we'd never be for any other reason). We all have chains and we all make cages. For the more often you *do* a thing, the more often you *think* a thing, the more often you *say* a thing, the thicker those bars get – the cage of our character. It is that kind of a cage which is the worst kind of prison, because when you speak to Christians who are in prison for the faith you discover that they are free.

Think of the book of Revelation. John was in prison and he was in the Spirit on the Lord's Day and he was in heaven. Notice that an open door was before him, and he walked through it and saw glory. He was free while his captors were still in prison. It is no wonder that this has marked Christian thought and Christian song.

Being free to walk with the Lord – that is freedom. You can have that freedom in a prison cell. But you can be free to travel anywhere in the world yet be "in prison" all the time. The prison of our character can not only shut us *in* with ourselves – and that's not very good company – it can shut us *out* from God.

18

PETER THE ELDER

We are now going to look at Peter in a very dull role. Sometimes the Lord calls us to do things for him that are not very exciting. We begin with Acts 6, and although Peter is not mentioned by name, he is here acting as one of the twelve leaders of the early church dealing with a problem, With the believers multiplying rapidly there were mumblings of discontent. How familiar that sounds – I am so glad that they had that problem in those days! The number was getting a bit unmanageable and that means people may get overlooked and neglected. Those who spoke only Greek complained that the widows among them were being discriminated against – that they were not being given as much food in the daily distribution as the widows who spoke Hebrew. So the twelve called a meeting of all the believers. "We should spend our time preaching and not administering a feeding program," they said. "Now look around among yourselves, dear brothers, and select seven men, wise and full of the Holy Spirit, who are well thought of by everyone and we will put them in charge of this business. Then we can spend our time in prayer, preaching and teaching. This sounded reasonable to the whole assembly and they elected the following: Stephen, a man unusually full of faith and the Holy Spirit, Philip, Procorus, Nicanor, Timon, Parmenus, Nicolas of Antioch a Gentile convert to the Jewish faith who had become a Christian. These seven were presented to the apostles who prayed for them and laid their hands on them in blessing.

Reads a bit like minutes of a church meeting, doesn't it? That is exactly what it is. There is a place in church life for such things. Now look at another such occasion – Acts 15. There is another crisis in the church:

While Paul and Barnabas were at Antioch, some men from Judea arrived and began to teach the believers that unless they observed the ancient Jewish custom of circumcision they could not be saved. Paul and Barnabas argued and discussed this with them at length, and finally the believers sent them to Jerusalem, accompanied by some local men, to talk to the apostles and elders there about this question. After the entire congregation had escorted them out of the city, the delegates went on to Jerusalem, stopping along the way in the cities of Phoenicia and Samaria to visit the believers, telling them, much to everyone's joy, that the Gentiles too were being converted. Arriving in Jerusalem, they met with the church leaders. All the apostles and elders were present, and Paul and Barnabas reported on what God had been doing through their ministry. But then some of the men who had been Pharisees before their conversions rose to their feet and declared that all Gentile converts must be circumcised and required to follow all the Jewish customs and ceremonies. So the apostles and church elders fixed a further meeting to decide this question.

At the meeting, after long discussion, Peter stood and addressed them as follows, "Brothers, you all know that God chose me from among you long ago to preach the good news to the Gentiles so that they also could believe. God, who knows men's hearts, confirmed that he accepts Gentiles by giving them the Holy Spirit in exactly the same way as he gave him to us. He made no distinction between them and us for he cleansed their lives through faith, just as he did ours. Now are you going to correct God by burdening the Gentiles with a yoke that neither we nor our fathers were able to bear? Don't you believe that all are saved the same way by the free gift of the Lord Jesus?"

There was no further discussion and everyone now listened as Barnabas and Paul told about the miracles God had done through them among the Gentiles. When they had finished, James took the floor.

"Brothers," he said, "Listen to me. Peter has told you about the time God had first visited the Gentiles to take from them a people to bring honour to his name. This fact of Gentile conversion agrees with what the prophets predicted. For instance listen to this passage from the prophet Amos: Afterwards, says the Lord, I will return and renew the broken contract with David so that Gentiles too will find the Lord. All those marked with my name, that's what the Lord says who reveals his plans made from the beginning. So my judgment is that we should not insist that the Gentiles who turned to God must obey our Jewish laws, except that we should write to them to refrain from eating meat sacrificed to idols, from all fornication, and from also eating un-bled meat of strangled animals. For these things have been preached against in Jewish synagogues in every city on every Sabbath for many generations."

Then the apostles, and the elders, and the whole congregation, voted to send delegates to Antioch with Paul and Barnabas to report on this decision.

In Galatians 2:11 there is a little bit of a fight between giants:

But when Peter came to Antioch, I, Paul, had to oppose him publicly, speaking strongly against what he was doing for it was very wrong. For when he first arrived he ate with the Gentile Christians who don't bother with circumcision and the many other Jewish laws, but afterwards, when some Jewish friends of James came, he wouldn't eat with the Gentiles any more because he was afraid of what these Jewish legalists who insisted that circumcision was necessary for salvation would say. Then all the other Jewish Christians and even Barnabas became hypocrites too, following Peter's example though they certainly knew better. When I saw what was happening and that they weren't being honest about what they really believed and weren't following the truth of the gospel, I said to Peter in front of all the others, "Though you are a Jew by birth you have long since discarded the Jewish laws so why all of a sudden are you trying to make these Gentiles obey them? You and I were Jews by birth, not mere Gentile sinners, and yet we Jewish Christians know very well that we cannot become right with God by obeying our Jewish laws but only by faith in Jesus Christ to take away our sins, so we too have trusted Jesus Christ that we might be accepted by God because of faith and not because we have obeyed the Jewish laws. For no one will ever be saved by obeying them."

Nobody is quite sure whether the second and the third events in the two passages occurred in that order. We don't know whether Peter put his foot in it before that Jerusalem church meeting or after it. Since it is not clear in scripture it is quite clear that it doesn't matter, but we are going to look at the three events and see just how Peter really had to sort out some of the difficult issues in church meetings where there was argument, long, wearisome discussion, and how God used this to bring about his will.

Most careers look much more glamorous and exciting to the onlooker than to those involved in them. Reality TV often shows this. That is also true of the ministry of the gospel. There are moments when you just don't know whether you are in the body or out of it. There are moments when God is performing miracles before your eyes. There are exciting moments. There is also a lot of humdrum work. One of the temptations is that we always want the sensational, the spectacular, the exciting. So we read the condensed accounts of people's lives in the Bible, and it is true that there are picked out key things, exciting things, but I am so glad the Bible is an honest book. It presents the humdrum as well as the heavenly, the mundane as well as the miraculous. It shows Peter grappling with church meetings, long discussions and decisions, as well as raising the dead and healing the lame man who had been forty years in that condition. If you are not prepared for both these sides of Christian ministry, don't respond to a call to God's service.

We need to look at Peter as an elder, the kind of thing he had to tackle as an elder, and some of the crises that went on in the church and in church meetings – meetings in which no miracles occurred, no words of prophecy were given, when believers just met together to do business, have discussion and make decisions. I thank God for those who are loyal to that side of the church's work because without that loyalty we would not get the exciting blessings either.

Examine your own heart if you want to get all the excitement but not share the daily round and the common task. Think of the work that is done behind the scenes. Think of all the telephone answering that goes on in a church office. Sometimes exciting messages come through that make us want to jump for joy, other times it's complaints, grumbles, tell so and so to do this or not to do that – but it is all part of the work and it is part of God's kingdom.

Indeed the fact that Jesus spent eighteen years in a very humdrum job in a little shop in a village before he spent three years doing very exciting things is our inspiration to keep things in balance.

The Bible shows us a church that is far from perfect, in

which there were grumblers and there was controversy, a church in which people did divide from one another, a church where there were long arguments, and a church which, thank God, had elders who could handle the situation and who could deal with it properly and wisely.

Let's take Acts 6 – complaints. Now complaining is a sign of spiritual immaturity, because godliness with contentment is great gain, and a person who is really godly is a person who is really content. Grumbling and complaining don't go with contentment and don't go with gratitude for blessings. When you are really grateful for your blessings and count all the good things there are, you don't become such a complainer or a grumbler.

But since we're not all perfect and since we are far from always thankful, I am afraid we do grumble and we do complain. That tends to increase the bigger a church gets, and it did in Acts 6. Because the believers multiplied there were those who felt neglected and those who felt lost in the crowd, and those who felt nobody was paying attention to them.

We understand this all too well. It is a natural thing to expect in an imperfect church. The church is imperfect because the people in it are imperfect. We are on our way to heaven and we are on our way to holiness. We are not there yet and so we get grumbles. That doesn't put me off the church or keep me away from it. It would put me off if people never got over their grumbles, if they never got more content, if they never grew up spiritually and it just went on and on year in and year out, the same old grumbles from the same people – that would worry me. I would say that's not a church where God is moving. So it is not the presence of complaints, it's how you deal with them.

Let's see how Peter and the other elders dealt with it. It arose over food. Now this is the church of God filled with the Holy Spirit a few months after Pentecost and arguing about food. Do you find that comforting? I do. It is an honest, realistic picture. We sometimes idealise the New Testament and say: "If only we get back to those days...." But you are in those days! The Spirit is moving today and people are grumbling today. So they had a situation which arose because of this: there were people who had been born in the place and people who had moved in. Wherever you get this you have got the potential for a grumble. It happens everywhere.

In Jerusalem, though, all of them were Jewish believers who actually spoke two different languages normally in their homes, though they worshipped together and worshipped in one language. But the Jews who had been born in the place spoke Hebrew, and others, who had been scattered around the world and came back from the places to which they had emigrated, spoke Greek, so they were called the Hellenists.

The church rightly had meals together and particularly looked after the widows. There were no pensions in those days, no social security, so the church had to undertake that. The days are coming when the church will have to take that up again. We are going to have needs that will not be able to be met by the government.

Now comes the grumble. The Hellenic widows said, "They get served first and they get the best food and they get rather more than we do because they are in, they belong. They know the people who are serving." It sounds childish but this is church life. This is human nature and so they were faced with it. Any sense of not being treated fairly because you don't belong to the "in" group soon comes out and causes grumbling – particularly any sense of unfair treatment in charity, I don't know why it should be, but when people don't deserve anything at all and somebody tries to give them something, they are even more angry if it is divided out wrongly. Isn't it strange? So if you set up a soup kitchen be sure that somebody will soon come and say, "He got half an inch more in his bowl than I did," even though you are doing it out of the goodness of your heart. Jesus told the parable of the labourers in the vineyard to illustrate this. He said there was an employer who out of the goodness of his heart deliberately gave jobs to the unemployed because he could see they were losing their self-respect. They needed jobs and – not because he had work for them but because he was sorry for them – he gave them jobs. He went out at different times of the day, and when he saw more unemployed he brought them in. At the end of the day he gave them what they needed out of the goodness of his heart. He gave them all a day's wage. He had the shop steward immediately – wage differential! They've only worked so long; we've worked so long. He was right into a trade union meeting. It was charity, it was the goodness of the employer that gave them work, but they grumbled. So these widows were grumbling even at that which they had no right to, which was being given out of the goodness of someone's heart. What a situation!

Peter and the other elders laid down three principles which we must remember. First, there must be *no dissension*. If grumble or complaint comes it has to be dealt with fairly, honestly. They have to rebuke the people making it, but it must be dealt with, with no dissension. For these things if they are not dealt with build up and up, and wreck a fellowship. A grieved, resentful people are just ripe for Satan, and it's Satan who gets hold of such people. Satan can never destroy the church from without. He has tried it. But he can from within through such people. The second principle is: there must be *no discrimination*. God has no favourites and therefore the church must never have favourites, and therefore there must be no discrimination between young or old, between those who have always been in the church and those who have just joined. Church must be colour blind and class-blind. A pastor wrote; "I always used to call people 'brother' – 'Brother Smith', 'Brother Brown' – and I suddenly realised that when I felt somebody really was my brother I didn't use the title." That is interesting. In your family, do you say "brother", "sister"? I never said "sister" to my sister. That pastor was challenged to ask just how far it was a *real* brotherhood with no special distinctions.

The third principle is: there must be *no distraction*. Satan has used grumbles and complaints to distract ministers of the gospel from their real job again and again. For time is swallowed up. You can spend a whole evening dealing with just one complaint. Peter very wisely said, "I am not going to deal with this." The other apostles said, "I am not going to deal with this. I'm called to preach the Word and to teach."

That is a very important principle, and Peter said, "Choose men to deal with the cause for this grumble." He said to the church meeting, "You choose them. Be sure you get men full of the Holy Spirit." Not just men who could serve food properly but full of the Holy Spirit and then they will be fair men. They chose men who were Greek-speaking Jews. What a tactful decision. They chose men who had the ability to deal with the situation and therefore the apostles were not distracted.

Satan would love to see preachers so busy sorting out grumbles and complaints that they have no real time to get with God, listen to him and get from his Word what the people need to feed on. One reason why we have so many seven-minute sermons is because ministers are so loaded with petty things to deal with, and the church meeting should be calling others to deal with them so that there may be no distraction from the essential work to which the leaders are called. That involves delegation of responsibility.

Let me move on to the second controversy. Now there is something much deeper here. There is a division among

277

Christians, and that happens. One reason is that we never quite grasp the whole truth. Said a minister of another denomination to me, "Do you think Baptists have the whole truth?" I said, "Yes." He really looked surprised at such conceit. I said, "Yes we do, and we believe that you have the whole truth too, and it's bound in leather and sitting on your lectern. But neither of us has fully grasped it yet."

That is the position because no one of us sees it all – though we have the whole truth in the Bible, in Jesus Christ who is the truth. All of us have blind spots, rather as you have a little spot at the back of the retina of your eye – and you can move a thing in front until suddenly it has gone and you realise there's a blind spot – you have spiritual blind spots and there are things you don't see, so you argue with your fellow Christians, you divide, you have controversy. Another reason why we have controversy is that we may have not seen the whole truth but what truth we have seen we have mixed with tradition. All of us have traditions (I don't care who you are) and this is what was happening in Acts 15. Not one Christian I have ever met is free from tradition – "the way we've done things in church". It is when we mix traditions and truth that we really run into trouble because somebody can see that what we are pressing for as truth is simply our tradition, and there is a division.

It happened over circumcision, which was a tradition of the Jews with a very long history. Originally it had been commanded by God for Jews, and they had always thought that if you are really going to walk with God you have got to be circumcised. So when the Gentiles came into the church, the Jews said, "Now you must accept this custom. It's part of being a Christian. If you're really going to be saved you've got to do this," and that's a really difficult situation. Peter was faced with it as were James and the other elders. They held a long church meeting with a lot of discussion. They listened to all points of view. You have got to be patient to have that. The Word of God does say they had a long discussion—that's got to be done first. But then Peter gave the breakthrough and James followed it up with the two things that settle such issues. Peter said, "What is the Spirit saying?" James said, "What is the Scripture saying?" In that way they got away from what men thought and they looked at what God does and what God says. That's the way to settle these controversies. What is God doing? What is God saying? What is the Spirit doing? What is the Scripture saying? If you can get a clear answer from both those together you are through and you are free as a church meeting.

Peter's message was like this: "May I say a word? You remember when I went to preach to those Gentiles? They weren't circumcised. God confirmed them by pouring his Holy Spirit out on them just as on us. Are you going to put God right now? Say now, 'God you shouldn't have done that, they weren't circumcised'? How dare you. How dare you impose a custom of your own on someone else whom God has already recognised." Be free.

James was saying (and remember they only had the Old Testament then): As I read my scripture it says here God is going to have a bigger family than the Jewish one and he's going to bring into it those who don't have Jewish customs.

So that settled it and the church meeting agreed. Now they got their principle clear, but then because the elders were wise they said, "But we will still say compromise in practice." Now here is the mark of a true, good elder who knows how to handle a situation. On the one hand he must get his principle very clear – what the Spirit and the scripture together say – and then he can compromise in practice.

Does that sound unchristian? No, because you still have to live together. They then said, "You Gentile believers when you are with Jews, will you observe the scruples that they have?" It's not a principle, it's not necessary to salvation, but it is advisable for fellowship, and it is a good elder who knows how to balance those two things – to get the principle right and then not be rigid in practice. Paul fought against circumcision as hard as he could and then he circumcised Timothy so that he could get into Jewish homes. There is no inconsistency there. Happy are the elders who can see what the clear principle is and get free from tradition and then say, "But we've still got to live together so let's observe for each other's sake the customs that are not necessary to salvation but can help."

Can I give you an example? I'm thinking now of a trip I had many years ago and the contrast one met. When I went to Kuala Lumpur I went to the Baptist church. I recognised immediately it was standing next to a Hindu temple. Then I went into the building next door and I thought I had stepped into a Southern Baptist church in Nashville, Tennessee. Everything was American – architecture, organ, robed choir, printed bulletin, the lot. There wasn't an American in the church and I thought, "What was exported here? American culture or Christianity?" Then I went a few miles up country to the church of God in Tapa. When I went in it was like going into a village church in Somerset, Anglican to its fingertips: gothic windows, Book of Common Prayer 1662. Again I thought: "What have we exported there?"

Then God led me on to the work of Brother Bakt Singh. There I saw something very different. I didn't see an American influence; I didn't see an English influence. I saw a pile of about two thousand sandals outside a building with no walls, and I took my own sandals off. I saw no pews and I saw men on one side, women on the other. I heard Indian music. I think I could grow to like it.

I was glad to take my shoes off and go in. It was their

culture. It was the way they showed reverence for a holy place. That place was holy to them not in itself but because of what God said to them and did among them in it. But if they ever came here and said, "You must take your shoes off to be a Christian," I would oppose them strongly, saying, "You have no right to say that." But after opposing them I would still go back and take mine off when I was with them.

Do you understand? Oh to get the right balance! You get some Christians who are all principle and just can't give way an inch in practice, and you get Christians who are so loose on practice and in principle that you never know where they are. Lord grant us elders like Peter and James who can see clearly what the Spirit says, what the scripture says, and say: "That's where we stand. But in practice for the sake of loving fellowship we'll adapt; we'll be flexible."

My last word here is that even Peter didn't always live up to this standard. There came a day when even Peter took his eyes off the Spirit in the scripture and he compromised.

The situation was totally different. He was among a crowd of Gentile believers now, therefore he behaved like a Gentile, quite rightly. He ate food without asking "Is this kosher?" Then a few of his Jewish pals came in and he made the fatal mistake. They were still in a majority of Gentiles and they should still have been prepared to eat non-kosher food and sit at the same table. But Peter got scared of what men would think. Do you know nearly all legalism in Christian fellowship comes from fear of man, not from fear of God? We start making rules for each other, and Peter, in a little embarrassed way, with insincerity and with hypocrisy for fear of the others, slipped away to the minority and didn't adapt. Paul had to pull him up and say: Peter, what are you doing? Peter, you are now compromising the principle not just your practice. You're now fearing men, not fearing God, you are now not practising what the Lord revealed to us –

that we are to be all things to all men if by any means we may save some. When we are among the Jews we behave as a Jew; when we are among the Gentiles we behave as Gentiles – as long as we are doing nothing immoral then we must be as adaptable as we can possibly be.

That was why the early missionaries to China from Cambridge grew pigtails. They were seeking to express their love, in a simple if naïve way. This is the kind of consideration that will mean we truly are one family: where we consider one another, get the principles clear and get free in everything else, but then can be flexible and consider one another and go along with each other in practice. We need elders, men who know how to practise love but who will never let go of holy truth. This is perhaps the most difficult thing to get in balance, and Peter found it difficult but he won through.

"Speaking the truth in love, grow up together into him who is the head, even Jesus Christ our Lord." Peter, writing years later, in 1 Peter 5:1 said, "I am Peter, a fellow elder." An elder's lot is not necessarily an exciting one. We see miracles from time to time. We have wonderful news to share and praise God for, but most of an elder's work is dealing with complaints, controversies, difficulties within the church, rebuking those who are not practising love – and just cementing people together. In church meetings, in the business, in humdrum discussions, in the decisions, in keeping the minutes – this is as much part of the Word of God and the church of God as all the sensational, exciting things that God is doing. God grant us elders like Simon Peter.

19

REFINED BY FIRE

Why was Peter able to face a violent death calmly, unafraid?

Read the following passages:
1 Peter 1:3–7; 1 Peter 2:19–25; 1 Peter 3:13–18
1 Peter 4:12–16; 1 Peter 5:10–11
2 Peter 1:10–21; 2 Peter 3:3–13

We have looked at Peter in so many different roles. He was an evangelist, able to win three thousand converts with one sermon. As a healer, he was able to say to a man crippled for forty years, "Get up and walk." As an elder he battled with all the problems that arise in church meetings. As a pastor he was a shepherd tending the flock of Christ.

He had many other roles too. I would love to know what he was like as a husband. There is a little about it. First I know that his wife was very beautiful because otherwise he would never have dared to give beauty hints to other wives, as he does in the third chapter of his first letter. Can you imagine, with an ugly wife in the congregation, Peter talking about how to be beautiful? But he spoke about beauty, not glamour, which is interesting. He said that you don't need to have lots of jewellery or fine clothes or a special hairdo to be beautiful. That's beauty that's stuck on. You need a beauty that comes from the inside. I can see him looking down at his wife as he spoke about real beauty.

The Lord called Simon Peter to leave his mother-in-law right at the beginning of his discipleship. Maybe to leave his wife behind for a time at that stage, I do not know. I know that later this wife, who had every wife's instinct to build a nest and to have a home of her home, gave it up and travelled with her husband. Paul used to say to people, "Have I not the right to lead about a wife as Peter does?" – showing that she travelled with him from country to country. This travelling pair went all over the then known world looking after Peter's converts, because on the day of Pentecost when three thousand were converted, do you read where they came from? They were from many different parts of the world.

Peter was the kind of evangelist who doesn't just get a decision and then forget all about the person. He wanted to know how they were getting on. So he not only travelled, this big fisherman, throughout the length and breadth of his own land, right to the sea coast – Joppa, Caesarea – he looked out across the sea and he thought of his converts far away, and he went to see them. Most of them were in what we now call Turkey, a region with five hundred cities and villages even in those days. There he went to his converts in Bithynia and Asia. He went further still, to Corinth, for a time. He was the minister of the church there, and that's unfortunately what led to a bit of split in that church because some of them liked Paul best and some of them liked Peter best.

That is how it is when different ministers come to minister in a place, and people have their favourites. Paul teaches them: Paul wasn't crucified for you and Peter wasn't either – so stop talking like this; you look at the Lord Jesus. But it went on until one day Peter arrived in Rome. Now think of it, this fisherman from a little fishing village in the obscure province away in the east, in Palestine, is now in the great metropolis, the most sophisticated city in the then known world. Peter the big fisherman is as far from home as he could be and he has come there to go home. Far from home and very near it, nearer than he thought. As far as we can make out, he came to Rome at Paul's request because there was division in the church at Rome between the Gentile believers and the Jewish believers trying to get on together in one church. Paul had a particular ministry to the Gentile believers and they took him to their side as it were, and the Jewish believers were feeling a bit disgruntled.

Little did that church realise that the conflict within the fellowship would cost the lives of both Peter and Paul, and that Peter, in coming to sort out the problem within the church, would die in the fires of Rome started by the emperor Nero. Now when Peter came to Rome he came in the swinging sixties. That's literally true – if you know your Roman history you know that in the middle of the first century in the sixties "swinging Rome" was a byword. You see, the main wars were past. They now had a period of peace and prosperity. They were affluent, and they were going in exactly the same way as the "swinging sixties" went in Britain.

It is almost uncanny to read the story of Roman society and compare it with Britain. If I can give you one illustration: sport and violence were getting closer and closer together in Rome. They were no longer content with just games. There had to be blood. At first animals, then gladiators. It wasn't long before it was the Christians being thrown into the arena for the crowds to watch them being killed.

Rome was cracking up. Whereas once a divorce in Rome was a social stigma and almost unheard of, now in the sixties in Rome there were more divorces than marriage each year. That is exactly what happened in the Western world in the mid 1970s. For the first time in the West there were countries reporting more divorces than marriage. The more you look into the pattern, the more you see the parallel. In Rome, family life was cracking up, sport was, everything was. There in the middle of the city of Rome was a church with problems, and Peter and Paul trying to cement them together, that the body of Christ might be one in that place and witness to the things of the Lord.

What about the emperor? A fine young man became emperor – a man who was creative, composing his own music, a man who was artistic in architecture, who loved classical buildings and who loved to see a new building go up that was beautiful, a man who did great things and had great ambitions, but a man whom power corrupted. His name was Nero. So corrupted did he become that this man's name is not remembered now for the creative and artistic achievements, nor for the good that he did, nor for the ideas he had which built up Roman society. We now think of the name "Nero" with shudders. If you saw the film *Quo Vadis* some years ago you saw a brilliant portrayal by Peter Ustinov, almost a caricature, of a man twisted, corrupted with his own bigness, his own power. It was into that Rome, under that Nero, that Peter came. Something happened while he was there, which comes out in all his letters. The whole city of Rome one morning was in flames. The buildings of stone did not burn but most of the houses were still wooden and close together, and the fire spread through that city. No-one really knows to this day who started it, but all the suspicions of the people were against Nero. They knew that he wanted to rebuild it, they knew that he had plans, models of new buildings, but he couldn't put them up because existing homes were there.

So when the city burned down the people said, "Nero did it. He has gone mad and he's destroying our city so that he can build his dreams." The same thing happened when the city of London burnt down in the year 1666, 19th July, having started in a baker's oven in Pudding Lane. In that dreadful fire of London 200,000 people were made homeless and 90 churches were burnt down including St. Paul's Cathedral. Many of the lovely London churches that replaced them were built by Sir Christopher Wren, following the fire. But when the fire was over and the hundreds of homeless people living in shacks looked around at their devastated city, they said, "Who started it? Who's to blame?" There's always a scapegoat needed for such situations, and in those days the French Roman Catholics were the unpopular people in London, and people said it must have been the Roman Catholics.

Back in the days of Rome they said, "Who's to blame?" Nero heard the rumours and said, "Well, we must find someone to blame quickly." Who are the most unpopular people around? Somebody said, "There's that little group of people called Christians. How about them?"

"Fine." That day Nero spread the rumour, "It was those dreadful Christians. They're dreadful people," he said. "They're cannibals. They eat bodies and drink blood." He said all manner of other things about them. He said, "They have love feasts. They're just orgies." He said, "I have heard that their preachers say the world will end in fire, so they're just trying to hurry up the day."

The rumours spread through the streets of Rome and the Christians were arrested and then were subject to indescribable tortures. Some of them were crucified, some of them had the skins of wild animals sewn around their bodies and were sent into the stadium and wild beasts were set on them to devour them, but the worst of all was Nero's own punishment. He covered Christians with tar and pitch, tied them to posts, set them alight to provide light for his garden parties—that's Nero.

Peter was not among those caught in the first batch of

Christians. Peter had to do some hard thinking and praying when this blew up. Out of the flames he realised that something terrible had been born, something that could wipe out thousands of Christians. He didn't know then how far it would spread. He did not know that the ripples of this persecution would go right out to the furthermost parts of the empire, even to Britain. He did not know that the persecution begun by Nero would last over two hundred years.

The first thing he thought of was this: "I must get the truth down in writing." Already at least one apostle was dead, probably more, and Peter realised he could die and Paul could die. The first thing he wanted to record in writing was the account of Jesus. Until this moment there was no Gospel written. It was an oral thing, passed on by word of mouth.

So Peter, who remember was an uneducated, illiterate fisherman, had to get hold of someone who could write. He got hold of a young man called John Mark and he said, "Mark, write down the account of Jesus." He dictated it to him. So we have the first, earliest Gospel written – Mark's Gospel. It is the shortest. The end of it is still missing, the last page is torn in two in the middle of a sentence and it finishes with these words, "The disciples were afraid for" – that's all. Looks as if it was torn even as they wrote it. So he got the story of Jesus written down, and it has survived to this day. That is why in Mark's Gospel Peter figures so largely and why it is in Mark's gospel we have Peter baring his soul and describing the betrayal, the denial, so honestly. It is Peter's Gospel, which Mark wrote down in Rome.

Peter realised that the ripples of this persecution, spreading out to Asia, to Greece, would reach his own converts, so what did he do? He said, "I must write a letter. I must write to them and tell them. I must prepare them for persecution. I must get them ready for suffering." Then he got hold of a secretary, an *amanuensis*, a man called Sylvanus, and said,

"Sylvanus, will you write this down for me: Dear exiles of the dispersion in Pontus, Galatia, I want to write to you." He wrote the first letter of Peter, and all the way through it the note that is struck is suffering. He is saying: I want to get you ready for all this. I want to get you ready for suffering.

How do you get people ready for persecution? The astonishing thing is Peter never tells them to get ready to run. He tells them one thing all the way through. He says, "Get your relationships right." Now isn't that interesting? That is the one thing he says from beginning to end. If your relationships are right then you will be able to rejoice when the suffering comes. If your relationships are wrong you won't be able to take it. He says make sure your relationship with the Lord is right before the suffering comes; make sure that, even though you have never seen him, you love him so that, when he comes, you just look for your eternal reward in glory. Make sure your relationship with the church is right – your brothers and sisters in Christ. If that is not right, you won't stand in persecution. Make sure your relationship with the government is right, that you are loyal to your state. Make sure that your relationship to your employer is right because if your relationship with your boss is not right, you won't stand in suffering. Make sure that your relationship to your husband or your wife is right, or you won't be able to stand. Now that is a profound message, and I believe that down through the centuries Peter's message comes home to us today because it is going to be tough. We are being warned increasingly clearly by the Lord himself that it is not going to be easier for Christians in this land of ours. The one way we can get ready for persecution is not panic, not to buy a little cottage somewhere in the Scottish highlands where we can run away, but to get relationships right with the Lord, with the church, with the government, with the boss, with the family. Then you will cope.

There was a total change in Peter's attitude to suffering, and, second, a total change in his attitude to death. You know what the world's attitude to these two things is. Peter's attitude to suffering once upon a time had been to refuse it, to have nothing to do with it, to run away from it. When Jesus said to Peter, "The Son of man must suffer", Peter said, "Never, forget it. You're not going to suffer. Don't talk about it." Jesus said, "Get behind me Satan. You're not thinking the things of God."

Now here is Peter in his letter saying rejoice when you suffer – not refuse to suffer, but rejoice to suffer. The heart of suffering is when you suffer unjustly. It's bad enough when you have done something wrong and you suffer for it, but when you have not done anything wrong, when you have been blamed for something you haven't done, can you cope with that? Can you take it? Peter says, "Rejoice." Now why had he switched in the attitude to suffering? Why could he rejoice to suffer instead of refusing to? What a change!

Why at the slightest hint that he might be crucified once upon a time he would have run a mile, but now he faces his own crucifixion calmly and says, "I'm going to die soon," and he knew he was going to die on a cross. How could he do it? The answer is very simple. First, he had the *example* of Jesus suffering. Now he knew that it was possible to turn the other cheek. Now he knew it was possible to remain forgiving when they spit on you. He now could see that it could be done. So he knew now what it was all about. He could look at the life of Jesus and say, "So that's what being like Jesus is." That is not enough to give a person a positive attitude to suffering, but it is partly enough. Once you look at the example of Jesus who, when he was reviled and insulted, did not revile or insult back – then you have an example of how to cope with it. More than that, Peter also thought of the *effect* of Jesus' suffering – which was to bring profound good into the world, because his suffering was not wasted, not useless. He bore the sins of many in his own body on the tree that he might bring us to God; that he might make us righteous – and it has worked.

Once pain does good you can put up with it. A woman bringing a baby into the world is in pain, struggling, but doing good. It is all going to be worthwhile, something will result from it that is positive and lovely. So Peter says, "Now you can be glad to suffer. You've got an example of how to take it and you've also got the knowledge that suffering in the Lord produces lovely results, good effect." So he has changed his attitude to suffering.

The other thing he changed was his attitude to death. Few things made Christians so different from everybody else in the ancient world as their attitude to death. In fact most people disliked it, didn't talk about it if they could help it. When it came, they accepted it reluctantly. Their tombstones were covered with words of doom and gloom, "All over now, finished." You feel the heaviness of death on ancient Roman society, but not so the Christians. Once upon a time Peter had run from death; he hated it. As soon as the storm came, as soon as the boat was being tossed and Peter was in danger of losing his life, he panicked. "Lord, don't you care?" When his own life was threatened, when Jesus was arrested after a feeble attempt to show resistance, when he cut off the servant's ear, Peter was on the run too. Now here is Peter calmly writing and saying, "I know I'm going to die very soon," and he was not going to die of old age.

He knew how he was going to die and when he was going to die. The Lord told him both those things. Could you cope with that knowledge? Not many people can cope positively if they are told how they will die and when they will die. Peter not only coped but he looked forward to it. What explains the change? He had the resurrection of Christ and the return of Christ, and given those two things he just couldn't wait to go. It is lovely when you meet a Christian like this.

I knew an old man called Joe who had been born within two weeks of Winston Churchill. When Churchill died at 92 they told old Joe and his reply was, "I'm not at all surprised, drinking all that whisky and smoking all those cigars!" Some years later, Joe was taken seriously ill. He lived near my home and I used to visit him almost every day during the most serious part of that illness, and every day he said a fond goodbye to me. He said, "I won't be here tomorrow." He was so excited about going! He said, "So it's been lovely to know you, goodbye." The next day he would say, "I'm still here."

It went on like that every day: "I'm still around, dreadful!" His dear, loving daughter, a missionary in Angola, was a relative of my wife. She nursed him through that illness (to his great disgust) and she saw how disgusted he was. He so looked forward to going! Why? Because he lived so close to the Lord on earth that to die was just to get a bit closer. We say, "They've gone," and heaven says, "They've come." We say, "Their place is empty"; heaven says, "Their place is filled." That's the difference. Peter had the resurrection of Jesus, and he said, "We've been begotten again to a living hope by the resurrection of Christ from the dead." In other words, death doesn't have the last word. I don't fear death, now that I have met the risen Jesus. He got through it, and I'm going to get through it.

The other thing Peter looked forward to was the return of Christ – the day when Christ comes back, and the day when Christians receive their inheritance. Peter says God will keep you on earth and keep the inheritance in heaven, and one day he will bring the two together. Christians are the only people I know who get their inheritance when they die. Everybody else gets an inheritance when somebody else dies. People will get my inheritance when I die, but as a Christian I can say, "I'll get my inheritance when I die."

I long to depart and be with Christ, which is better. "To die is to gain," so on the day when he appears I gain so much. So, between the resurrection and the return of Christ, Peter had a changed attitude to death; between the example and the effect of Christ's suffering, Peter had a changed attitude to suffering. This is a new Peter, so now he faced death.

From this point onwards in Peter's life we are dependent on legend and tradition, so what follows here is not the Word of God. I give it to you as legend which grew up around Simon Peter and his last days in Rome. It is almost certain that that is where he met his death. Some archaeological excavations under under the Vatican, just a few years ago, revealed some very early traces of his name right underneath that vast basilica of St. Peter's, which is built on the site of the largest stadium in which Christians were put to death in those days. So we can say it is almost certain, but here are the legends and I give them to you for what they are worth. I believe they point to his character. Paul died at about the same time in the same place—Peter and Paul the two great missionaries.

The first legend is "Quo Vadis" and I remember walking down the Appian Way to the little fork in the roads where Peter (so the legend goes, and there is a good deal of ground for believing it) had fled. He had been arrested and he was running down the Appian Road to escape. As he ran down the road he met the Lord Jesus on the way back in. He said, "Domine, quo vadis?" for that is the Latin rendering of, "Lord, where are you going?" The Lord replies, "I go to Rome to be crucified again."

Peter said, "But I thought you had been crucified once for all?"

Jesus said, "Yes, but I saw your flight from death and I go to be crucified in your stead."

Peter said, "Lord, I will return to obey your command."

The Lord said, "Fear not, I am with you."

You can take that as it is – a legend. I believe it points to two things. It points to the vacillating temperament Peter had. It points to the fact that even at the last stage of your earthly pilgrimage the old self can come in. But it points also to the Lord's firm hand, his stable control of his disciple – Peter, back in there to die. For the time had come now when Peter had been told there will be no angel to open prison doors, not this time, this time you die. The second legend comes from the writings of Clement of Alexandria, an early Christian. One of the things they did in those days to increase the anguish of a victim in the stadium was this: they killed his wife first in front of his eyes. Clement of Alexandria records this:

"They say that when Peter beheld his wife led out to death he rejoiced at her calling in the Lord, and he cried out to encourage and comfort, addressing her by name, 'Oh remember the Lord.' Such was the marriage of that blessed pair and their perfect agreement in those things that were dearest to them."

A third legend is that when they finally brought Peter out after his wife, they put a cross up for him and he felt unworthy to die in the same way as his Lord died, so he asked to be crucified in a way which was not uncommon in those days. It increased the pain but it shortened the length of crucifixion. He asked to be crucified upside down, and so they pinned him to the cross upside down and thus he died.

I think Peter would be astonished and even hurt at all that has surrounded his name ever since. He would be shattered at being called the first Pope. He would say, "I'm just a fellow elder." I think he would wonder what on earth they were doing to put up a massive building and call it St. Peter's. The most I could get out of that when I looked at it was to say, "Well at least this great building has made this fisherman famous, when you can see the wrecks of the tombs of emperors."

Then there is the idea that Peter is standing up there outside the pearly gates to let us in. But if you want Peter you will have to look inside the city, and when you meet him you will find that he has nail prints in his hands. When I meet Peter I want to look at his hands. He will have nail prints, like Jesus.

In his first letter, Peter calls himself an elder, then writes: "I am also a witness of Christ's sufferings." Now that doesn't just mean that he saw them, in fact he didn't see all of them – he ran away. He saw Gethsemane, but he ran after that. But he was not only speaking about the trial of Jesus when he saw him spat upon and reviled. The word "witness" in Greek is the same as the English word "martyr". Where Peter says, "I am a witness of his sufferings," if you read it in the Greek it is, "I am a martyr of his sufferings." You can witness to something by saying "I've seen it in him." You can also witness to something by being that something yourself, and Peter's final role was a witness, a martyr of Christ's sufferings.

As you read through the first and the second letter of Peter which he got written before he died, where he talks about his departure, he says calmly: "I am soon to die but I'm going to keep on reminding you of these things so that when I have gone you will remember them." When I read those two letters there is one word keeps coming out at me and I want to ring it with red: "fire". Have you ever noticed it? That is what convinces me those letters were written out of the great fire of Rome when he saw a city destroyed. He remembered people scrabbling through the ruins after the fire, trying to find anything of value left there. One thing remaining was gold, and there was a lot of gold in Rome. Furniture and homes were destroyed, but as you went through that fire the one thing not destroyed, but even better and purer after the fire than before, was the gold melted and refined in that holocaust. Peter wrote, "When these fiery trials come, your faith, which is more precious than gold, is like that gold, and it will be refined and purer afterwards." When the fire comes, it refines; and, as Peter looked at the devastated city of Rome, he knew that it would be rebuilt. He saw that fire not only leads to refining, it leads to re-building. He could see that God was going to re-build the universe and that the heavens and the earth – the planets, the stars, this planet earth, everything – would disappear in a gigantic bonfire and go back to the energy from which it was created. Peter saw that two thousand years ago, and it is only in recent years that scientists have admitted its possibility, for now we know that energy holds the world together, and that when we split an atom, fire is released. This truth was revealed to Peter long ago: the whole universe is going to burn up in fire. What a day! God will then build a world in which there is only goodness. As far as we know, the last thing Peter wrote or dictated to his secretary was, "I want to remind you about that day, and as things were once destroyed with water they will one day be destroyed in fire and there will be a new heaven and a new earth" – and that is what we look forward to, and we can go through the fire knowing that we will be refined.

No wonder Peter could face suffering and death in a new way. Isn't it amazing? This man, when Jesus found him, was only a fisherman, and had Jesus not met him he would have lived and died in Capernaum and you would never have heard his name. Yet today there are hundreds of millions of people who know the name of Peter. How did it start? Very simply, when Jesus stepped into his life and looked at a fisherman and said to him: "Follow me, and I will make you...." If he can do that for Peter he can do it for you.

Lightning Source UK Ltd.
Milton Keynes UK
UKOW02f2328260916

283895UK00001B/30/P